Bloom's Modern Critical Interpretations

Bloom's Modern Critical Interpretations

Bloom's Modern Critical Interpretations

EMERSON'S ESSAYS

Edited and with an introduction by
Harold Bloom
Sterling Professor of the Humanities
Yale University

CHELSEA HOUSE
P U B L I S H E R S
An imprint of Infobase Publishing

Bloom's Modern Critical Interpretations: Emerson's Essays

©2006 Infobase Publishing

Introduction © 2006 by Harold Bloom

Chelsea House
An imprint of Infobase Publishing
132 West 31st Street
New York NY 10001

Library of Congress Cataloging-in-Publication Data
Emerson's essays / Harold Bloom, editor.
    p. cm. — (Bloom's modern critical interpretations)
  Includes bibliographical references (p.   ) and index.
  ISBN 0-7910-8118-4 (hardcover)
  1. Emerson, Ralph Waldo, 1803-1882—Criticism and interpretation.
I. Bloom, Harold. II. Series.
  PS1638E4225 2006
  814'.3—dc22   2005038036

You can find Chelsea House on the World Wide Web at http://www.chelseahouse.com

Contributing Editor: Jesse Zuba
Cover design by Keith Trego
Cover photo Ralph Waldo Emerson / © Hulton-Deutsch Collection/CORBIS

Printed in the United States of America

Bang EJB 10 9 8 7 6 5 4 3 2 1

This book is printed on acid-free paper.

All links and web addresses were checked and verified to be correct at the time of publication. Because of the dynamic nature of the web, some addresses and links may have changed since publication and may no longer be valid.

Contents

Editor's Note

My Introduction centers upon Emerson's essays, "Experience" and "Self-Reliance" and then traces their American Sublime in Walt Whitman's *Song of Myself*.

Stephen Whicher examines the dialectics of Freedom and Fate in "Circles," after which Lawrence Buell demonstrates Emerson's coherent artistry throughout his essays.

"Circles" returns in David Wyatt's celebration of Emersonian re-centering, while Barbara Packer analyzes the splendor of "Experience," doubtless the best of all the essays.

My essay on Emerson's invention of the American Religion relies upon his "Self-Reliance," after which Sharon Cameron returns us to "Experience" and finds there the profound mourning of the essayist for his son.

David Bromwich reads "Self-Reliance" by the illumination of Wordsworth's Immortality Ode, while David M. Robinson ranges widely through *Essays: Second Series*, following the ambiguities of "the amphibious self."

Emerson's Gnostic-Hermetic view that each of us is in a sense hermaphroditic is meditated on by George Kateb in "Self-Reliance," after which Pamela Schirmeister broods upon Emerson's evasions of merely discursive thought.

In this volume's final essay, Kerry Larson defines Emersonian "justice" as being difficult to distinguish from experiential conflict.

My Afterthought reflects upon the place of Emerson and Whitman in the cultural and political labyrinth of our Evening Land.

HAROLD BLOOM

Introduction: The American Sublime

Parable—Those thinkers in whom all stars move in cyclic orbits are not the most profound: whoever looks into himself as into vast space and carries galaxies in himself also knows how irregular all galaxies are; they lead into the chaos and labyrinth of existence.

NIETZSCHE

What is the American Sublime, and how does it differ from its European precursor? When Emerson set out to define *The American Scholar*, in 1837, he began with "the old fable" of One Man, taking this vision of a primordial being from Plutarch's Platonizing essay on "Brotherly Love." Characteristically, Emerson saw the division and fall of man as a reification and as an undoing by the trope of metonymy:

Man is thus metamorphosed into a thing, into many things. The planter, who is Man sent out into the field to gather food, is seldom cheered by any idea of the true dignity of his ministry. He sees his bushel and his cart, and nothing beyond, and sinks into the farmer, instead of Man on the farm. The tradesman scarcely ever gives an ideal worth to his work, but is ridden by the routine of his craft, and the soul is subject to dollars. The priest becomes

a form; the attorney a statute-book; the mechanic a machine; the
sailor a rope of the ship.

Parallel to these metonymic reductions is the undoing of the scholar as
"the delegated intellect" whereas: "In the right state he is *Man Thinking*." To
account for the scholar's fall, Emerson first considers the scholar as a
problem in influence. The main influences directed upon the scholar—who
for Emerson, as for Stevens, comprises also the poet—are (1) Nature, (2)
Books, (3) Action. But Nature is revealed to be only the print of the scholar's
seal. As for Books: "One must be an inventor to read well." Finally, Action
turns out to be "instinct," the world of will and drive. The three precursors
of the scholar thus fade away, leaving "self-trust," freedom or wildness. His
ground cleared, Emerson attains to the center of his oration: "It is a
mischievous notion that we are come late into nature; that the world was
finished a long time ago." The wild or free notion is that: "This time, like all
times, is a very good one, if we but know what to do with it." From this
follows the prophecy that made possible the drastic grandeur of the
American Sublime: "A nation of men will for the first time exist, because
each believes himself inspired by the Divine Soul which also inspires all
men."

Emerson delivered *The American Scholar: An Oration*, at Harvard on
August 31, 1837. A few months before, in the spring of 1837, there was a
business crash, banks suspended nearly all payments, and a general economic
depression dominated society. It is noteworthy, and has been noted, that
Emerson's two great outbursts of prophetic vocation coincide with two
national moral crises, the Depression of 1837 and the Mexican War of 1846,
which Emerson, as an Abolitionist, bitterly opposed. The origins of the
American Sublime are connected inextricably to the business collapse of
1837. I want to illustrate this connection by a close reading of relevant
entries in Emerson's journals of 1837, so as to be able to ask and perhaps
answer the invariable question that antithetical criticism learns always to ask
of each fresh instance of the Sublime. *What is being freshly repressed?* What has
been forgotten, on purpose, in the depths, so as to make possible this sudden
elevation to the heights? Here is the seer, apparently stimulated to an ascent,
by a meditation upon a business depression:

Behold the boasted world has come to nothing. Prudence itself is
at her wits' end. Pride, and Thrift, and Expediency, who jeered
and chirped and were so well pleased with themselves, and made
merry with the dream, as they termed it, of Philosophy and
Love,—behold they are all flat, and here is the Soul erect and

unconquered still. What answer is it now to say, It has always been so? I acknowledge that, as far back as I can see the widening procession of humanity, the marchers are lame and blind and deaf; but to the soul that whole past is but one finite series in its infinite scope. Deteriorating ever and now desperate. Let me begin anew. Let me teach the finite to know its master. Let me ascend above my fate and work down upon my world.

The Yankee virtues, as internalized by Emerson himself, no longer triumph over the Transcendental vision, which indeed now turns transumptive, projecting all the past as a lame, blind, deaf march, and introjecting a Sublime future, mounted over fate, the finite, the cosmos. What Emerson represses is *Ananke*, the Fate he has learned already to call "compensation." His vision of repetition is a metonymic reduction, an undoing of all other selves, and his restituting *daemonization* renders him solipsistic and free. That a poetic repression brings about the Sublime wildness of freedom is almost the most Emersonian of all Emersonian rhetorical paradoxes; and one that he himself carried to its apocalypse eventually in the grand death-march of the essay *Fate*, in *The Conduct of Life*:

> But Fate against Fate is only parrying and defence: there are also the noble creative forces. The revelation of Thought takes man out of servitude into freedom. We rightly say of ourselves, we were born again, and many times. We have successive experiences so important that the new forgets the old, and hence the mythology of the seven or the nine heavens. The day of days, the great day of the feast of life, is that in which the inward eye opens to the Unity in things, to the omnipresence of law:—sees that what is must be and ought to be, or is the best. This beatitude dips from on high down on us and we see. It is not in us so much as we are in it. If the air come to our lungs, we breathe and live; if not, we die. If the light come to our eyes, we see; else not. And if truth come to our mind we suddenly expand to its dimensions, as if we grew to worlds. We are as lawgivers; we speak for Nature; we prophesy and divine.

I want to defer comment on this magnificent instance of the American Sublime by first comparing Emerson, as a moral theorist of interpretation, to Freud and to St. Augustine. Augustine, as Peter Brown says, parallels Freud by speaking of a "Fall" in consciousness:

Augustine ... produced a singularly comprehensive explanation of why allegory should have been necessary in the first place. The need for such a language of 'signs' was the result of a specific dislocation of the human consciousness. In this, Augustine takes up a position analogous to that of Freud. In dreams also, a powerful and direct message is said to be deliberately diffracted by some psychic mechanism, into a multiplicity of 'signs' quite as intricate and absurd, yet just as capable of interpretation, as the 'absurd' or 'obscure' passages in the Bible. Both men, therefore, assume that the proliferation of images is due to some precise event, to the development of some geological fault across a hitherto undivided consciousness: for Freud, it is the creation of an unconscious by repression; for Augustine, it is the outcome of the Fall.

Augustine's vision of the Fall, as Brown also shows, had changed from an early, quasi-Plotinian belief, which was that Adam and Eve had "fallen" into physicality: "that the prolific virtues they would have engendered in a purely 'spiritual' existence had declined, with the Fall, into the mere literal flesh and blood of human families." In the mature Augustinian doctrine, the dualizing split in human consciousness is no technical descent to a lower degree of being, but is the most wilful and terrible of catastrophes. How does this compare with catastrophe theory in Freud, and in Emerson? Do all three doctors-of-the-soul, Augustine, Emerson, and Freud agree fundamentally that consciousness, as we know it, cannot inaugurate itself without a catastrophe? The Christian Augustine and the Empedoclean-Schopenhauerian Freud do not surprise us in this regard, but why should the Idealizing quasi-Neoplatonist Emerson insist upon catastrophe as the invariable inaugural act for consciousness?

Here is Emerson's equivalent of the Augustinian or psychoanalytic division into consciousness, from his greatest essay, *Experience*:

It is very unhappy, but too late to be helped, the discovery we have made that we exist. That discovery is called the Fall of Man. Ever afterwards we suspect our instruments. We have learned that we do not see directly, but mediately, and that we have no means of correcting these colored and distorting lenses which we are, or of computing the amount of their errors. Perhaps these subject-lenses have a creative power; perhaps there are no objects. Once we lived in what we saw; now, the rapaciousness of this new power, which threatens to absorb all things, engages us.

This is surely the authentic vision of the daemonic in Emerson, the apocalyptic frenzy of an American Sublime. The mystery of this passage; as of the other rhapsodies I have quoted from Emerson, is in the paradox of repression, of the power brought into being by an enormous fresh influx of repression. More even than the British Romantic Sublime, Emerson's American Sublime exposes what I am tempted to call the deep structure of rhetoric, by which I mean the defensive nature of rhetoric. I oppose myself here not only to what passes for "Freudian literary criticism" but to the much more formidable "deconstructive" literary criticism in which de Man and Derrida follow Rousseau and Nietzsche. De Man, analyzing Nietzsche, concludes that between rhetoric as a system of tropes and rhetoric as persuasion there is an *aporia*, a limit or doubt that cannot be defined. I venture an analysis now of this *aporia*, for what relates one trope to another in a systematic way, and carries each trope from evasion to persuasion, is that trope's function as defense, its imagistic maskings of those detours to death that make up the highway map of the psyche, the drives from anterior fixations to entropic self-destructions.

Emerson followed Vico in declining to confuse meaning with signification, a confusion still evident even in the most advanced models of post-Structuralist thought. For Emerson, meaning is concerned with survival, and signification is only an instrumentality of meaning, this being a distinction in which Peirce followed Emerson. What holds together rhetoric as a system of tropes, and rhetoric as persuasion, is the necessity of defense, defense against everything that threatens survival, and a defense whose aptest name is "meaning." Vico named poetic defense as "divination," which in our vocabulary translates best as "over-determination of meaning." But here I must allow myself a digression into theory-of-misprision.

The poetic defense of repression is always a ratio of representation (the Lurianic *tikkun* or restitution) because in poetic repression *you forget something in order to present something else*. Whereas, poetic sublimation is always a ratio of limitation (*zimzum* or contraction) because by it *you remember something (concentrate it) in order to avoid presenting that something, and you choose to present something else in its place*. Substitution or breaking-of-the-vessels between poetic repression and poetic sublimation is a transformation from the unconscious to consciousness just as the movement from poetic sublimation to poetic introjection or projection restores or returns representations to the unconscious. Tropes, defenses, images, ratios of limitation withdraw representations from the unconscious without replenishing the unconscious, while the countermovements of representation restitute the unconscious. When Emerson experiences and describes his influxes of the American Sublime, he is at work creating the great trope of the specifically American Unconscious, or what he himself in *Self-Reliance* calls "Spontaneity or Instinct":

> The magnetism which all original action exerts is explained when we inquire the reason of self-trust. Who is the Trustee? What is the aboriginal Self on which a universal reliance may be grounded? What is the nature and power of that science-baffling star, without parallax, without calculable elements, which shoots a ray of beauty even into trivial and impure actions, if the least mark of independence appear? The inquiry leads us to that source, at once the essence of genius, of virtue, and of life, which we call Spontaneity or Instinct. We denote this primary wisdom as Intuition, whilst all later teachings are tuitions. In that deep force, the last fact behind which analysis cannot go, all things find their common origin.

How does the Freudian Unconscious contrast with this Emersonian American Sublime? Freud's concept of the unconscious was first obtained from his theory of repression, and was intended to explain *discontinuities* in the psychic life of every individual. But these were active discontinuities, so that Freud's notion of the unconscious rapidly became a dynamic conception, and not merely a descriptive one. Ideas had been repressed and then continued to be shut out from consciousness, by an ongoing process of repression. Unconscious ideas that could break back through into consciousness, Freud referred to as "preconscious" and distinguished sharply from repressions that could never return, which constituted the unconscious proper. These latter repressions, according to Freud, are ideas and not affects. If they *seem* affects, then they are "potential beginnings which are preventing *by* developing." Yet even these permanently repressed ideas do not make up the whole of the Freudian unconscious. Mysteriously, there is an original unconscious; indeed Freud finally thought that the mind originally was totally unconscious, and that gradually part of the mind became preconscious and part conscious, with yet another part always remaining unconscious. To this unrepressed unconscious, the augmenting ego added materials through fresh repressions.

Emerson's version of the unconscious is a purer instance of poetic or hyperbolical repression. Whatever one may want to say about the structure of the Freudian unconscious (and I do *not* believe it is structured like a language), I think that Emersonian "Spontaneity or Instinct" *is* structured like a rhetoric, that is, is both a system of tropes and also a mode of persuasion. Like Freud's unconscious, it is originary, and again like Freud's giant trope, it is augmented by fresh and purposeful forgettings, by evasions that are performed in order to present something other than the something that is being evaded. But, in Freud, the something evaded is any drive objectionable to ego-ideals, whereas in Emerson the something must take the name of a single drive, the thrust of anteriority, the mystifying strength of the past, which is profoundly objectionable to Emerson's prime ego-ideal, Self-Reliance. Emerson's pugnacity on this theme is in the Optative Mood; as he says: "When we have new perception, we shall gladly disburden the memory of its hoarded treasures as old rubbish." As for what became Nietzsche's "guilt of indebtedness," which is so profoundly analyzed in *Towards the Genealogy of Morals*, Emerson dismisses it with a Sublime shrug, a shrug directed against Coleridge: "In the hour of vision there is nothing that can be called gratitude, or properly joy."

With so daemonic an unconscious as his support, Emerson cheerfully places the spirit wholly in the category that Kierkegaard called only "the aesthetic." I turn again to "The Rotation Method" in *Either* of *Either/Or*, so as to illuminate Emerson's kind of repression:

> Forgetting is the shears with which you cut away what you cannot use, doing it under the supreme direction of memory. Forgetting and remembering are thus identical arts, and the artistic achievement of this identity is the Archimedean point from which one lifts the whole world. When we say that we *consign* something to oblivion, we suggest simultaneously that it is to be forgotten and yet also remembered.

Kierkegaard is playing upon his own notion of "repetition," which is his revision of the Hegelian "mediation" into a Christian conception "of the anxious freedom." Emerson's Transcendental equivalent is his famous declaration in the journal for April 1842: "I am *Defeated* all the time; yet to Victory I am born." Less than a year later, Kierkegaard wrote: "The difficulty facing an existing individual is how to give his existence the continuity without which everything simply vanishes.... The goal of movement for an existing individual is to arrive at a decision, and to renew it." I think we can remark on this that Kierkegaard does not want us to be able to distinguish between the desire for repetition, and repetition itself, since it is in the blending of the two that the "anxious freedom" of "becoming a Christian" truly consists. But Emerson was post-Christian; for him that "Great Defeat" belonged totally to the past. What Kierkegaard called "repetition" Emerson called by an endless variety of names until he settled on Fate or Necessity, and he insisted always that we had to distinguish between our desire for such reality, and the reality itself. In the grand passage from the essay *Fate* that I quoted earlier, the emphasis is sublimely upon what Emerson calls successive rebirths, while meaning successive re-begettings of ourselves, during this, our one life. Perpetually, Emerson insists, our new experience forgets the old, so that perhaps Nietzsche should have remarked of Emerson, not that he did not know how old he was already or how young he still was going to be, but only that Emerson did know that always he was about to become his own father. This, I now assert, is the distinguishing mark of the specifically American Sublime, that it begins anew not with restoration or rebirth, in the radically displaced Protestant pattern of the Wordsworthian Sublime, but that it is truly past even such displacement, despite the line from Edwards to Emerson that scholarship accurately continues to trace. Not merely rebirth, but the even more hyperbolical trope of self-rebegetting, is the starting point of the last Western Sublime, the great sunset of selfhood in the Evening Land.

But what does this hyperbolical figuration mean, or rather, how are we to transform its signification into meaning? We all of us go home each evening, and at some moment in time, with whatever degree of overt consciousness, we go back over all the signs that the day presented to us. In those signs, we seek only what can aid the continuity of our own discourse, the survival of those ongoing qualities that will give what is vital in us even more life. This seeking is the Vichian and Emersonian making of signification into meaning, by the single test of aiding our survival. By such a test, the American Sublime is a trope *intending* to forget the father in order to present the son or daughter. In this trope, the father is a limitation or what Stevens called a reduction to a First Idea, an idea of an origin, and the son or daughter intends to be a restituting representation in which a First Idea is reimagined, so as to become the idea of an aim. But what is a First Idea, unless it be what Freud termed a primal fixation or an initial repression? And what did that initial repression forget, or at least intend to forget? Here Freud touched his *aporia*, and so I turn beyond him to Kabbalah again, to seek a more ultimate paradigm for the Scene of Instruction than even Kierkegaard affords me, since here too Kierkegaard touched his *aporia*, and accepted the Christian limit of the Incarnation. The Orphic Emerson demands an ultimate paradigm which is beyond the pleasure-principle, yet also beyond these competing reality-principles.

Lacan, in his revision of Freud, tells us that the ego is essentially paranoid, that it is a structure founded upon a contradictory or double-bind relationship between a self and an other, or relationship that is at once an opposition and an identity. I reject this as interpretation of Freud, and reject it also as an observation upon the psyche. But Lacan, as I remarked in another context, joins himself to those greater theorists, including Nietzsche and Freud, who talk about people in ways that are more valid even for poems. I do not think that the psyche is a text, but I find it illuminating to discuss texts as though they were psyches, and in doing so I consciously follow the Kabbalists. For, in poems, I take it that the other is always a person, the precursor, however imagined or composite, whereas for Lacan the other is principle, and not person.

The fourth of the six *behinot* or aspects of each *sefirah*, according to Moses Cordovero, is the aspect of a particular *sefirah* that allows the *sefirah* above it to give that particular *sefirah* the strength enabling it, the later *sefirah*, to emanate out further *sefirot*. Or to state it more simply, yet still by a Kabbalistic trope, *it is from a son that a father takes the power, that in turn will enable the son to become a father.* This hyperbolical figuration is a rather complex theory of repression, because the son or, later poem initially needs to forget the autonomy of its own power in order to express any *continuity* of power. But this is very close also to the peculiar nature of Sublime representation, where there is an implication always that what is being represented is somehow absent, and so must be restituted by an image. But the image, which in Sublime representation tends to be of a fathering force, as it were, remains distinct from what it represents, at least in the Continental and British Sublime. This is where I would locate the *difference* in the Emersonian or American Sublime, which is closer to the Kabbalistic model of Cordovero in its reversal between the roles of the fathering force and the new self of the son, that is, of the later or belated poem. In Emerson and in his progeny from Whitman, Thoreau, Dickinson on through Hart Crane, Stevens, and our contemporaries, the fathering force and the poetic self tend to merge together, but the aim of self-presentation is not defeated, because the fathering force or representative tends to disappear into the poetic self or son, rather than the self into the image of the fathering force.

I turn to *The Divinity School Address* for a proof-text here, and offer an Emerson cento of the American Sublime from it:

> That is always best which gives me to myself. The sublime is excited in me by the great stoical doctrine, Obey thyself. That which shows God in me, fortifies me. That which shows God out of me, makes me a wart and a wen....
>
> Wherever a man comes, there comes revolution. The old is for slaves. When a man comes, all books are legible, all things transparent, all religions are forms....
>
> Let me admonish you, first of all, to go alone; to refuse the good models....

I look for the hour when that supreme Beauty which ravished the souls of those Eastern men, and chiefly of those Hebrews, and through their lips spoke oracles to all time, shall speak in the West also.... I look for the new Teacher that shall follow so far those shining laws that he shall see them come full circle....

There are the two central Emersonian images of the Sublime: "all things transparent" and the Central Man who shall see the transparency and thus see also the laws of reality "come full circle." That transparency, to appear again in Whitman and in Stevens, can be interpreted two ways, transumptively or reductively. The second would relate it to Anna Freud's observation, in *The Ego and the Mechanisms of Defense*, that: "The obscurity of a successful repression is only equalled by the transparency of the repressive process when the movement is reversed." The first would relate it to the Hebrew idea of God as avoiding the Greek notions either of immanence or of transcendence. Thorlief Boman, in his *Hebrew Thought Compared with Greek*, shows that the Hebraic image of transparency, as a trope for God, sees the Divine as being neither *in* the world nor *over* the world, but rather *through* the world, not spatially but discontinuously. Let us allow both meanings, this Hebraic transumption and the Freudian reduction, and combine both with Emerson's bringing-forth a father-god out of himself, even as we examine again the two most famous of all American Sublime passages, the epiphanies in the first and last chapters of Emerson's *Nature*:

I become a transparent eyeball; I am nothing; I see all; the currents of the Universal Being circulate through me; I am part or parcel of God.

The problem of restoring to the world original and eternal beauty is solved by the redemption of the soul. The ruin or the blank that we see when we look at nature, is in our own eye. The axis of vision is not coincident with the axis of things, and so they appear not transparent but opaque.

Reductively, the first passage represents a partial return of the repressed, while the second appears to be what Anna Freud calls "the obscurity of a successful repression." But transumptively, the first passage records a successful repression, and the second the failed perspectivism of sublimation. The Emersonian repressiveness attains to a discontinuity with everything that is anterior, and in doing so it accomplishes or prepares for a reversal in which the self is forgotten ("I am nothing") and yet through seeing introjects the fathering force of anteriority. By seeing the transparency, the poet of the American Sublime *contains* the father-god, and so augments the poetic self even as he remembers to forget that self. Wordsworth celebrated the continuities of hearing, and dreaded the discontinuities of seeing. Emerson, in the defensive discontinuities of seeing, found a path to a more drastic, immediate, and total Sublime than European tradition wished or needed to discover. His greatest disciple, Whitman, an American bard at last, illustrates better than his master, the seer, both the splendor and the disaster of so aboriginal a repression.

My proof-text in Whitman is inevitably *Song of Myself*, but of its fifty-two sections I will concentrate only upon some Sublime centers, though I want to give a mapping-out of the revisionary pattern of the entire poem, for Whitman's romance of the self does follow essentially the model of the British Romantic crisis-poem, though with revealing, Emersonian, further distortions of the model. Employing my own shorthand, this is the pattern of ratios in *Song of Myself*:

Sections: 1–6   *Clinamen*, irony of presence and absence
            7–27   *Tessera*, synecdoche of part for whole
            28–30   *Kenosis*, metonymy of emptying out
            31–38   *Daemonization*, hyperbole of high and low
            39–49   *Askesis*, metaphor of inside vs. outside
            50–52   *Apophrades*, metalepsis reversing early and late

To adumbrate this pattern fully would take too long, but the principal contours can be sketched. The opening six sections are overtly a celebration, and what they celebrate presumably is a return of the repressed, an ecstatic union of soul and self, of primary and antithetical, or, more simply, they celebrate the American Sublime of influx, of Emersonian self-recognition and consequent self-reliance. What ought to be overwhelmingly present in the first six sections is what Whitman, criticizing Keats, referred to as the great poet's "powerful press of himself." But in these opening sections, the reader confronts instead images of absence rather than of presence; indeed, the reader is led inevitably to the bewildered observation that the poet's absence is so sacred a void that his presence never could hope to fill it. Defensively, Whitman opens with a reaction-formation against his precursor Emerson, which rhetorically becomes not the digressiveness or "permanent parabasis" of German Romantic irony, but the sharper, simpler irony of saying one thing while meaning another. Whitman says "I celebrate" and he cunningly means: "I contract and withdraw while asserting that I expand." Thus in section 2, he evades being intoxicated by an outward fragrance, narcissistically preferring "the smoke of my own breath." This characteristic and beautiful evasiveness intensifies in section 4, where the true self, "the Me myself," takes up a stance in total contradiction to the embracings and urgings that the poet only ostensibly celebrates:

> Apart from the pulling and hauling stands what I am,
> Stands amused, complacent, compassionating, idle, unitary,
> Looks down, is erect, or bends an arm on an impalpable certain rest,
> Looking with side-curved head curious what will come next,
> Both in and out of the game and watching and wondering at it.

If this dialectical evasion is a *clinamen* away from Emerson, then precisely what sort of guilt of indebtedness does it seek to void? Is there a crucial enough difference between the Emersonian and Whitmanian versions of an American Sublime so as to allow Whitman enough breathing-space? I need to digress again, upon antithetical theory and the American Sublime, if I am to answer this question and thus be able to get back to mapping *Song of Myself*. What I want to be able to explain is why Whitman, in section 5, resorts to the image of transparency when he describes the embrace between his self and his soul, and why in section 6 he writes so firmly within the materialist tradition of Epicurus and Lucretius. Epicurus said: "The what is unknowable," and Whitman says he cannot answer the child's question: *What is the grass?* Poetically, he does answer, in a magnificent series of tropes, much admired by the hesitant Hopkins, and progressing from the Homeric: "And now it seems to me the beautiful uncut hair of graves" until we are given the astonishing and very American: "This grass is very dark to be from the white heads of old mothers."

In the 1856, Second Edition of *Leaves of Grass*, Whitman addressed Emerson directly, acknowledging that "it is yours to have been the original true Captain who put to sea, intuitive, positive, rendering the first report, to be told less by any report, and more by the mariners of a thousand bays, in each tack of their arriving and departing, many years after this." But Whitman aspired after strength, and so could not abide in this perfectly accurate tribute. In 1863, in a private notation, full of veneration for the precursor, he subtly described Emerson, perhaps better than even Nietzsche was to describe him:

America in the future, in her long train of poets and writers, while knowing more vehement and luxurious ones, will, I think, acknowledge nothing nearer [than] this man, the actual beginner of the whole procession—and certainly nothing purer, cleaner, sweeter, more canny, none, after all, more thoroughly her own and native. The most exquisite taste and caution are in him, always saving his feet from passing beyond the limits, for he is transcendental of limits, and you see underneath the rest a secret proclivity, American maybe, to dare and violate and make escapades.

By the time he wrote *Specimen Days* (1882), the consequences of misprision had triumphed in Whitman. Emerson was then condemned as having only a gentleman's admiration of power, and as having been an influence upon Whitman just "for a month or so." Five years later, Whitman lied outright, saying: "It is of no importance whether I had read Emerson before starting *L. of G.* or not. The fact happens to be positively that I had *not*." Rather desperately, Whitman went on to say: "*L. of G.'s* word is the body, including all, including the intellect and soul; E's word is mind (or intellect or soul)." Though I will return to this last remark of Whitman's later, in studying his opening swerve away from Emerson, I wish to end these citations from Whitman-on-Emerson by quoting the truest of them, again from *Specimen Days*:

> The best part of Emersonianism is, it breeds the giant that destroys itself. Who wants to be any man's mere follower? lurks behind every page. No teacher ever taught, that has so provided for his pupil's setting up independently—no truer evolutionist.

Here, Whitman has provided antithetical theory with the inevitable trope for Emersonianism or the American Sublime: "it breeds the giant that destroys itself." We need not be surprised to discover that the trope was, however, Emerson's own invention, crucial in the essay *Self-Reliance* (which Whitman certainly *had* read before he wrote *Song of Myself*):

> I affect to be intoxicated with sights and suggestions, but I am not intoxicated. My giant goes with me wherever I go.

We can contrast another Emersonian-Whitmanian giant, a double one indeed, that dominates the opening section of the most Emersonian poem in our literature, *An Ordinary Evening in New Haven*:

I

The eye's plain version is a thing apart,
The vulgate of experience. Of this,
A few words, an and yet, and yet, and yet—

As part of the never-ending meditation,
Part of the question that is a giant himself:
Of what is this house composed"if not of the sun,

These houses, these difficult objects, dilapidate
Appearances of what appearances,
Words, lines, not meanings, not communications,

Dark things without a double, after all,
Unless a second giant kills the first—
A recent imagining of reality,

Much like a new resemblance of the sun,
Down-pouring, up-springing and inevitable,
A larger poem for a larger audience,

As if the crude collops came together as one,
A mythological form, a festival sphere,
A great bosom, beard and being, alive with age.

"The question that is a giant himself" is a late version of the
Stevensian reduction to the First Idea, while the second giant who kills the
first is another reimagining of the otherwise intolerable First Idea or
winter vision. This second giant is the Emersonian giant or daemonic
agent of the American Sublime, a "giant that destroys itself." A
transumption of these giants, difficult as it was to accomplish, is one of the
beautiful achievements of our contemporary master of this tradition, A.R.
Ammons, when he concludes an early venture into the American Sublime
by saying:

that is the
    expression of sea level, the talk of giants,
of ocean, moon, sun, of everything,
spoken in a dampened grain of sand.

Those giants carry me, at last, into my promised theoretical digression, after which I intend to make a return to *Song of Myself* where I left it, in its first six sections. Giantism, as a trope, whether in Milton, or in Emerson and his descendants, is related to sightlessness, or rather to a repressive process that substitutes itself for tropes and defenses of *re-seeing*, which I take as a synonym for *limitation*, in my particular sense of the Lurianic *zimzum* or "contraction." To recapitulate a distinction made at the start of *A Map of Misreading*, "revisionism" as a word and as a notion contains the triad of re-seeing, re-esteeming or re-estimating, and re-aiming, which in Kabbalistic terms becomes the triad of contraction, breaking-of-the-vessels, and restitution, and in poetic terms the triad of limitation, substitution, and representation. In these terms, sublimation is a *re-seeing* but repression is a *re-aiming*, or, rhetorically, a metaphor re-sees, that is, it changes a perspective, but an hyperbole *re-aims*, that is, redirects a response.

Even so, an irony re-sees, but a synecdoche re-aims; a metonymy reduces a seeing, but a metalepsis redirects a purpose or desire. In re-seeing, you have translated desire into an act, but in re-aiming, you have failed to translate, and so what you re-aim is a desire. In poetic terms, *acting is a limitation, but desiring is a representation.* To get back from an act to a desire, or to translate a desire into an act, you must re-estimate and re-esteem either act or desire, and by preferring one to the other, you substitute and so shatter the vessels, break and remake the forms again. Another way of putting this is that a revisionary ratio (trope, defense, image) of limitation is closer to an act than to a desire, but a ratio of representation is closer to a desire or repurposing. To use Kenneth Burke's rhetorical terms, of his four Master Tropes, three (irony, metonymy, metaphor; or dialectic, reduction, perspective) are acts of re-seeing, or simple revisionism, while the fourth (synecdoche or representation) is a desire that redirects purpose, and so is a more complex revisionism. Hyperbole and transumption, as successively more heightened representations, are even more strongly tropes of desire.

Expanding Burke to my purposes, I would say that the prime poetic acts are to make presence more dialectical, to reduce differences, and to change our sense of otherness, of being elsewhere, by perspectivizing it. But the prime poetic desires are to be elsewhere, to be different, and to represent that otherness, that sense of difference and of being elsewhere. I would add, as a surmise, that all of us tend to value poetry more for its desires than for its acts, more for its re-aimings or purposiveness, than for its re-seeings. The Sublime, and particularly the American Sublime, is not a re-seeing but rather is a re-aiming. To achieve the Sublime is to experience a greater desire than you have known before, and such an achievement results from a failure to translate anterior or previous desires into acts. As the Emersonian, American sense of anteriority was greater, ours being the Evening Land, even so the Sublime heightened, or repression augmented, if only because there was more unfulfilled desire to repress.

Emerson forgets English poetic tradition, in his most Sublime prose passages, because his purpose is to present something else, an American individuality. This forgetting is not primarily a limitation, that is, a calling attention to a lack both in language and in the self. Rather, this forgetting aims to reinforce a potentiality for response in the self, though unfortunately no act of forgetting can do much to reinforce a potentiality in language. Emerson therefore founds his Sublime upon a refusal of history, particularly literary history. But no poetic Sublime can be so founded without a compensating isolation and even a crippling sublimation of the self, as Wordsworth's Sublime already had demonstrated. Emerson's new desire forgets the old desire, only at the expense of increasing the distance between desire and act, which is probably the psychic reason why Emerson's prose style is so discontinuous. More even than Nietzsche, Emerson's unit of thought and expression tends to be the aphoristic, single sentence. Yet Emerson, unlike Nietzsche, was primarily an orator, a proud and knowing continuator of the Oral Tradition. Nietzsche is consistent with his own deepest purposes in so emphasizing the aphoristic energy of *writing*, whereas Emerson gives us the endless paradox of a mode of inspired "speech" that resorts always to aphorisms, which is what we can accept happily in Oscar Wilde, yet bewilders us in the American moralist.

The Emersonian or American Sublime, I am asserting, differs from the British or the Continental model not by a greater or lesser degree of positivity or negativity, but by a greater acceptance or affirmation of discontinuities in the self. Only Emerson could permit himself, within one page of the same essay (*Circles*), first to say: "There is no outside, no inclosing wall, no circumference to us," but then to cry out: "Alas for this infirm faith, this will not strenuous, this vast ebb of a vast flow! I am God in nature; I am a weed by the wall," and then outrageously to add: "The only sin is limitation." At the end of so discontinuous a Sublime, so strong yet so uncertain a repression, there must be also a heightened sense of the void, of the near-identity between the Sublime as a solitary ecstasy and the terrible raptures of nihilism, Nietzsche's *unheimlich* guest hovering by the door. Emerson's odyssey did not end in madness, and yet Emerson burned out, soon after the Civil War. Nietzsche became insane, Emerson became prematurely senile, Wordsworth merely became very boring, and so alas did Whitman, after *Drum-Taps*. In thirty years punctuated by many influxes of sublimity, Emerson went from saying: "It is a mischievous notion that we are come late into nature; that the world was finished a long time ago" to saying, in 1866: "There may be two or three or four steps, according to the genius of each, but for every seeing soul there are two absorbing facts,—*I and the Abyss.*" For "the Abyss," we can read: tradition, history, the other, while for "I" we can read "any American." The final price paid for the extreme discontinuities of Emersonian vision is that we are left with a simple, chilling formula: the American Sublime equals *I and the Abyss.*

I return finally to the opening six sections of *Song of Myself*, with their defensive swerve away from Emerson, even as they appear to celebrate an Emersonian realization of the self. Whitman, not a poet-of-ideas like Emerson, but more traditionally a poet (however odd that sounds), seems to have known implicitly that a poetic representation of a desire tends to be stronger (that is, less limiting) than a poetic representation of an act. *Song of Myself*, in its beginnings, therefore substitutes the desires for union between split parts of the self, and between self and soul, for the acts of union proper, whatever those might be. Whitman wishes to originate his own mode, but he cannot do so without some discontinuity with Emerson, a prophet of discontinuity, and how do you cast off an influence that itself denounces all influence? Emersonianism urges itself to breed a giant that will destroy itself, but this most gigantic of its giants painfully found himself anticipated in nearly every trope, and in every movement of the spirit, a pain that Whitman shared with Thoreau.

It is evident, both from the opening emphases in *Song of Myself*, and from Whitman's comments in *Specimen Days*, on the rival words of precursor and ephebe, that Whitman's intended swerve from Emerson is to deny Emerson's distinction between the Soul and Nature, in which Nature includes all of the NOT ME, "both nature and art, all other men and my own body." Whitman's ME must include his own body, or so he would persuade us. He writes what in 1881 he would title at last *Song of Myself*, and not *Song of the Soul* or even *Song of My Soul.* But the embrace between his soul and his self in section 5, which makes the axis of things appear not opaque but transparent, oddly makes "you my soul" the active partner, and the self, "the other I am," wholly passive in this courtship. If we translate soul as "character" and self as "personality," then we would find it difficult to identify so passive a personality with "Walt Whitman, a kosmos, of Manhattan the son, / Turbulent, fleshy, sensual, eating, drinking and breeding" of section 24. Clearly, there is a division in Whitman between two elements in the self, as well as between self and soul, and it is the first of these divisions that matters, humanly and poetically. Indeed, it was from the first of these divisions that I believe Emerson initially rescued Whitman, thus making it possible for Whitman to become a poet. The "real me" or "me myself" in Whitman could not bear to be touched, ever, except by the maternal trinity of night, death, and the sea, while Walt Whitman, one of the roughs, learned from Emerson to cry: "Contact!" There is a sublime pathos in Whitman making his Epicurean *clinamen* away from Emerson by overproclaiming the body. Emerson had nothing to say about two subjects and two subjects only, sex and death, because he was too healthy-minded to believe that there was much to say about either. Emerson had no sexual problems, and was a Stoic about death.

I return to mapping *Song of Myself*, with its implicit contrast that Whitman, gloriously and plangently, always had much too much to say about sex and death, being in this the ancestor not only of Hart Crane and, perhaps surprisingly, of Wallace Stevens and, these days, of Ammons and Ashbery, but also of such prose obfuscators of sex and death as Hemingway and his egregious ephebe, Norman Mailer. Whitman, surpassing all his descendants, makes of a linked sex–and–death a noble synecdoche for all of existence, which is the figurative design of sections 7–27 of *Song of Myself*. A universalizing flood tide of reversals-into-the-opposite reaches a great climax in section 24, which is an antithetical completion of the self without rival in American poetry, astonishing both for its dignity and its pathos, and transcending any other modern poet's attempt to think and represent by synecdoche. The reader cannot know whether to admire this proclamation more for its power or for its precision:

> Unscrew the locks from the doors!
> Unscrew the doors themselves from their jambs!
>
> Whoever degrades another degrades me,
> And whatever is done or said returns at last to me.
>
> Through me the afflatus surging and surging, through me the current and index.
>
> I speak the pass-word primeval, I give the sign of democracy,
> By God! I will accept nothing which all cannot have their
>   counterpart of on the same terms.
>
> Through me many long dumb voices,
> Voices of the interminable generations of prisoners and slaves,
> Voices of the diseas'd and despairing and of thieves and dwarfs,
> Voices of the threads that connect the stars, and of wombs and of
>   the father-stuff,
> And of the rights of them the others are down upon,

Of the deform'd, trivial, flat, foolish, despised,
Fog in the air, beetles rolling balls of dung.

We can say of this astonishing chant that as completing synecdoche it verges on emptying-out metonymy, reminding us of the instability of all tropes, and of all psychic defenses. Primarily, Whitman's defense in this passage is a fantasy reversal, in which his own fear of contact with other selves is so turned that no outward overthrow of his separateness is possible. It is as though he were denying denial, negating negation, by absorbing every outward self, every outcast of society, history, and even of nature. To say that one will accept nothing which all cannot have their counterpart of on the same terms is indeed to say that one will accept no overthrow from outside oneself, no negation or denial. Whitman, with the genius of his enormous drive towards antithetical completion, can be judged to end the *tessera* phase of his poem in the remarkable triad of sections 25–27. For in section 25, nature strikes back against the poet, yet he is strong enough to sustain himself, but in 26–27 he exhaustedly begins to undergo a kind of passive slide-down of spirit that precludes the fierce *kenosis* or emptying-out of his poethood in sections 28–30. At the end of 27, Whitman confesses: "To touch my person to some one else's is about as much as I can stand." The Whitmanian *kenosis*, in 28–30, appears to make of masturbation a metonymic reduction of the self, where touch substitutes for the whole being, and a pathetic salvation is sought through an exaltation of the earth that the poet has moistened:

A minute and a drop of me settle my brain,
I believe the soggy clods shall become lovers and lamps,
And a compend of compends is the meat of a man or woman,
And a summit and flower there is the feeling they have for each other,
And they are to branch boundlessly out of that lesson until it
    becomes omnific,
And until one and all shall delight us, and we them.

This is the prelude to the most awesome repression in our literature, the greatest instance yet of the American Sublime, sections 31–38. Rather than map the glories of this Sublime, I will examine instead the violent descent into the abyss that culminates it in section 38. Having merged both the fathering force and the universal brotherhood into himself, with terrifying eloquence ("I am the man, I suffer'd, I was there"; and "Agonies are one of my changes of garments"), Whitman pays the fearful price of Emersonian Compensation. Nothing indeed is gotten for nothing:

Enough! enough! enough!
Somehow I have been stunn'd. Stand back!
Give me a little time beyond my cuff'd head, slumbers, dreams, gaping,
I discover myself on the verge of a usual mistake.
That I could forget the mockers and insults!
That I could forget the trickling tears and the blows of the
    bludgeons and hammers!
That I could look with a separate look on my own crucifixion and
    bloody crossing.

I remember now,
I resume the overstaid fraction,
The grave of rock multiplies what has been confided to it, or to
    any graves,
Corpses rise, gashes heal, fastenings roll from me.

Emerson had prophesied a Central Man who would reverse the "great Defeat" of Christ, insisting that "we demand Victory." Whitman, more audacious even than his precursor, dares to present himself both as a repetition of the great Defeat and as the Victory of a Resurrection: "I troop forth replenish'd with supreme power, one of an average unending procession." What are we to do with a hyperbolical Sublime this outrageous? Whitman too is saying: "*I and the Abyss*," despite the self-deception of that "average unending procession." But Whitman's repression is greater, as it has to be, since a crucial part of its anteriority is a primal fixation upon Emerson, a fixation that I want to explore in the conclusion of this chapter once I have concluded my sketchy mapping of the later ratios in *Song of Myself*.

Sections 39–49 are an attempt at a sublimating consolidation of the self, in which Whitman presents us with his version of the most characteristic of High Romantic metaphors, his self as inside reciprocally addressing the natural world as a supposedly answering outside. The final or reductive form of this perspectivizing is summed up in an appropriately entitled poem of Wallace Stevens, *The American Sublime*:

But how does one feel?
One grows used to the weather,

The landscape and that;
And the sublime comes down
To the spirit itself,

The spirit and space,
The empty spirit
In vacant space.

That is to say: the Sublime comes down to the Abyss in me inhabiting the Abyss of space. Whitman's version of this coming down completes his great *askesis*, in section 49:

I hear you whispering there O stars of heaven,
O suns—O grass of graves—O perpetual transfers and promotions,
If you do not say any thing how can I say any thing?
. . . .
Of the turbid pool that lies in the autumn forest,
Of the moon that descends the steeps of the soughing twilight,
Toss, sparkles of day and dusk—toss on the black stems that decay
    in the muck,
Toss to the moaning gibberish of the dry limbs.

I ascend from the moon, I ascend from the night,
I perceive that the ghastly glimmer is noonday sunbeams reflected,
And debouch to the steady and central from the offspring great
    or small.

The steadiness of the central is reached here only through the rhetorical equivalent of sublimation, which is metaphor, the metaphor of two lights, sun and moon, with the sun necessarily dominating, and taking as its tenor the Emersonian "steady and central." I return to the formula for poetic sublimation ventured earlier in this discourse. The sublimating ratio is a limitation because what it concentrates is being evaded, that is, is remembered only in order *not* to be presented, with something else substituted in the presentation. Whitman does not present what he is remembering, his dream of divination, of being a dazzling sunrise greater than the merely natural sun. Instead of this autonomous splendor, he accepts now a perspectivizing, a balancing of "sparkles of day and dusk." His restitution for this *askesis* comes in his great poem's close, in sections 50–52, which form a miraculous transumption of all that has gone before. Yet the Whitmanian metaleptic reversal differs crucially from the Wordsworthian-Tennysonian model, in that it places the burden upon the reader, rather than upon the poet. It is the reader, and not the poet, who is challenged directly to make his belatedness into an earliness. Whitman was to perfect this challenge in *Crossing Brooklyn Ferry*, appropriately called *Sun-Down Poem* when it first appeared in the second *Leaves of Grass*, in 1856. Here, in *Song of Myself*, the challenge is made explicit at the close of section 51: "Will you speak before I am gone? will you prove already too late?" Nowhere in Emerson (and I concede to no reader in my fanatical love of Emerson) is there so strong a representation of the Central Man who is coming as there is in Whitman's self-presentation in section 52. I would select this as the greatest of Emerson's prophecies of the Central Man, from the journals, April 1846:

> He or That which in despair of naming aright, some have called the *Newness*,—as the Hebrews did not like to pronounce the word,—he lurks, he hides, he who is success, reality, joy, power,—that which constitutes Heaven, which reconciles impossibilities, atones for shortcomings, expiates sins or makes them virtues, buries in oblivion the crowded historical past, sinks religions, philosophies, nations, persons to legends; reverses the scale of opinion, of fame; reduces sciences to opinion, and makes the thought of the moment the key to the universe, and the egg of history to come.
>
> ... 'Tis all alike,—astronomy, metaphysics, sword, spade, pencil, or instruments and arts yet to be invented,—this is the inventor, the worth-giver, the worth. This is He that shall come; or, if He come not, nothing comes: He that disappears in the moment when we go to celebrate Him. If we go to burn those that blame our celebration, He appears in them. The Divine Newness. Hoe and spade, sword and pen, cities, pictures, gardens, laws, bibles, are prized only because they were means He sometimes used. So with astronomy, music, arithmetic, castes, feudalism,—we kiss with devotion these hems of his garment,— we mistake them for Him; they crumble to ashes on our lips.

The Newness is Influx, or fresh repression, lurking and hiding, imaged in depth, in burying and in sinking. This daemonic force then projects the past and introjects the future, and yet *not now*, but only in the realm of what *shall come*: "He ... disappears in the moment when we go to celebrate Him," and more than his garment would crumble to ashes on our lips. Whitman, as this Newness, is even more splendidly elusive:

> The spotted hawk swoops by and accuses me, he complains of my gab and my loitering.

I too am not a bit tamed, I too am untranslatable;
I sound my barbaric yawp over the roofs of the world.

The last scud of day holds back for me,
It flings my likeness after the rest and true as any on the shadow'd
wilds,
It coaxes me to the vapor and the dusk.

I depart as air, I shake my white locks at the runaway sun,
I effuse my flesh in eddies, and drift it in lacy jags.

I bequeath myself to the dirt to grow from the grass I love,
If you want me again look for me under your boot-soles.

You will hardly know who I am or what I mean;
But I shall be good health to you nevertheless,
And filter and fibre your blood.

Failing to fetch me at first keep encouraged,
Missing me one place search another,
I stop somewhere waiting for you.

The hawk accuses Whitman of belatedness, of "loitering," but the poet is one with the hawk, "untranslatable" in that his desire is perpetual, always transcending act. There, in the twilight, Whitman arrests the lateness of the day, dissolving the presentness of the present, and effusing his own presence until it is air and earth. As the atmosphere we are to breathe, the ground we are to walk, the poet introjects our future, and is somewhere up ahead, waiting for us to catch up. So far ahead is he on our mutual quest, that he can afford to stop, though he will not tell us precisely where. His dominant trope remains the grass, but this trope is now transumptive, for it is grass not yet grown but "to grow." Implicit in such a trope is the more-than-Emersonian promise that *this* Central Man will not disappear "in the moment when we go to celebrate him."

I end by returning to Whitman's American Sublime of sections 31-38, with specific reference to the grand march of section 33, where the poet says: "I am afoot with, my vision." Here is a part of this audacious mounting into the Sublime:

Solitary at midnight in my back yard, my thoughts gone from me a
long while,

Walking the old hills of Judaea with the beautiful, gentle God by
    my side,
Speeding through space, speeding through heaven and the stars,
Speeding amid the seven satellites and the broad ring, and the
    diameter of eighty thousands miles,
Speeding with tail'd meteors, throwing fire-balls like the rest,
Carrying the crescent child that carries its own full mother in its
    belly,
Storming, enjoying, planning, loving, cautioning,
Backing and filling, appearing and disappearing,
I tread day and night such roads.

I visit the orchards of spheres and look at the product,
And look at quintillions ripen'd and look at quintillions green.

I fly those flights of a fluid and swallowing soul,
My course runs below the soundings of plummets.

I help myself to material and immaterial,
No guard can shut me off, no law prevent me.

As an hyperbolical progression, this sequence is matched only by its
misprision or sublime parody, the flight of the Canon Aspirin in *Notes Toward
a Supreme Fiction*. Whitman's angelic flight breaks down the distinction
between material and immaterial, because his soul, as he precisely says, is
"fluid and swallowing." Similarly, the Canon's angelic flight breaks down the
limits between fact and thought, but the Canon's soul being more limited,
the later angelic flight fails exactly where Whitman's cannot fail. The Canon
imposes orders upon reality, but Whitman discovers or uncovers orders,
because he is discovering himself (even though he does not uncover himself,
despite his constant assertions that he is about to do so). I vary an earlier
question in order to conclude this discourse. Why is Whitman's American
Sublime larger and stronger than either the Sublime of his precursor,
Emerson, or the Sublime of his ephebe, Stevens? In the language of
misprision, this means: why and how is Whitman's poetic repression greater
and more forceful than that of the other major figures in his own tradition?

Whitman's ego, in his most Sublime transformations, wholly absorbs
and thus pragmatically forgets the fathering force, and presents instead the
force of the son, of his own self or, in Whitman's case, perhaps we should say
of his own selves. Where Emerson *urges* forgetfulness of anteriority,
Whitman more strenuously *does* forget it, though at a considerable cost.

Emerson says: "*I and the Abyss*"; Whitman says: "*The Abyss of My Self.*" The second statement is necessarily more Sublime and, alas, even more American.

STEPHEN WHICHER

Circles

About 1840, Emerson entered a period of comparative unsettlement in his thoughts from which proceed some of his most interesting essays. Numerous indications, in them and in his journals, betray his disturbed awareness that the pattern of his first convictions is undergoing an unforeseen modification, and that the various truths he has come to recognize are in radical and permanent conflict with each other. This new mood marks, for example, the most unsettled and unsettling of his *Essays, First Series*, the essay 'Circles.' Largely written new for this volume, it stands on the edge between the earlier and later periods in his thought and shows internal evidence that his thought is in a state of transition.

Its main theme, that 'Intellect is progress forevermore,' is by no means a new thought to him. As his son Edward Emerson suggests, the essay should be read in connection with 'Uriel,' for it also, like the poem, celebrates the subversive power of a new idea. Both say, in effect, 'Beware when the great God lets loose a thinker on this planet.' Both speak for Emerson's pride in the explosive properties of his thought, and his ill-concealed delight at the thought of the havoc he could wreak—if people were once to listen to him. It thus emphatically belongs among his revolutionary utterances. 'I unsettle all things,' he says, by way of warning; but no one can miss the ring of pride.

Yet intermingled with this celebration of the power of thought to

From *Freedom and Fate: An Inner Life of Ralph Waldo Emerson*. © 1953 by the University of Pennsylvania Press.

destroy the routine of society is another note of a less assured kind—a fresh consciousness of impermanence in his own thought. His own convictions too are unsettled. The familiar principle that no belief or institution is final, which he accepted easily as long as he felt himself the innovator, has acquired a new import for him, now that he finds some of his own beliefs losing substance. 'Our life is an apprenticeship,' he begins, 'to the truth that around every circle another can be drawn; ... that there is always another dawn risen on mid-noon, and under every deep a lower deep opens'—a confession whose full force we catch when we recall the use of the same reminiscence of Milton earlier in the journals: '... the common life is an endless succession of phantasms; and long after we have deemed ourselves recovered and sound, light breaks in upon us and we find we have yet had no sane hour. Another morn rises on mid-noon'; and notice also the possible allusion to a line by his young friend, W.E. Channing, that was to become a favorite with him:

If my bark sinks, 'tis to another sea.[1]

A little later we find the exhortation, clearly applicable to his own case: 'Fear not the new generalization. Does the fact look crass and material, threatening to degrade thy theory of spirit? Resist it not; it goes to refine and raise thy theory of matter just as much.' This recalls a similar adjuration in his journals of the same period: 'The method of advance in nature is perpetual transformation. Be ready to emerge from the chrysalis of today, its thoughts and institutions, as thou hast come out of the chrysalis of yesterday.

'Every new thought which makes day in our souls has its long morning twilight to announce its coming.'

The upshot is a renewed stress on the active soul. The thought in the strength of which he took up his revolutionary position—that positive power was all—is now in turn shaken by the growing realization that negative power, or circumstance, is half. As a consequence he feels momentarily thrown back on the perception of the moment. 'No facts are to me sacred; none are profane; I simply experiment, an endless seeker with no Past at my back.' In a similar spirit he wrote that part of the essay 'Self-Reliance' which he afterwards said would have been better written, 'Damn consistency!' What matters is not any thought, but the thinking. In the immortal energy of mind lies the compensation for the mortality of truth. 'Valor consists in the power of self-recovery, so that a man cannot have his flank turned, cannot be out-generalled, but put him where you will, he stands. This can only be by his preferring truth to his past apprehension of truth, and his alert acceptance of it from whatever quarter; the intrepid conviction that his laws, his relations to society, his Christianity, his world, may at any time be superseded and decease.'

'Life only avails, not the having lived.... Neither thought nor virtue will keep, but must be refreshed by new today.' This more personal and urgent application of Emerson's old recommendation to live in the present accounts for the unusually restless mood of this essay. He comes for the moment to echo a strain of Romantic thought not generally characteristic of him, the ideal of striving as an end in itself, the Browningesque moral ideal of a *Strebung nach Unendliche*. Life was a pursuit 'of the Unattainable, the flying Perfect, around which the hands of man can never meet, at once the inspirer and the condemner of every success.' It demanded a 'continual effort to raise himself above himself, to work a pitch above his last height....' At whatever human cost, one must keep growing, or die on the vine.

The restlessness of this essay infects even his conception of the Soul itself. The incessant creative energy of the World-Soul, conspicuous in his later evolutionary thinking, appropriately governs this essay. 'Whilst the eternal generation of circles proceeds, the eternal generator abides.... Forever it labors to create a life and thought as large and excellent as itself, but in vain, for that which is made instructs how to make a better.' Its incessant creative labor sets man a strenuous example. To live in the soul, to follow nature, is to be continuously creative, and never to pause or rest. 'In nature every moment is new; the past is always swallowed and forgotten; the coming only is sacred. Nothing is secure but life, transition, the energizing spirit.... People wish to be settled; only as far as they are unsettled is there any hope for them.'

This essay shows signs that Emerson at the time of writing was appreciably unsettled; but that there is any hope for him, in the sense in which he means it here, is more doubtful. The eternal generator is always alive and changes only in his works. But the radical defect of man, the creator in the finite, is his incapacity to maintain his creative force. 'The only sin is limitation'—but this is original sin beyond the power of grace. A limitary instinct opposes the expansive one, and the counteraction of the two forms the chequered pattern of human life. Here Emerson stresses the expansive force, the ground of hope. But the weight of his experience as a whole told on the other side. Every man believes that he has a greater possibility—but every man learns that it is beyond his reach. 'Alas for this infirm faith, this will not strenuous, this vast ebb of a vast flow! I am God in nature; I am a weed by the wall.'

Here is Emerson's deepest disillusionment, deeper than his disaffection with the ideal of great action, though bound up with it: the infirmity of faith. The experience of the Deity in the soul, that seems when present to 'confer a sort of omnipresence and omnipotence which asks nothing of duration, but sees that the energy of the mind is commensurate with the work to be done, without time,' is inherently and necessarily transient and confers in the long run nothing but a tantalizing promise and a glorious memory. It lifts one above circumstances, beyond all limits, out of time; yet it is itself subject to time, limits, and circumstance and obeys its own insurmountable laws of ebb and flow. Time and experience are teaching Emerson to respect their dominion. His transcendentalism is steadily giving way to a basic empiricism—one which, though it includes and stresses man's peculiar experience of the Soul, nevertheless pragmatically recognizes the priority of experience over 'Reality.'

At the heart of this later empiricism is a new respect for time. Originally, part of the revolution to which he had looked forward was a release from subjection to time. As he wrote in 1838: 'A great man escapes out of the kingdom of time; he puts time under his feet.' His revolt against tradition had been designed to cut the traces that bound him to history and bring him to live, not in the kingdom of time, but in direct contact with the divine life beyond and above time. 'Man ... cannot be happy and strong until he ... lives with nature in the present, above time.'

'A moment is a concentrated eternity,' he wrote in 1836. The phrase points up the paradox implicit in his ambition to live in a present above time. He did not wish to be rapt into eternity, but to live in an Eternal Now. He at first thought of his Eternal Now as a permanent condition of poise and self-sufficiency, like the motionless center of a moving wheel. But actually, since his eternity was a moment, at every moment eternity slipped away from him. His ambition to live in the present, above time, meant that every present moment was a new crisis, without support from the one just past nor help for the one to come. Eventually, Emerson was brought to admit the fallacy of his notion of an Eternal Now, and to concede that all his life, ecstasies as well as prosaic details, was and must be subject to the passage of time.

From the 1840's onward dates his intense consciousness of the unceasing onward flow of time, a flowing that comes to signify to him, not the perpetual creative revolution celebrated in 'Circles,' but rather the stream of everything that runs away. He was often understandably distressed by this incessant flux. 'If the world would only wait one moment, if a day could now and then be intercalated, which should be no time, but pause and landing-place, a vacation during which sun and star, old age and decay, debts and interest of money, claims and duties, should all intermit and be suspended for the halcyon trance.... But this on, on, forever onward, wears out adamant.' The evanescence and lubricity of all objects is lamented in 'Experience' as the most unhandsome part of our condition.

Yet 'even in the midst of his moods of regret,' F. O. Matthiessen has pointed out, 'that the days were slipping past without fulfillment, he did not doubt that his course was right. Out of the depth of his consent to his lot welled up the opposite mood, his dilation in response to the flux.' Perhaps the best expression of this consent to the universal flowing is his poem 'Two Rivers.' The finished poem is only a dilution of the first impromptu prose 'thought':

'Thy voice is sweet, Musketaquid, and repeats the music of the rain, but sweeter is the silent stream which flows even through thee, as thou through the land.

'Thou art shut in thy banks, but the stream I love flows in thy water, and flows through rocks and through the air and through rays of light as well, and through darkness, and through men and women.

'I hear and see the inundation and the eternal spending of the stream in winter and in summer, in men and animals, in passion and thought. Happy are they who can hear it.'

An admission that his spiritual life was subject to time may seem a small concession, particularly as in a part of his mind he had always known that it was so. 'As the law of light is, fits of easy transmission and reflexion, such is also the soul's law,' he had written in 1833, and quoted Wordsworth:

'Tis the most difficult of tasks to keep
Heights which the soul is competent to gain.

Forty years later, in his essay 'Inspiration,' he was still quoting the same lines from Wordsworth and conceded, as the sun of a lifetime's wisdom, that 'what we want is consecutiveness. 'T is with us a flash of light, then a long darkness, then a flash again.' And in this essay, as at previous times, he explores the means of cultivating inspiration and suggests some nine disciplines or circumstances favorable to it. In his search for the 'modus' of inspiration faith and scepticism were always mixed and changed only in their proportions. But that small change made all the difference.

The extent of that change becomes more apparent when we notice that, in this late essay, two of the primary conditions he lays down for inspiration are health and youth. 'We must prize our own youth. Later, we want heat to execute our plans: the good will, the knowledge, the whole armory of means are all present, but a certain heat that once used not to fail, refuses its office, and all is vain until this capricious fuel is supplied.' And again, 'Health is the first muse....' So in 1845 he speaks of genius as before he spoke of heroism: 'Genius consists in health, in plenipotence of that "top of condition" which allows of not only exercise but frolic of faculty.'

He has come almost to concede the natural basis of inspiration. As he notes in this essay, 'It seems a semi-animal heat; as if tea, or wine, or sea-air, or mountains, or a genial companion, or a new thought suggested in book or conversation could fire the train, wake the fancy and the clear perception.' In the 1840's he more and more often ascribes the power of performance, not to an influx of the divine, but to animal spirits; and, whereas he speaks of the first with hope, of the last he uses almost a valetudinarian tone. 'The capital defect of my nature for society ... is the want of animal spirits. They seem to me a thing incredible, as if God should raise the dead. I hear of what others perform by their aid, with fear.' There is some pathos in Emerson's never wholly daunted quest for the means to stir an instinct which at the same time he knew to depend on a vital force which he could never win. The note is perceptible in such a poem as 'Bacchus.' It is epitomized in a wry entry in his Journal for 1842: 'I have so little vital force that I could not stand the dissipation of a flowing and friendly life; I should die of consumption in three months. But now I husband all my strength in this bachelor life I lead; no doubt shall be a well-preserved old gentleman.'

Emerson's recognition of the affinity of the natural vigor of youth and inspiration appears surprisingly early, in one of the most enlightening of his unpublished lectures, the sixth of his course on *Human Life*, called 'The Protest.' Here he expounds, already a little reminiscently, his own protest against the actual. He speaks of it not as his own, but as that of the Youth, and we infer from the lecture that the youth's protest against society is not altogether Emerson's. He is already too old to share the youth's single-minded zeal; he is an 'old stager of society,' the youth 'fantastic' and 'extravagant.' Yet Emerson's tone is not one of superiority, but rather one of envy. 'The heart of Youth is the regenerator of society; the perpetual hope; the incessant effort of recovery.... Well for it if it can abide by its Protest.... The world has no interest so deep as to cherish that resistance....

'[The young] alone have dominion of the world, for they walk in it with a free step.... Each young soul ... represents the Soul and nothing less.'

The lecture should be read together with 'Circles,' of which it is a forerunner. There also Emerson praises 'Infancy, youth, receptive, aspiring, with religious eye looking upward,' which 'counts itself nothing and abandons itself to the instruction flowing from all sides.' In 'Circles' youth is the condition of creative energy; correspondingly, 'old age seems the only disease.... We call it by many names,—fever, intemperance, insanity, stupidity and crime; they are all forms of old age; they are rest, conservatism, appropriation, inertia; not newness, not the way onward. We grizzle every day.'

In the essay, youth and age are not a matter of birthdays, but are spiritual principles that divide life between them. When we live with the soul, we are young; when we fall away from it, we fall again into the power of time. Yet the metaphor is a powerful one, since it recalls the power of time at the moment that it denies it. If the presence of the soul always brings youth, yet youth is the time when the soul best loves to be present. Time is the enemy of faith. In the same manner Emerson contrasted morning and evening, as when he spoke of his morning wishes in 'Days.' 'That is morning, to cease for a bright hour to be a prisoner of this sickly body, and to become as large as nature.'

In 'Circles' Emerson defies time. 'This old age ought not to creep on a human mind,' he asserts. 'I see no need of it. Whilst we converse with what is above us, we do not grow old, but grow young.' And the original journal entry continues, 'Is it possible a man should not grow old? I will not answer for this crazy body. It seems a ship which carries him through the waves of this world and whose timbers contract barnacles and dry-rot, and will not serve for a second course. But I refuse to admit this appeal to the old people we know as valid against a good hope. For do we know one who is an organ of the Holy Ghost?' 'The World-Soul' echoes this denial of age.

> Spring still makes spring in the mind
>> When sixty years are told;
> Love wakes anew this throbbing heart,
>> And we are never old ...

Courageous words! But in 'The Protest' we find a different and less happy account of the part played in life by 'old age.' The lecture attempts to explain the opposition the youth encounters and in so doing elaborates an Emersonian version of the Fall of Man. For once Emerson blames, not society and the slavish actual, but a failure of force, complementary to inspiration, inherent in every individual.

> What is the front the world always shows to the young Spirit? Strange to say, The Fall of Man....
> ... There is somewhat infirm and retreating in every action; a pause of self-praise: a second thought. He has done well and he says, I have done well, and lo! this is the beginning of ill. He is encumbered by his own Past. His past hour mortgages the present hour. Yesterday is the enemy of Today....

This Pause is fatal. Sense pauses: the soul pauses not. In its world is incessant onward movement. Genius has no retrospect. Virtue has no memory. And that is the law for man. Live without interval: if you rest on your oars, if you stop, you fall. He only is wise who thinks now; who reproduces all his experience for the present exigency; as a man stands on his feet only by a perpetual play and adjustment of the muscles....

This old age; this ossification of the heart; this fat in the brain; this degeneracy; is the Fall of Man.

Here Emerson recognizes that the life of the Soul must be without interval, as he does in 'Circles'; but he recognizes, too, the impossibility of such a life for man, subject as he is to an 'old age' that must keep him from ever becoming part or parcel of God. We can see in this lecture that he has begun to notice an effect of time more inexorable than the quick end it brings to any particular moment of inspiration—the long slow ebb of his power to rise to inspiration at all. The process of growing old was a long declension from his birthright. Read autobiographically, the lecture has considerable poignancy.

With this submission to time and fate, all that Emerson called condition came to assume a reality for him that rivaled that of the Soul. From identifying his real self primarily with the divine Self within him and dismissing the rest as outer shell, temporary and apparent, he came to recognize that his real self was his whole contradictory nature, divine potentiality and mortal limits together. 'Then the fact that we lie open to God, and what may he not do!

'But no, we can predict very well that, though new thoughts may come, and cheer, and gild, they shall not transport us. There are limits to our mutability. Time seems to make these shadows that we are, tough and peaked.' As F. I. Carpenter has wisely remarked, 'He changed his allegiance from the world of pure thought to that of experience.'

This change marks the end of any real belief on Emerson's part in the rationality of life. Always baffled by the problem of the Individual, he now found himself so inextricably involved in contradictions that he made inconsistency the test of true speech. 'We must reconcile the contradictions as we can, but their discord and their concord introduce wild absurdities into our thinking and speech. No sentence will hold the whole truth, and the only way in which we can be just, is by giving ourselves the lie.... All the universe over, there is but one thing, this old Two-Face, creator-creature, mind-matter, right-wrong, of which any proposition may be affirmed or denied.'

Once he had accepted the defeat of his first hopes, he regularly took for granted the inherent absurdity of the human situation.

But the defeat of his early dreams of victory must not be overstated. The promise of the Soul remained, though all experience told against it. With the loss of his immediate expectations he appealed to the indefinite future; he retreated in good order to a prepared position. The individual seeks for the means to rise to a heroic life—in vain; he abstains from routine, ceases to put up bars and impediments, and waits for the rightful flood of Power. Nothing happens. What then? 'Our philosophy is to *wait*. We have retreated on Patience, transferring our oft-shattered hope now to larger and eternal good.' 'Patience,—patience,' was the counsel even of the American scholar. The transcendentalist had learned the same lesson: 'Patience, and still patience.' This was still the last word in Emerson's report on 'Experience': 'Patience and patience, we shall win at the last.' He had to concede, 'We have no one example of the poetic life realized, therefore all we say seems bloated.' Yet 'to my soul the day does not seem dark, nor the cause lost.... Patience and truth, patience with our own frost and negations, and few words must serve.... If our sleeps are long, if our flights are short, if we are not plumed and painted like orioles and Birds of Paradise, but like sparrows and plebean birds, if our taste and training are earthen, let that fact be humbly and happily borne with.... Perhaps all that is not performance is preparation, or performance that shall be.'

And beneath this consent to his long sleep we can still hear mutterings of the old defiance. Emerson's faith in the greatness of man was not destroyed, but driven underground. If he came to concede the inescapable power of the actual, to believe in fate, he never accommodated his claims to this acknowledged fact. He recognized his empirical limitations but, like a deposed monarch, gave up none of his pretensions to sovereignty, for all that he could perceive no way to attain his throne. '... there ought to be no such thing as Fate,' he wrote one year after the above passage. 'As long as we use this word, it is a sign of our impotence and that we are not yet ourselves.... whilst this Deity glows at the heart, and by his unlimited presentiments gives me all Power, I know that to-morrow will be as this day, I am a dwarf, and I remain a dwarf. That is to say, I believe in Fate. As long as I am weak, I shall talk of Fate; whenever the God fills me with his fulness, I shall see the disappearance of Fate.'

One ground at least of his never-waning interest in great men was his hope to see achieved in him 'that shall come' the success to the senses which his lack of vital force forbade in him. And the basis of this hope of a vicarious success to the senses is the fact that, to the soul, he is a victor now. No concessions to the actual can affect or dim the Deity that glows at the heart and gives him all power. Emerson was thinking of that 'Religious Intellect,' Charles King Newcomb, but also speaking for himself, when he quoted 'Benedict' in 'Worship': 'I am never beaten until I know that I am beaten.... in all the encounters that have yet chanced, I have not been weaponed for that particular occasion, and have been historically beaten; and yet I know all the time that I have never been beaten; have never yet fought, shall certainly fight when my hour comes, and shall beat.'

'I am *Defeated* all the time; yet to Victory I am born.'

Note

1. A more hopeful expression in its context than it seems by itself:

I am not earth-born, though I here delay;
Hope's child, I summon infiniter powers,
And laugh to see the mild and sunny day
Smile on the shrunk and thin autumnal hours.
I laugh, for Hope hath happy place with me:
If my bark sinks, 'tis to another sea.

LAWRENCE I. BUELL

Reading Emerson for the Structures: The Coherence of the Essays

Emerson has never been taken very seriously as an artist of wholes. Even some of his best friends, like Alcott, claimed that he could be read as well backwards as forwards, and the best recent critic of his style agrees that he was primarily "a worker in sentences and single verses."[1] Indeed, Emerson himself admitted that his essays lacked continuity. Nor did this disturb him greatly, for in his study of other authors he himself "read for the lustres";[2] and in his critical theory he made much of the importance of symbolism and analogy but had little to say about form. Likewise, as a lecturer he was apt to make up his discourse as he went along, shuffling and reshuffling his papers as he spoke. Even if he had wanted to compose an orderly lecture, his method of composition by patching together passages from his journals would seem to have been an almost insuperable handicap.

This weight of evidence, however, has not kept a growing minority of Emerson's readers from insisting that there is an authentic and sophisticated unity to at least some of his prose. "The Poet," "Self-Reliance," "Art," and especially Nature and "Experience" have all been defended as intricately-structured wholes.[3] Unfortunately, these defenses have labored under two sorts of disadvantages, which have kept their conclusions from carrying the weight they deserve. First, they have usually emphasized very general and abstract patterns in the essays: "dialectical unity," Plato's twice-bisected line,

---

From *The Quarterly Journal of Speech* 58, no. 1 (February 1972). © 1972 by the Speech Communication Association.

"upward" movement, and the like. *Nature* treats its topics on an ascending order in the scale of being; the chapters in *Essays, First Series* are organized on the principle of complimentary pairs—few would dispute such claims as these. What is at issue, rather, is Emerson's control over his subject from section to section, paragraph to paragraph, especially after *Nature*, which is much more explicitly blocked out and argued than the essays. A student of mine put the problem exactly when he said that it's easy enough to see Emerson clearly from a distance but as you get close everything becomes foggy.

Secondly, previous studies of Emersonian structure have not taken into account the process of composition from journal to lecture to essay. Therefore they have not been able to speak directly to the assumption that Emerson failed to synthesize his raw materials where Thoreau, in *Walden*, succeeded. To know where Emerson succeeds and fails in composition, one has to catch him in the act.

This paper, accordingly, will attempt to pin down the extent to which Emerson's essays have continuity, taking their genesis into account when it is useful, and disregarding for the moment the metaphysical implications of Emersonian structure (*Nature* as scale of being, "Nominalist and Realist" as bi-polar unity, etc.), important as these implications are. I do not mean to argue that Emerson mastered form as he did the aphorism; but I would contend that he was far more in control than at first appears, and that the appearance of formlessness is to a large extent a strategy on Emerson's part calculated to render his thoughts more faithfully and forcefully than direct statement would permit. The same holds true, I suspect, for a number of other literary artists who also seem positively to cultivate haphazardness as a stylistic attribute: e.g., Montaigne, Hazlitt, and Robert Burton.

1

In Emerson's case it is certainly clear that the dense, obscure style for which he is best known was a deliberate choice. Most of his early sermons are plain and lucid, sometimes to the point of formula, and in later life he was quite capable of the same style when he pleased, as in the "Historical Discourse at Concord," a number of his printed lectures, and most of *English Traits*. Whereas there is a real doubt whether Walt Whitman could have written a decent poem in conventional metre, there is no question that Emerson knew, and could use, all the techniques of conventional prose style.

As to the organization of Emerson's mature essays, it is likewise fair to say: (1) that there is usually more order than we at first notice, and (2) that Emerson provides enough clues to ensure continuity, though in a studiously offhand, and sometimes downright misleading manner. We read the first nine pages of "Intellect" with a sense of wandering, when all at once appears the general proposition which snaps the essay into a degree of focus: "In the intellect constructive ... we observe the same balance of two elements as in intellect receptive" (*W*, II, 334), and we see that Emerson has been developing this general distinction all the while. Or in "Self-Reliance" we come upon: "The other terror that scares us from self-trust is our consistency" (*W*, II, 56). The *other* terror? Oh yes—conformity. But it was introduced, six pages before, in simple antithesis to self-reliance, with no indication to the effect "now, reader, we shall discuss the two threats to self-reliance." But presently comes the conclusion: "I hope in these days we have heard the last of conformity and consistency" (*W*, II, 60), and the ten pages spring together as a unit—not clarifying all the vagaries therein, but reassuring us that the Ariadne's thread is still in hand. Emerson could easily have guided his reader somewhat more, but of course he could not spend the day in explanation.

These intimations of order, which are continually turning up in the essays, encourage us to search for more. "If you desire to arrest attention," Emerson writes in his journal, "do not give me facts in the order of cause & effect, but drop one or two links in the chain, & give me with a cause, an effect two or three times removed."[4] This is a far better description of his method, overall, than "infinitely repellent particles,"[5] for upon close examination of the essays one can find a number of recurring devices used by Emerson both to supply and to conceal continuity.

The one just illustrated might be called the "buried outline." The key is either withheld for several pages, as in the two essays above, or thrown out so offhandedly that one is likely to miss it, as in "The Poet," where the plan for the essay is tucked into a part of the last sentence in the long exordium. "Experience" is an especially provoking case. "Where do we find ourselves?" the essay begins (*W*, III, 45). Where indeed? Not until the beginning of the second section do we learn that the first has been about "Illusion"; indeed, a previous hint suggests that "Surface" is the subject (*W*, III, 48). And the final organization of the essay is not clarified until near the end, when Emerson draws up a list of the seven topics he has covered (*W*, III, 82).

Actually, the reader is most fortunate to get such an exact list from Emerson; not only do all the items apply, they are even given in the right order. Possibly he is atoning for the prefatory motto (*W*, III, 43), which also contains a sevenfold list, but one which corresponds only in part to the essay's structure. The reader who approaches the essay with it as a guide is bound to be misled. This is a second typical Emersonian tactic for "providing" structure—the careless list. Along with his passion for drawing up rosters of great men, immortal books, natural facts, and the like, seems to have gone an abhorrence for following them up. "Self-Reliance," he predicts, will work revolutions in men's "religion," "education," "pursuits," "modes of living," "association," "property," and "speculative views" (*W*, II, 77), and he starts to go down the list. But he gets through only four items, of which the last three turn out to be "travel," "art," and "society." In "Culture" Emerson is a little more accurate: he lists four antidotes to "egotism" ("books," "travel," "society," "solitude") (*W*, VI, 139) and covers all of them. But they might just as well have been called "education," "travel," "city," and "country."

Even if one concedes the worst to Emerson's detractors, it is inconceivable that the sloppy way he uses lists could be accidental. The device is too simple. He could have done better as a schoolboy. Surely Emerson is inexact on purpose, either to suggest that demonstration of his principle is endless (as in the long list in "Self-Reliance," which is only half followed up), or, more commonly, to give a tentativeness to his subject. "I dare not assume to give their order, but I name them as I find them in my way," he says of the lords of life in "Experience" (*W*, III, 83). The motto proves his point—there they simply occur to him in a different way. The inaccurate list gives Emerson the fluid framework he needs to suggest both that his ideas have a coherence and that they are in a state of flux. Even when he categorizes precisely, as in *Nature*, he likes to add a disclaimer. Nature's "multitude of uses," he says, "all admit of being thrown into one of the following classes ..." (*W*, I, 12). As if the act of classification, though necessary, were distasteful to him.

A third way in which Emerson uses and conceals structure is to develop a point without ever stating it. Consider this progression from "Spiritual Laws." (Brackets indicate material adapted from lectures and journals.)

[... 'A few strong instincts and a few plain rules' suffice us.]

[My will never gave the images in my mind the rank they now take. The regular course of studies, the years of academical and professional education have not yielded me better facts than some idle books under the bench at the Latin School. What we do not call education is more precious than that which we call so. We form no guess, at the time of receiving a thought, of its comparative value. And education often wastes its effort in attempts to thwart and balk this natural magnetism, which is sure to select what belongs to it.]

In like manner our moral nature is vitiated by any interference of our will. People represent virtue as a struggle, and take to themselves great airs upon their attainments, and the question is everywhere vexed when a noble nature is commended, whether the man is not better who strives with temptation. But there is no merit in the matter. [Either God is there or He is not there.] [We love characters in proportion as they are impulsive and spontaneous. The less a man thinks or knows about his virtues the better we like him. Timoleon's victories are the best victories, which ran and flowed like Homer's verses, Plutarch said. When we see a soul whose acts are all regal, graceful and pleasant as roses, we must thank God that such things can be and are, and not turn sourly on the angel and say 'Crump is a better man with his grunting resistance to all his native devils.']

[Not less conspicuous is the preponderance of nature over will in all practical life.] (*W*, II, 132–134).[6]

Not until the end of this sequence, if at all, do we begin to see how well-controlled it is. At first the initial paragraph transition comes as a shock—seemingly one of those instances in which Emerson was unable to dovetail two blocs of thought taken from lectures. His argument, a defense of total spontaneity, reinforces this suspicion. So may the next transition ("In like manner ..."), which is almost as baffling as the one before. It is not clear to what "moral nature" is being compared. Like what? Like education? Like the Latin School? But eventually one sees that Emerson is developing a familiar threefold sequence: never explicitly stated, as, e.g., "The mind grows by nature, not by will." Had Emerson written this, he would have been almost pedantically straightforward—which is probably why he didn't.

As it is, the clues in the opening sentence of the next paragraph probably will not suffice to enlighten the reader as to what Emerson is about, because he immediately goes off on another tack. Rather than develop his second point at once, he turns back to dispense with the popular view ("People represent ..."), and his attack takes the form of a battery of aphorisms which are sufficiently oblique to the opening sentence and to each other as to force the reader to strain for the connection. The statement, "Our moral nature is vitiated by any interference of our will," is vague and self-contradictory, and the vatic pronouncement, "Either God is there or he is not there," hardly clarifies matters. Both the tactic of veering away from an initial statement and then working back to it, and the tactic of fanning out from a statement with a barrage of apothegms (to be brought back abruptly, oftentimes, at the start of a new paragraph) are also typical of Emerson. Since the first three sentences of the paragraph have no apparent antecedent in journal or lecture, it would seem that the former strategy was deliberately manufactured for the occasion.

But is the rest of the paragraph under control? To be sure, some of it is memorable, but is it any more than a bag of duckshot? Even where a connection may be traced from point to point there may be no real development. In much of the passage Emerson seems to repeat himself rather than move forward. But again a close look shows more sophistication than at first appears. Though the last five sentences could be rearranged, there is a logic to their order: from the divine to the homely and back again, from "God" to "characters" in general, to a representative man, to a specific historical example, to a contemporary example which is more earthy and concrete and yet at the same time, by contrasting Crump with a great "soul" or "angel," brings us back to God and clinches Emerson's point about the divine quality of spontaneity. The previous paragraph unfolds with equal delicacy in a reverse fashion. A sudden and particular perception of the speaker's is given perspective by a parallel from his schooldays, which in turn suggests a general theory of education.

Not all passages in the essays will serve my case as well as the one just discussed. On the other hand, there are passages far more intricately designed. Here is one from "Self-Reliance."

> [I suppose no man can violate his nature.] All the sallies of his will are rounded in by the law of his being, as the inequalities of Andes and Himmaleh are insignificant in the curve of the sphere.] Nor does it matter how you gauge and try him. A character is like an acrostic or Alexandrian stanza;—read it forward, backward, or across, it still spells the same thing.] In this pleasing contrite wood-life which God allows me, [let me record day by day my honest thought without prospect or retrospect, and, I cannot doubt, it will be found symmetrical, though I mean it not and see it not.] My book should smell of pines and resound with the hum of insects. [The swallow over my window should interweave that thread or straw he carries in his bill into my web also.] We pass for what we are. [Character teaches above our wills.] Men imagine that they communicate their virtue or vice only by overt actions, and do not see that virtue or vice emit a breath every moment (*W*, II, 58).[7]

Upon first reading, this paragraph seems to consist simply of variations on the theme of the topic sentence. What it says about achieving formal unity without conscious intent sounds like wishful thinking; the speaker seems to be hoping that he built better than he knew. One is tempted to substitute "paragraph" for "character" and take Emerson as encouraging the reader to read him as Alcott suggested. And yet the passage will indeed "be found symmetrical," if we look closely, and the way to see this is by making that very substitution, by seeing a double meaning in "character." The paragraph turns on the pun "character" equals "writing." Every man is defined by his nature, as a landscape in nature is limited by the horizon; and that nature can be read in his "character," as a poem is read. The poet, too, is defined by his landscape (and here Emerson brings the senses of nature as character and nature as countryside together), which if he is true to himself will be found, down to the last straw, in what he writes. For "character," whatever our conscious intention, "communicates" itself in our every "breath" or utterance.

In order to create this impressive piece of double-entendre, Emerson, as my notations show, drew on two and perhaps three lectures, and two journal passages, adding several new aphorisms. And in none of those individual passages is the eventual design more than adumbrated. But surely in synthesizing them Emerson must have known what he was about, judging not only from the effect of the ensemble but the fact that he added the sentence about "my book" and went back to *JMN*, V, after using the same passage in abbreviated form twice previously, to retrieve the metaphor of character as poem.

2

I hope that by now I have succeeded in showing that at his best Emerson was capable of full control over his materials, even when they were very diverse. How consistent that control was throughout a given essay remains to be seen, however. Undoubtedly Emerson had some clear-cut failures, especially in his old age, when like Thoreau he lost the power to synthesize. "Books" is an obvious example; it is little more than a catalogue. Another instance is "Poetry and Imagination," for which manuscripts also survive. These suggest that except for the introductory section, no part of the essay has a fixed and authentic order. The "essay" cannot, for the most part, be considered as much more than a collection of sayings. The last ten pages especially seem to have undergone a last-minute re-shuffle before publication, involving a dozen or so thought-units.

But it is unfair to pick on Emerson in his old age, when Cabot was beginning to take over his editorial work. All the texts arranged by Cabot and Edward Emerson are more or less corrupt anyway, and more than the footnotes of the Centenary Edition indicate, because of the amount of silent cutting and patching that was done to prepare Emerson's lecture notes for publication.[8] Of course, the fact that the unusual desultoriness of "Poetry and Imagination" and other late works does not seem to have bothered critics is a sign that this is what one expects from Emerson.

Nevertheless, close scrutiny of his earlier prose reveals that he did pay a considerable attention to organization, even in some essays which are usually assumed to be formless. A discussion of two such hard cases, "History" and "The Over-Soul," should support this statement.

"History" is Emerson's most ambitious essay. Its scope is wider even than Nature, inasmuch as it traces the operation of cosmic unity-in-diversity in man's past as well as in his present environment. The vastness of this subject leads Emerson to a diffuseness of illustration extraordinary even for him, and practically overwhelming for the reader. The first page or so is highly explicit; the rest seems a maze of redundancy. Still, it has a plan, though with characteristic nonchalance Emerson puts off a direct statement of it until near the close, and even then is misleadingly vague: "... in the light of these two facts, namely, that the mind is One, and that nature is its correlative, history is to be read and written" (W, II, 38). This indicates, hazily, the essay's structure. After a long prologue which treats his themes in miniature (paragraphs 1–6), Emerson shows first that to the perceiving mind, the diverse manifestations of nature and history are governed by the same laws as itself (pars. 7–18) and then the converse proposition, that everything in individual experience is writ large in history and nature (pars. 19–44). In somewhat more detail, the essay can be summarized as follows:

> *Prologue.* The individual mind partakes of the universal mind common to all men (par. 1). Therefore, while in order to understand the mind one must know all of history, which is the record of the mind, the whole of history can be explained from individual experience (2–3). Every experience of ours is duplicated in history; every fact in history is applicable to us (3). This principle of universality in the particular explains our reverence for human life and the laws of property, our identification with what we read (4) and with the "condition" of the great and the "character" of the wise (5); let us then apply this principle to the theory of history as well and take it as a commentary on us, rather than the reverse (6).
>
> *First Proposition* (Unity-in-Diversity). All history has its counterpart in individual experience (7). We must therefore go over the whole ground of history and internalize it to learn its lesson (8–9). All study of antiquity—e.g., ancient and medieval

architecture—is the attempt to reduce "then" to "now" (11–12). Just as man (12) and external nature (13) manifest a unity amid diversity of temperaments and forms, so with history, as in the diversity of Greek culture (14). Further instances of the cosmic principle of unity-in-diversity are the resemblance between human and natural forms (15–16), the similarity of the creative process in diverse areas (17), and the similarity with which great souls and great art affect us (18).

Second Proposition (Diversity-in-Unity). Everything in and of us has its counterpart in the not-me (19). For instance, common experience sometimes takes on cosmic significance (20); everyday objects supply civilization with models for its great architecture (21–24); the conflict in human nature between love of adventure vs. repose has caused the dispute throughout history between nomads and settlers (25). Each individual experiences in himself the primeval world (27), a Grecian period—i.e., a state of natural innocence (28–29), an age of chivalry and an age of exploration (30). Likewise with religious history (30–31): Christianity (32), ancient religion (33), monasticism (34–35), the reformation and its aftermath (36) all express various intuitions and moods in the individual. The same is also true of literature from Greek fable (38) to Goethe (39), from medieval romance (40–41) to Sir Walter Scott (42). Finally, man has affinities with all of nature as well as history. Men like Napoleon need the whole of nature in which to operate (43); and the endeavors of geniuses, and even ordinary people as well, have universal implications (44).

Conclusion (45)—quoted above.

Peroration (46–48).

This précis hardly captures the greatness of Emerson, but it may be argued that an awareness of what it does convey is essential to a just appreciation of that greatness. Otherwise one must picture Emerson simply as a talented aphorist who ran wild for forty pages.

As the summary shows, Emerson did not have total control over his subject. Paragraphs 16–18 are anti-climactic. The peroration is too diffuse. More seriously, Emerson feels obliged to go over his whole ground twice; that at least is the impression created by the preface, whose first three paragraphs splice together the pivotal passages of his 1838 lecture on history, which contains all his essential thoughts on the subject (*EL*, II, 11–15 passim). The sense of redundancy is increased by Emerson's nonchalance in distinguishing between his two propositions (cf. pars. 7, 19, 24, 26), nor is it clear whether some parts of the essay are "about" history, or nature, or the principle of unity-in-diversity underlying both. Finally, need it be said that Emerson never really confronts the question of history's importance? On the one hand, it is all-important, as a clue to our nature; on the other, it is superfluous, since we contain all history within ourselves. One should be prepared for ambivalence on so abstract a point, but he may justly expect at least an explicit statement of the problem.

When all this is deducted, though, it remains that the essay has method. After the first three paragraphs of lecture-in-miniature, Emerson prepares for his first proposition, as he often does, by appeals to common sense experience: the way we regard property, reading, etc., should prepare us for the philosophical view which he is about to outline. He begins proposition two in the same manner, with four personal anecdotes which bear witness to his point. The "argument" in both sections moves, roughly speaking, from this existential level to a variety of limited examples (e.g., Gothic architecture) to something like a comprehensive statement (12–14; 27–44). The nature of that statement differs according to the point. Proposition one, unity-in-diversity, can be stated more simply than proposition two, diversity-in-unity, which necessitates short sketches of the history of society, religion, literature, and science. If this portion of the essay seems prolix it is because as in *Nature* Emerson is trying to apply his principle to all main branches of his subject. Altogether, then, while structure is not Emerson's strongest point in "History," the essay does have a form distinct enough for the careful reader to perceive.

So too, I think, does "The Over-Soul," despite the fact that it has been singled out as an arch-example of discombobulated afflatus. As I shall explain later, I think that the essay does fall apart about three-quarters of the way through, but until then Emerson has his materials well in hand.

The essay begins with a long and stately exordium (pars. 1–2), stitched together mainly from two passages from lectures and one directly from the journals, which supply its three stages of movement: the initial paradox, "our vice is habitual," yet we hope; the question, what is the ground of this hope?; and the preliminary answer, "man is a stream whose source is hidden."[9] The way in which the passage converges to a focus on this metaphor is emphasized by the switch from the general "we" and "man" to the personal "I": "*Man* is a stream whose source is hidden. *Our* being is descending into us from *we* know not whence. The most exact *calculator* has no prescience that somewhat incalculable may not balk the very next moment. I am constrained every moment to acknowledge a higher origin for events than the will I call *mine*" (*W*, II, 268; italics mine). Emerson's supposed reticence and Thoreau's greater self-assertiveness have distracted us from the fact that

Emerson too was adept at the subjective mood, and this is a good instance. The device of funneling in from the abstract to the personal, used now and again in other essays too, makes the passage fall somewhat as a leaf falls, circling, zigzag, into one's hand. Then, as the first-person mood continues for another paragraph, along with the metaphor, it adds a sense of urgency to the previous questions, the urgency of a personal witness.

The essay now proceeds to identify the mysterious source of power (par. 3). It is the Over-Soul, which inheres in everyone and everything and is always accessible to us whether we sense it or not. Again the speaker ends his definition on a personal note: "I dare not speak for it"; but he will try to give some hints.

In the next section, as I see it (pars. 4–13), Emerson tries to indicate the signs of the Soul's operation—how it feels, some of the ways we can identify it, and so forth. The orientation here is mainly empirical ("If we consider what happens in conversation ..."; "Of this pure nature every man is at some time sensible," etc.) At first the discussion is carried on in very general terms: the Soul animates all the faculties (par. 4); it is ineffable but everyone has felt it (5). Then Emerson attempts to particularize: its onset is marked by a suspension of the sense of limitations of time, space, and nature (6–7); it comes not by gradation but in a sudden access of power (8), both in virtue (9) and in intellect (10); it reveals itself through other people, humble as well as lofty (11–12), young as well as old (13). Though Emerson's handling of continuity is not unexceptionable, altogether he manages successfully to co-ordinate the large blocs from three different lectures which furnished him with most of his text for this section. For instance, the paragraph sequences 4–5 and 12–13, each of which involves a juxtaposition of passages from different lectures, sustain the motif of affirmation followed by pietistic diffidence.[10]

After the second of these semi-withdrawals Emerson strikes out in a different direction: "The soul is the perceiver and revealer of truth." Here is another case of the buried outline (even more elusive than in "History," since it is defective as well as soft-pedaled—more of which in a moment). The statement announces a shift of emphasis in the next section (14–24) from the experience of the holy to analysis of the Soul's powers. The shift is by no means total, for at one point Emerson gives a glowing account of the emotion of the sublime (16) and later he describes how to identify the tone of an inspired person (22–23); still, the basic framework of discussion is an anatomy of the Soul's attributes. Emerson distinguishes four. The Soul enables us to perceive truth beneath appearance (14); it reveals Absolute Truth (15–19); it reveals our character to others and vice-versa (20–23); it inspires the acts of genius and, potentially, those of all other men as well (24).

Only the first two of these points, we note, are prefigured in the outline. It is hard to know whether to ascribe this to subtlety or incompetence. That Emerson held them distinctly in his own mind is suggested by the fact that points corresponding to one, three, and four are explicitly distinguished and spelled out in his lecture, "The Doctrine of the Soul" (1838), which is the chief source for this section, while the bulk of point two comes from one short sequence in "Religion" (1840). On the other hand, some of the material from the former work appears in support of a different point in the essay, and the last category in the lecture version, "action," bears but a partial resemblance to "genius." Other features of this section of the essay also suggest a loss of direction: the paragraphs are longer than before, the transitions are weaker (cf. 17–18, 21–22, 23–24), the lecture passages are less spliced.[11] And yet a distinguishable framework is still maintained, as is the former tactic of qualifying the grand claims for the Soul with the enjoinment of personal humility (19, 23).

Until the section's end, that is. At this point, in conclusion to his discussion on genius, Emerson rises to an unexpectedly insistent note: "Why then should I make account of Hamlet and Lear, as if we had not the soul from which they fell as syllables from the tongue?" As usual, pride goes before a fall, for at this point the essay definitely does fall apart, at least temporarily (25–28), under the rising tide of feeling. Beginning with the passage on enthusiasm (16), Emerson's prose has taken on an intoxication which now seems to carry it away. Perhaps this is inevitable, since the subject is now precisely the imperativeness of abandonment: "This energy does not descend into individual life on any other condition than entire possession." The soul must cast off all pretense and open itself humbly and totally to God. For several pages Emerson celebrates this point, reaching a crescendo in paragraph 28:

> Ineffable is the union of man and God in every act of the soul. The simplest person who in his integrity worships God, becomes God; yet for ever and ever the influx of this better and universal self is new and unsearchable. It inspires awe and astonishment. How dear, how soothing to man, arises the idea of God, peopling the lonely place, effacing the scars of our mistakes and disappointments! When we have broken our god of tradition and ceased from our god of rhetoric, then may God fire the heart with his presence. It is the doubling of the heart itself, nay, the infinite enlargement of the heart....

And so on, for another page and a half. Much of the writing here is very fine, notably the next-to-last sentence, but the effect of the whole is chaotic: hyperbolic affirmation ("The simplest person ... becomes God"), heightened by the sense of awe and ineffableness, but shot through also with a sense of longing ("How dear, how soothing ..."; "may God fire the heart with his presence"), so that finally one is conscious both of an exuberance and a desperation in the passage. It is a doxology, but also a *de profundis*, a passionate prayer for the fulfillment of the soul's need. In suggesting, then, that pride led the speaker to a lapse of coherence, I was not being entirely facetious. Once he has swelled to the thought "Why shouldn't I come into my own?", "In what way am I inferior to Shakespeare?" it is quite understandable that he should fall victim to the dualism which he has been holding in check by the affirmation-resignation device previously described. To put the matter in the language of New England theology, Emerson wants to assert, in the Arminian tradition, that preparation (in this case, simplicity and sincerity) will ensure grace; but secretly he senses as well as Jonathan Edwards did that grace is of God and man has no control over its workings. And so the rhetoric of Emerson's hymn to the "entire possession" of the soul by the Soul becomes turbid with undercurrents of frustration.

In the conclusion, however, and the peroration which follows, the essay regains its composure (29–30). "Let man then learn the revelation of all nature and all thought to his heart; this, namely; that the Highest dwells with him"—the tone here is calm, and the problem of dualism is resolved by two sorts of backings-off. First, primary emphasis is placed on an uncontroversial (for Emerson) point: faith is to be determined by experience and not by authority. And second, the very real problem of how inspiration is to come to the soul is circumvented by resorting to generalizations about the process of spiritual growth. "I, the imperfect, adore my own Perfect.... More and more the surges of everlasting nature enter into me.... So come I to live in thoughts and act with energies which are immortal," etc. Logically this is inconsistent with what was said about the soul's onsets being sudden and unpredictable, but emotionally and structurally it provides a graceful conclusion to the essay, which in retrospect is seen to flow like this: exordium; statement of subject; signs of the Soul; attributes of the Soul; preparation for grace; prospects.

3

We have seen that Emerson's prose preserves at least the semblance of order even in many places where it seems aimless. But how much importance should we attach to this fact? After all, it is no compliment to regard the two essays just discussed as attempts at systematic thought, inasmuch as Emerson obscures the central issues of the relation of self to history and soul to Soul.[12] Emerson's vitality, especially for the modern reader, lies in the provocativeness of his *obiter dicta*, not in his powers of reasoning. Yet the impact of his orphic sayings, as I have already suggested, depends partly upon the structure which loosely sustains them. For one thing, the sense of totality enhances one's pleasure in the individual detail, as Emerson himself well knew. "Nothing is quite beautiful alone; nothing but is beautiful in the whole" (*W*, I, 24). Furthermore, the way in which structure appears in Emerson—faintly adumbrated, often concealed, rarely very explicit— happens to be an excellent representation of the peculiar sort of ambivalence Emerson maintained, all his life, toward the idea of totality. Mainly he held to the simple principle of the microcosm, which underlies his theory of symbolism and which is often blamed for aggravating his tendency toward formlessness.[13] But he also entertained at least three other models of universal order, all of which are more specific than the microcosmic principle: 1) nature as operating on a principle of polarity ("Compensation"); 2) nature as an upward flowing through "spires of form" ("Woodnotes," "Nature"); and 3) nature as a book of meanings ("Language"). In short, Emerson's thought ran the whole gamut from complete open-endedness ("In the transmission of the heavenly waters, every hose fits every hydrant" *W*, IV, 121) to complete schematicism ("Natural objects ... are really parts of a symmetrical universe, like words of a sentence; and if their true order is found, the poet can read their divine significance orderly as in a Bible" *W*, VIII, 8). He desires to claim the utmost liberty for the imagination, on the one hand, and to preserve the prospect of a coherent world-order on the other. Against this background, his use of structure is most significant anal appropriate. It furnishes the essays with the same combination of abandonment and unity that he observed in nature.

Indeed many of the essays derive their structures from one or another of Emerson's models of universal order, such as the principle of polarity or the principle of upward flowing, as those who have defended his coherence have pointed out. The two propositions in "History," for instance, are in a sense polar, being opposite ways of viewing the same thing. But I would not want to claim that this pale abstraction is the "subject" of "History," nor, again, that the subject of Nature is the six-fold hierarchy of nature from commodity to spirit. Rather I take it that the subject is the process of discovering the method of history or nature as Emerson sees it. In reading him, one seems meant to feel as he himself felt in reading nature, that "every one of those remarkable effects in landscape which occasionally catch & delight the eye, as, for example, a long vista in woods, trees on the shore of a lake coming quite down to the water, a long reach in a river, a double or triple row of uplands or mountains seen one over the other ... must be the rhetoric of some thought not yet detached for the conscious intellect" (*JMN*, VII, 405). Emerson's rhetoric gives off intimations of order, which the reader seeks to follow up without withering them into formulae.

Though it may be praising Emerson overmuch to compare his structures to those of nature, it remains that his achievement in the area of form has been underrated. In particular, more attention needs to be paid to his habits of composition. Thoreau scholarship is ahead in this respect, doubtless because of the currency of the half-truth that he was the more dedicated artist. As the volumes of Emerson's journals, miscellaneous notebooks, and lectures continue to appear, making the record of his revisions more available than it has been, we may expect a general reappraisal of Emerson as an artist of wholes as well as parts.

Such a reappraisal, however, should not be apologetic, should not make the mistake of seizing upon the ordering elements in Emerson's prose as if they were the sole thing which saves his essays from disaster. We must also accept the validity, at least for him, of the open-ended kind of discourse Emerson was attempting. It was his temperamental preference to be suggestive, rather than definitive; this was also what was expected in the lyceum; and the empirical fact is that his mode of communication succeeded. In retrospect it may seem a bit amazing that a man of such intellectual sophistication, speaking in such an elusive style, with virtually no attempt at crowd-play, should have been regularly received with "something close to veneration" in a forum where popular entertainment was the norm.[14] The paradox largely resolves itself when one realizes that Emerson's admirers were looking for stimulation and elevation rather than rigorous thought or hard data. The same spiritual malaise which led Emerson into skepticism and out of the church, in search of alternative ways to express religious sentiment, was widely shared by his audiences; indeed it was one of the main reasons for the rise of the whole lyceum movement. In such a spiritual climate, vague moral uplift seemed much more appropriate than rational precision, which was fast becoming discredited in matters of belief.

No man is totally a product of his times, least of all a genius. The prevailing reverence for Emerson did not mean universal understanding or approval, as this record of an 1857 lecture in Emerson's home town suggests: "Friday Eve Jany 2, 1857 R. W. Emerson lectured. Subject, *The times: politics, preaching, bad boys, clean shirts &c &c.*"[15] But the important point is that after some initial hesitation over Emerson's heresies, most of New England did accept him on his own terms, as a poet, whose proper role was not to explain but to inspire. Had Emerson descended more often to the former, much of the sense of the poetic and the mysterious which was responsible for his charisma would have been lost.

NOTES

Mr. Buell is Assistant Professor of English at Oberlin College. The research for this paper was conducted with the assistance of a Howard Foundation Fellowship, which the author acknowledges with gratitude.

1. Jonathan Bishop, *Emerson on the Soul* (Cambridge: Harvard Univ. Press, 1964), p. 106.

2. *The Complete Works of Ralph Waldo Emerson*, ed. Edward Emerson (Boston: Houghton, 1903–4), III, 233. Abbreviated below as *W*.

3. See for instance W. T. Harris, "The Dialectic Unity in Emerson's Prose," *Journal of Speculative Philosophy*, 18 (1884); 195–202; Walter Blair and Clarence Faust, "Emerson's Literary Method," *Modern Philology*, 42 (1944), 79–95; Sherman Paul, *Emerson's Angle of Vision* (Cambridge: Harvard Univ. Press, 1952), pp. 117–118; Richard Francis, "The Architectonics of Emerson's *Nature*," *American Quarterly*, 19 (1967), 39–53; Enno Klammer, "The Spiral Staircase in 'Self-Reliance,'" *Emerson Society Quarterly*, No. 47 (1967), 81–83; Richard Tuerk, "Emerson's *Nature*—Miniature Universe," *American Transcendental Quarterly*, 1 (1969), 110–113.

4. *The Journals and Miscellaneous Notebooks of Ralph Waldo Emerson*, ed. William Gilman *et al.* (Cambridge: Harvard Univ. Press, 1960–) VII, 90. Abbreviated below as *JMN*.

5. *The Correspondence of Emerson and Carlyle*, ed. Joseph Slater (New York and London: Columbia Univ. Press, 1964), p. 185.

6. The sources of the bracketed passages are, respectively, *The Early Lectures of Ralph Waldo Emerson*, ed. Robert Spiller, *et al.* (Cambridge, Mass.: Belknap Press, 1959–), II, 145; "School" (unpublished 1838 lecture), p. 11; *JMN*, VII, 442; *JMN*, VII, 66–67; "School," p. 10. "School" and all other unpublished Emerson lectures cited below are in Houghton Library, Harvard University. Emerson's *Early Lectures* hereafter cited as *EL*.

7. The sources of the bracketed passages are, *EL*, II, 171 ("I suppose ... sphere"); *JMN*, V, 184 ("I suppose ... same thing"); "Tendencies" (unpublished 1840 lecture), p. 33 ("I suppose .. nature"; "let me record ... see it not"); *JMN*, VII, 364 ("The swallow ... my web also"); "Religion" (unpublished 1840 lecture), p. 41 ("Character ... wills").

8. Sometimes excerpts from many different lectures are brought together, as in "Powers and Laws of Thought" (*W*, XII, 3–64). When only one lecture is used in the text, as with "Instinct and Inspiration" (*W*, XII, 65–89), long passages are often excised (sometimes without notice), usually because Emerson has used them in other essays. Some passages which in manuscript are little more than rough jottings are deceptively organized in neat paragraphs. And there are copying errors as well.

9. The three chief sources are *JMN*, VII, 505–506; "Doctrine of the Soul" (unpublished 1838 lecture), pp. 31–32; and *EL*, II, 343.

10. Emerson's sources in this section are "Doctrine of the Soul," pp. 37–38 (for par. 4, entire); *EL*, II, 85 (for par. 5, entire), "School," pp. 14–15 (for par. 7, "See how the deep divine thought ... she is clothed"); "Tendencies," p. 42 (for par. 8, "The growths of genius populations, of men"); *EL*, II, 84 (for par. 9, "The soul requires purity ... becomes suddenly virtuous"); "School," p. 25 (for par. 11, "One mode of the divine teaching ... cities and war") and pp. 27–28 (for par. 11, "Persons are supplementary ... higher self-possession");

"Doctrine of the Soul," pp. 39–40 (for most of par. 11, "It shines for all ... seek for it in each other") and p. 53 (for the rest of par. 11 and par. 12, entire); "Religion," p. 40 (for par. 13, entire).

11. "Doctrine of the Soul," p. 52, contains the three-part distinction of the Soul's powers, from which I have quoted by permission of the Ralph Waldo Emerson Memorial Association and the Harvard College Library. Emerson's sources in pars. 14–24 are "Doctrine of the Soul," pp. 40–41 (for par. 14, entire); *EL*, II, 87–92 (for most of par. 16); "Religion," pp. 19–22 (for most of pars. 18–19); "Doctrine of the Soul," pp. 49–50, 51 (for pars. 20–21 entire); *JMN*, VII, 217 (for par. 22, "That which we are ... over our head"); "Doctrine of the Soul," pp. 56–57 (for the remainder of par. 22); *JMN*, VII, 157 (for par. 23; entire); "Doctrine of the Soul," pp. 43–45 (for par. 24, "There is in all great poets ... syllables from the tongue").

12. Cf. Roland Lee, "Emerson's 'Compensation' as Argument and as Art," *New England Quarterly*, 37 (1964), 291–304, which argues that the essay fails as art because it is too much of an argument.

13. See Charles Feidelson, Jr., *Symbolism and American Literature* (Chicago: Univ. of Chicago Press, 1953), pp. 119–161, and René Wellek's section on Emerson in *A History of Modern Criticism* (New Haven: Yale Univ. Press, 1965), III, 163–175.

14. Quotation from Carl Bode, *The American Lyceum: Town Meeting of the Mind* (New York: Oxford Univ. Press, 1956), p. 226. The best contemporary account of Emerson's aura as a lecturer is James Russell Lowell, "Emerson, the Lecturer," *My Study Windows* (Boston: Houghton, 1886), pp. 375–384. Lowell shared in the veneration of Emerson, at least in public, almost to the point of idolatry. For a modern and more balanced view, synthesizing a number of nineteenth-century reports of Emerson both favorable and adverse, see Herbert A. Wichelns, "Ralph Waldo Emerson," *A History and Criticism of American Public Address*, ed. William Norwood Brigance (New York: McGraw-Hill, 1943), II, 501–525.

15. Concord Lyceum minutes, quoted in Kenneth W. Cameron, *Transcendental Climate* (Hartford: Transcendental Books, 1962), III, 712.

DAVID M. WYATT

Spelling Time:
The Reader in Emerson's "Circles"

> In stripping time of its illusions, in seeking to find what is the heart of
> the day, we come to the quality of the moment, and drop the duration
> altogether.   —"Works and Days"

For Emerson the effect of his place in time has everything to do with the timing of effects in his prose. As the self-proclaimed originator of a tradition, he cannot help hoping to activate in his reader a sense of being at the beginning—in the first presence—of things. To the question "What will we have?" he swiftly answers "This only—a good timing of things."[1] Because Emerson is so concerned with giving his own measure to time, the documents which fully register this project are the finished ones. The Journals never engage time through a form which tests the human power to account for it even as it is being dismissed. As a source of our sense of the man they remain invaluable; as a realization of his will resisting the element it must work in, they tell us little.[2] Emerson's greatest temptation—to risk becoming nothing by trying to be All—knows no bounds in the Journals, as it finds nothing formal there to oppose it. Works always *in medias res*, they risk neither the arbitrariness of a beginning nor the curtailment of an end. It is rather while constructing performances addressed to an audience that Emerson does attend to the timing of effects within a limited stretch of

From *American Literature* 48, no. 2 (May 1976). © 1976 by Duke University Press.

discourse. While composing *Nature* Emerson distinguishes between the demands of private thought and public saying: "that statement only is fit to be made public which you have got at in attempting to satisfy your own curiosity. For himself, a man only wants to know how a thing is; it is for other people that he wants to know what may be said about it" (*JMN*, IV, 52). Only when Emerson risks descent into a public form which, according to its own laws, must end, does he ever make a beginning.

The decision to write in sentences constitutes Emerson's primary submission to form. Within them (rather than the poetic line) he fights his battle against time. Meanwhile he embeds his sentences within a structure—the essay—continually struggling to make of its parts a whole. "Unity" hardly results. The tension between his sentences and the structure they compound never resolves itself into that marvelous and mythic entity, "organic form," which "shapes, as it develops, itself from within."[3] While this may seem a critical failure, it simply reflects Emerson's practical insight into the limited workings of language. With Coleridge he can endlessly dilate upon the mind as "essentially *vital*," while recognizing that "all objects"—even works of art—(as objects) are "essentially fixed and dead."[4] He understands that the vital power in his mind must submit to connection with and activation of power in his audience through the wholly mediate form of words. So he argues in 1835:

> There is every degree of remoteness from the line of things in the line of words. By & by comes a word true & closely embracing the thing. That is not Latin nor English nor any language, but *thought*. The aim of the author is not to tell truth—that he cannot do, but to suggest it. He has only approximated it himself, & hence his cumbrous embarrassed speech: he uses many words, hoping that one, if not another, will bring you as near to the fact as he is. (*JMN*, V, 51)

With the "line of words" Emerson always falls knowingly, if reluctantly, into step.

The decision to write in order to be read thus becomes for Emerson an acceptance of limitation, a descent into time. He values form, including literary form, insofar as it permits a release of power. He knows that "there is no action of any physical organism [even less an essay] that remotely approaches the power of the human mind to reverse and recast *itself*, constantly to reaffirm or to cancel its own precedent action, in whole or in part."[5] To preserve this power it is necessary to appeal as directly as possible to the reader's consciousness through (rather than to) the work. While lacking the esemplastic nature of its source, the work which results need not remain inert. It consists of a discontinuous or veiled structure which reading can enliven. "This is that law," Emerson argues in "Spiritual Laws," "whereby a work of art, of whatever kind, sets us in the same state of mind wherein the artist was when he made it." The unique resource which Romantic theorists reserve for the imaginative artist Emerson presumes and develops in his audience. Our active involvement in the form as proceeding is intentionally provoked by the entire American symbolist tradition. Its works, often noticeably incomplete in themselves, inspire the trust that they can, should, and will be by us completed. It becomes difficult to speak of such works, especially Emerson's, as anything but pretexts for events, for direct transactions between the soul of the author and the soul of the reader.

Trans action—the exchange of power from one mind to another—this is the essential experience of Emerson's essays. The best ask us to make our own way, to answer the question with which "Experience" begins: "Where do we find ourselves?" This way typically resolves into a "stairway of surprise" ("Merlin"), a perambulation through "a series of which we do not know the extremes" ("Experience"). "Step by step we scale this mysterious ladder; the steps are actions, the new prospect is power" ("Circles"). As we emerge onto the landings which such essays periodically provide it is ourselves in the act of becoming capable readers we are always finding. Jonathan Bishop has given us this Emerson of the verb. His book's central noun—"soul"—continually resolves into a procedure—"active soul." And acting proves more definitive of his version of Emerson than being soulful. For the soul lives in change: "metamorphosis of circumstances into consciousness is the consummation of the Soul's great act."[6] Bishop attempts to define the "Soul," and succeeds; I would like to define further the definer. For, as Bishop admits, it is Emerson's reader *as reader* who best realizes and preserves the meaning of the word "Soul." "It must mean the mind of the reader understanding what is before it, following some verbal action upon the page. This literary action is all that an author can be sure he will share with his reader."[7] As a prospectus for Emerson criticism, this will prove definitive. In following the verbal action of "Circles," we can discover ourselves becoming active souls. We are processed by a structure aspiring at once to closure and continuity. While reading "Circles" we enjoy a sense of resolved being and unstayed becoming. The patterns we spell while moving through the essay grant simultaneous access to "the quality of the moment" and to "duration" and so illuminate the temporal dimensions whose usually alternating interchange forms the tension sending up Emerson's work.

Emerson concentrates "Circles" into a microcosm of itself in its first sentence: "The eye is the first circle; the horizon which it forms is the second; and throughout nature this primary figure is repeated without end." The immediate impression conveyed here is one of compression, authority, wholeness. In no other essay are we asked to admit and condense so much at the outset, to "scan the profile of the sphere" in miniature before reading through its more "copious sense." We feel that something—maybe everything—has been said, that what remains to be read may dilate upon, but will not diverge from, the senses this unit circumscribes. Yet the essay's primary "analogy"—"that every action admits of being outdone"—quickly intrudes to counsel against acceptance of finality, sphericity, closure. Fundamentally at odds with itself, "Circles" addresses a reader no less capable of balancing opposing rhythms and claims.

This first sentence has in fact already engaged us with the argument, or "analogy," its apparent formal roundedness opposes. Composed of three stages of statement, each stage absorbs and enlarges—"outdoes"—the preceding. The eye moves through larger and larger arenas. The semicolons create a pause rather than a stay, permitting the reader, without marked delay, to move unhindered from one circumscription to the next. And the sentence ends with a denial of the very closure it enacts and describes—with an admission that the formal entities it defines proliferate "without end." Thus endlessness intrudes into a semantic unit seemingly committed to its opposite. For the sentence contains an abundance of fixities and definites: "eye," "circle," "horizon," "figure." Predication merely brings them into relation, not into activity. Of all these nouns only the "eye" "forms." Such passivity can suggest a world more static than "self-evolving." As for the propositional form of the sentence, it can be read as casting these entities into discrete, logical steps, steps as additive as they are supersessive. So we are also led into an orderly, reflexive universe, one with "primary" and secondary figures, one governed by repetition. The extent of this repetition—it is endless—can be interpreted as always confirming, rather than ever-opening, the confines of this world. Reading this sentence, we cannot help wavering between the conflicting experiences at once offered by it.

Are we to be exposed then to a static or a developing essay? To both, as the paragraph goes on to demonstrate. "We are all our lifetime reading the copious sense of this first of forms." Even more gracefully than in his opening sentence, Emerson here confounds the dimensions of our project. This sentence first sentences us to an unvarying task, a spending of "all our lifetime." But the task assigned, we quickly discover, is "reading," the pursuit of the evanescence of meaning itself. The object of this constantly inconstant attention is next admitted to be a multiplicity: "copious sense." But such historical variety derives from a singular priority, from a "first" which has developed into "forms." We emerge from such an interval alerted to the presence of the one within the many, to the possibility of recovering during history ("our lifetime") a sense of originality (apprehending the "first"). In such a context the reader has no choice but too many options.

But before proceeding to multiply our options, the essay deflects us into the memory of another one. The reader is addressed as if he had just finished "Compensation." "One moral we have already deduced in considering the circular or compensatory character of every human action." We are meant to turn aside here, for the last time, into a consideration of this companion piece. In each of his essays Emerson seeks a fitting style through which, as James Cox argues, the character of his thought can "eventuate."[8] In "Compensation" he typically casts his sentences into antitheses. They become in that context the formal vehicles the experience of which embodies the principle they deduce. The essay's larger structure also betrays a compensatory pattern. Its second movement asks us to balance the "affirmative" force of "Being" against the indifferency of all action argued in the first. The reversion to "Compensation" at the beginning of "Circles" alerts us to the deconstruction of the former mode about to be carried out. "Circles" renders simultaneous the this and the that, the More and the Less between which the earlier essay had us alternate. "The radical tragedy of nature seems to be the distinction of More and Less"; this is the imbalance which "Compensation" mechanically seeks to redress. "Circles" converts this seeming tragedy into an outright comedy by denying from the outset the experience of a certain distinction between more and less, completion and beginning, arrest and motion. The allusion to the former essay thus functions as proof of the "analogy" now being traced. As a literal re-vision of "Compensation," "Circles" demonstrates that "every action"—especially outmoded literary action—"admits of being outdone."

But Emerson jettisons more than the mode of an earlier essay here. The period leading up to the composition of this work had been dominated, in Harold Bloom's phrase, by the "three anti-influence orations-essays of 1837–1840."[9] This prolonged struggle with his relation to the thoughts and acts of forebears finds relief in "Circles." Emerson discovers through the essay an original style, one which acknowledges and incorporates the forces he had wished, especially in *Nature*, to exclude. These are the forces of history and continuity. "His revolt," Stephen Whicher argues, "had been designed to cut the traces that bound him to history and bring him to live, not in the kingdom of time, but in direct contact with the divine life beyond and above time."[10] His compromise, in "Circles," is to evolve a style which eventuates in a reading experience both continuous and arrested, one with a developing memory of itself (a history), and one continually fulfilling itself in single moments.

Thus "Circles" simultaneously spells and dispells time. Standing midway between the full acknowledgment of duration in "Experience" and the early expansion into the moment won in *Nature*, it fuses the prevailing temporal mode of each essay. It is at once a pulsation and an artery. More pointedly, it flows and stays its flow throughout. Its sentences repeatedly ask us to complete, while at the same time to extend, a syntactic and argumentative motion, as if to enact the basic pattern which is its subject: spiraling and staying. We can experience this double pattern at work in the following: "There are no fixtures in nature. The universe is fluid and volatile. Permanence is but a word of degrees. Our globe seen by God is a transparent law, not a mass of facts. The law dissolves the fact and holds it fluid." One could go on; there is no need to. Here each sentence seems to forget its dependence on those around it. This epigrammatic "shower of bullets" ("Montaigne") strikes us at first as though unsubordinated to a single argumentative source. The curt propositional thrust of each sentence gets abruptly stayed by each period. The temporary arrest any period naturally provides is so marked here as to fix each proposition into separate, momentous intervals. Syntax and punctuation create a rhythm suggestive of a world of isolated facts. Meanwhile, the paragraph's argument—for fluidity—attempts to cohere into an eddy of implication, one which strains against the consistently stayed rhythm which bears it. The infinitely repellant particles of Emerson's diction are negated or qualified into locutions that keep dissolving hard distinctions. "Fixtures," "Permanence," and "facts" surface only to be denied existence or stability. Those terms allowed to stand—"degrees," "transparent," "fluid"—suggest a flowing interconnectedness. As the connections within each sentence emerge, attention strains to dissolve its steps into a more fluid motion. But to see through (render "transparent") the isolated status of these sentences to their underlying unity is to adopt "God's" perspective, to operate through the knowledge of a "law" presently unavailable to us. In the tension *between* fixity and flowing we have our being. The combined effects of this passage render up not a portable subject, but an acute knowledge of the limits and powers of an attention operating in time.

In "Circles" Emerson's prose dissolves successive distinctions between spiraling and staying. We may stop with each sentence, or follow out the paragraph's ongoing movement. Reading becomes an experience of single, separate moments as "Step by step we scale the mysterious ladder" of this prose. At the same time, it moves through a duration like the "life of man," through a "self-evolving circle, which, from a ring imperceptibly small, rushes on all sides outwards to new and larger circles, and that without end." This doubleness of experience accounts for the overpowering sense of freedom, of choice between two modes of being which surrounds us while reading "Circles." Its title is only half a title: "Circles" also describes "Spirals." We remain free to metamorphose between the perfected circle of timelessness, of a completed thought, and the ongoing spiral of time, of Man Thinking. But such a choice becomes a burden: to be at once in time and out of it may be more freedom than we can bear.

The doubleness of this achievement in the essay's opening we have already deduced. What larger patterns are generated by reading the essay as a whole? It is one of Emerson's shortest. Memory of the essay as it is being read is thereby encouraged. It is not surprising therefore that we proceed by way of repetition. As each "new generalization" meets its echo the reader discovers that to advance he must remember. Emerson admits that in "my daily work I incline to repeat my old steps." This inclination sends up the steps which compose the essay. The will to choose a "straight path" continually revealing new perspectives is chastened into a spiraling course.

The essay proper begins with two propositions to be repeated almost verbatim. "There are no fixtures in nature" and "Permanence is but a word of degrees" soon find echo in "Permanence is a word of degrees" and "There are no fixtures to men." Such recurrences are the fixtures of the essay. They provide a permanent path of reference, a staying of the outrunning argument. While each paragraph counsels against limitation and fixity, these "old steps" hold a steady sound. As the argument proceeds, the repetitions abide. Thus "Fear not the new generalization" encourages abandonment of the old, only to deliver us over to a rehearsal—of the phrase itself—in "all are at the mercy of a new generalization." The frequent restatement of the essay itself argues for the difficulty of advancing a vision wholly new. This is acknowledged in "Yet is that statement approximate also, and not final," an acceptance of limited verbal resources which itself bears repeating and revision: "There is no virtue which is final; all are initial." Perhaps Emerson's unwillingness to have us settle into one path issues most succinctly in "I unsettle all things." But the will to undo is shadowed even here by the urge to re-do: "People wish to be settled; only as far as they are unsettled is there any hope for them." Through such repetitions the reader is stayed and gathered in again, as his progression curves into a circumlocution.

If the repetitions arrest the shoves given by the argument, the reverse is also true. The effect of a return can be, as we have seen, to create a sense of timelessness, of being still in the presence of an unchanged truth. Or it can create a sense of connection with and dependence upon the past, a sense of historical awareness. The essay's repetitions have such a bipolar effect. Any attempt to describe one pole of this effect cannot escape implying the other. What is true of the essay's repetitive structure is also true of its argument. I have characterized it as urging newness, a continuous present, discontinuity. But a continuous argument against continuity acquires a history of its own. As its author acknowledges, he shall one day "wonder who he was that wrote so many continuous pages." The point to be made is that on every level of its realization "Circles" involves us in contradiction. It employs form in order to attack form.[11] Its sentences can be read as a "plenteous stopping at little stations" ("Powers and Laws of Thought"). But they also can be taken as nudges forward on the "self-evolving circle" of discovery. We negotiate in "Circles" an "at once" world, one which plunges us into "incessant movement and progression" even while manifesting a "principle of fixture or stability."

The image of man generated by "Circles" is consequently of a figure still *and* moving. The linearity of the writing process receives much more elaboration than in *Nature*, and through the same metaphor employed so frugally there: walking. Statements and thoughts are imaged not as transcendental leaps but as a horizontal series of moves, "step by step," through the essay's prose. Intellectual pursuits here depend upon strolling. "Each new step we take in thought reconciles twenty seeming discordant facts." The steps may be forward, or "farther back"; the point is that insight is to be found along the way. For this walker—and his reader—temporality resolves into an "anxiety that melts / In becoming, like miles under the pilgrim feet."[12]

At the same time "Circles" induces a motionless heroism: "Valor consists in the power of self-recovery, so that a man cannot have his flank turned, cannot be out-generated, but put him where you will, he stands." Character also serves which only stands and looks. The need for a vantage point "to command a view" tempts one into such arrest. Rather than submit to the passage of time, "Character makes an overpowering present." But the will to stand in a moment of our own making may be doomed as we continually discover that "this surface on which we stand is not fixed, but sliding." The axis of vision cannot be coincident with the axis of things until both are stilled.

The very context which creates such contradictions—the essay— apprises us of itself as the platform from which they can be resolved. Literature here recommends "Literature" as a "point outside of our hodiernal circle through which a new one may be described. The use of literature is to afford us a platform whence we may command a view of our present life, a purchase by which we may move it." Here the context in which we are "present" speaks out to us to recommend itself as something on which we might stand to move, or view, the world. In what sense can an experience we are having be conceived as a platform or lever? Can we extricate ourselves from immersion in the essay being read to consider it as an "It"? Again "Circles" attempts to double our experience, asking us to read it and to read *about* it. We must move—walk—through it in order to conceive of staying to use—stand on—it. We must be here in order to think of being *on* here. So Emerson fulfills his theory of complementarity: "a sentence causes us to see ourselves. I be & see my being, at the same time" (*JMN*, V, 278). This is the essay's ultimate confounding of its reader's singleness—to urge the necessity of our absence while we are still in the essay's presence.

In "Circles" motion and arrest, duration and the moment, all become dimensions of power *and* loss. In motion we can scale the mysterious ladder on which "the steps are actions" and "the new prospect is power," or we can too quickly bypass "that central life somewhat superior to creation."[13] Arrest can "confer a sort of omnipresence and omnipotence which has nothing of duration," or it can "solidify and hem in the life." But the experience of the essay recommends a paradoxical combination of both dimensions, a life in an "overpowering present," but a present on the move. This precarious and "sliding" nick of time neither Emerson nor his reader can forever isolate from the influence and anxieties of the past and future. For in reading the later "Experience" we find ourselves in a "series of which we do not know the extremes," rather than in the ever "new position of the advancing man." The moving bead reveals itself as part of a string of beads. Our horizon begins to expand, and as the visible distance increases from our beginning and our end, so too recedes the presence of memory and hope.

Any center or present occupied in "Circles" is superseded and must be continually reimagined. As attention to this process of redefinition frees us from the gravity of any and each new-found center, our career is given over to "freeplay" rather than to a fixed locus. Jacques Derrida describes the movement from *Nature* through "Circles" as a "decentering." This rupture of his traditional notions of structure and metaphysics is the "central" event in Emerson's career. It occurs to his readers most dramatically while negotiating "Circles." As its every circle devolves into a spiral, its every center permanently shifts. Derrida argues that whenever belief in a fixed transcendental center collapses, it becomes "necessary to begin to think that there was no center, that the center could not be thought in the form of a being-present, that the center had no natural locus, that it was not a fixed locus but a function, a sort of nonlocus in which an infinite number of sign-substitutions came into play. This moment was that in which language invaded the universal problematic."[14] This records the death of the circle. Emerson's "Circles" asks us to pursue and deny its lost heart. In "Experience" we eventually give up any hope of capture, consigning ourselves simply to the disciplines of pursuit.

Emerson never fully abandons, however, the nostalgia for a sustaining center, for a solitary moment of stay. It is impossible for him to do so, for he pursues his project by way of terms evocative of the very centeredness and timelessness he comes to know better than to seek. Bloom claims that "Emerson had come to prophecy not a de-centering, as Neitzsche had, and as Derrida and de Man are brilliantly accomplishing, but a peculiarly American *re-centering*."[15] That this re-centering ends in what Bloom calls the "transparency of solipsism" is a claim we should accept and lament, since such a restoration of meaning is won only at the cost of its being common to more than one center. Knowing this, Emerson finds himself drawn down, in "Experience," into the limitations of a continual and communal dialectic. Certainly the old superhuman language of presence persists in reappearing as he speaks of "Godhead": "though not in energy, yet by presence, this magazine of substance cannot be otherwise than felt." Yet the will and power to re-present such experience for the reader, rather than simply to invoke it, the essay fully chastens. This most concessive, least arresting essay demands and creates in its audience more self-reliance than does *Nature* by asking it to relinquish belief in, if not the use of, the traditional language of divination upon which that seemingly original essay finally relies. The first answer "Experience" gives—that there is no *arche* and no *telos*—destroys the limits *Nature* strives to define (if only for the liberated self) and calls the soul into time without beginning or end. To find ourselves in a series of which we do not know the extremes is disorienting: to "believe that it has none" is to accept responsibility for discovering whatever form the series affords. As it develops, "Experience" becomes Emerson's most structuring essay. It structures the reader's power to recognize, to interrogate—to accept the absence of—structures in an ongoing duration. Although he warns, near the end of "Experience," that "We must be very suspicious of the deceptions of the element of time," it is into this element that an aging Emerson, no longer able to come to the quality of the moment, increasingly delivers his reader.

NOTES

1. *The Journals and Miscellaneous Notebooks of Ralph Waldo Emerson*, ed. Ralph H. Orth and Alfred R. Ferguson (Cambridge, Mass., 1971), IX, 303. Hereafter *JMN* in the text.

2. Jonathan Bishop forwards this claim: "The key is still to be looked for in the familiar texts. No one who grasps a part of Emerson's meaning there should find himself

seriously altering his view through a study of the antecedent or secondary material," *Emerson on the Soul* (Cambridge, Mass., 1964), p. 7.

3. Coleridge, *Essays and Lectures on Shakespeare*.

4. Coleridge, *Biographia Literaria*, Chapter 73.

5. William Wimsatt, "Organic Form: Some Questions about a Metaphor," in *Romanticism: Vistas, Instances, Continuities*, ed. David Thorburn and Geoffrey Hartman (Ithaca, N.Y., 1973), p. 22.

6. Bishop, p. 23.

7. Bishop, p. 24.

8. James M. Cox, "Emerson and Hawthorne: Trust and Doubt," *Virginia Quarterly Review*, XLV (Winter, 1969), 93.

9. Harold Bloom, "The Freshness of Transformation or Emerson on Influence," *American Transcendental Quarterly*, No. 21 (Winter, 1974), 58.

10. Stephen E. Whicher, *Freedom and Fate* (Philadelphia, 1953), p. 98.

11. Carolyn Porter, in "Form and Process in American Literature," unpublished dissertation, Rice University, 1973, p. 72, argues that "Circles" "illustrates Emerson's increased awareness of the need for form as well as his reduced ambitions toward final form."

12. John Ashbery, "The Task" in *The Double Dream of Spring* (New York, 1970), p. 13.

13. Todd M. Lieber, in *Endless Experiments* (Columbus, Ohio, 1973), pp. 27–28, elaborates the complementarity inherent in Emerson's experience of motion: "Emerson, however, recognizes two very different types of motion. These may be differentiated by calling the first, which involves a sense of the constant presence of divinity and yields continual affirmation, process, and the second, flux, to denote an aimless, purposeless, unachieving drift."

14. Jacques Derrida, "Structure, Sign and Play in the Discourse of the Human Sciences" in *The Structuralist Controversy*, ed. Richard Macksey and Eugenio Donato (Baltimore, 1970), p. 249.

15. Harold Bloom, *A Map of Misreading* (New York, 1975), p. 176.

BARBARA PACKER

"Experience"

How shall we face the edge of time? We walk
In the park. We regret we have no nightingale.
We must have the throstle on the gramophone.
Where shall we find more than derisive words?
When shall lush chorals spiral through our fire
And daunt that old assassin, heart's desire?
　　Wallace Stevens, "A Duck for Dinner"

Emerson's final version of the Fall story is his shortest and most epigrammatic. It is remarkable not so much for its content as for its tone, and the startling nature of the "facts" it is invented to explain. The voice we hear in "Experience" has neither the rhapsodic intensity of the Orphic chants, nor the chill impersonality of the axis-of-vision formula, nor the militancy of "The Protest" or "Circles." It is instead the voice of a man of the world: urbane, rueful, a little weary. "It is very unhappy, but too late to be helped, the discovery we have made that we exist. That discovery is called the Fall of Man."

Equating self-consciousness with the Fall is of course one of the commonest Romantic ways of allegorizing the story of Genesis. And the

From *Emerson's Fall: A New Interpretation of the Major Essays.* © 1982 by B.L. Packer.

myth of ossification, with its insistence that the conscious intellect was the
enemy of that central power accessible only by surprise or abandonment,
may be regarded as containing or at least implying this final myth (which we
may call the myth of *reflection*).

But this new version differs from its predecessors in two significant
respects. It is considerably more pessimistic in its implications (there is no
suggestion that the catastrophe of self-consciousness is either potentially or
temporarily reversible), and the evidence adduced to support it is more
shocking, in its quiet way, than anything Emerson had ever written. In
Nature he had based his argument for the original divinity of the Self on its
surviving capacity for ecstasy; in "Circles," on its refusal to accept limitation.
In "Experience" what is taken as proof of the "ill-concealed Deity" of the Self
is neither its joy nor its zeal but simply its ruthlessness:

> There are moods in which we court suffering, in the hope that
> here at least we shall find reality, sharp peaks and edges of truth.
> But it turns out to be scene-painting and counterfeit. The only
> thing grief has taught me, is to know how shallow it is. That, like
> all the rest, plays about the surface, and never introduces me into
> the reality, for contact with which we would even pay the costly
> price of sons and lovers.

> We believe in ourselves as we do not believe in others. We permit
> all things to ourselves, and that which we call sin in others is
> experiment for us. It is an instance of our faith in ourself that men
> never speak of crime as lightly as they think; or that every man
> thinks a latitude safe for himself which is nowise to be indulged
> to another.... No man at last believes that he can be lost, or that
> the crime in him is as black as in the felon.

Emerson had once wanted to write a book like the Proverbs of Solomon;
"Experience" sounds more like the *Maxims* of La Rochefoucauld.

The necessary ruthlessness of the Self had been a corollary of the
doctrine of self-reliance from the beginning, of course; it is implicit in
Emerson's exhortation to "shun father and mother and wife and brother"
when genius calls, even if it causes them pain. And it is avowed even more
frankly in "Circles," where Emerson argues that "men cease to interest us
when we find their limitations. The only sin is limitation. As soon as you
once come up with a man's limitations, it is all over with him." As individuals,
we are always in the position of the disappointed child in "Experience" who
asks his mother why the story he enjoyed yesterday fails to please him as

much the second time around. And the only answer Emerson can give us is the one he offers the child: "will it answer thy question to say, Because thou wert born to a whole and this story is a particular?" This information is hardly an unmixed blessing. If our hunger for "sphericity" is on the one hand the only defense we have against the soul's tendency to ossification, it is on the other hand the restlessness that "ruins the kingdom of mortal friendship and of love."

Emerson's deliberate emphasis in essays like "Circles" and "Experience" on the ruthlessness and secret cruelty of the Self shocks us, and is meant to. It is not merely (as Firkins guesses) "that a parade of hardness may have seemed to him a wholesome counterpoise to the fashionable parade of sensibility,"[1] though that was doubtless an added attraction. Emerson says these unpleasant things chiefly because he thinks they are true. Of course it would be easier for us and for society as a whole if they were not true, if there were some way of living without the ruinous ferocity of desire, which never ceases to torment us in thought, even if our outward behavior is decorous. Our mortal condition would be easier to endure if the divine Providence had *not* "shown the heaven and earth to every child and filled him with a desire for the whole; a desire raging, infinite; a hunger, as of space to be filled with planets; a cry of famine, as of devils for souls"—as Emerson puts it in a memorable passage in "Montaigne." That desire sends us off on a perpetual quest through the world of experience, and at the same time foredooms the quest to failure, since each particular satisfaction can only frustrate a being whose desire is for the whole. As questers, we are partly like Tennyson's Ulysses—

.... all experience is an arch wherethrough
Gleams that untravelled world whose margin fades
For ever and for ever when I move ... [2]

but even more like Tennyson's Percivale—

"Lo, if I find the Holy Grail itself
And touch it, it will crumble into dust."[3]

Romance—the glamour or beauty that could transmute life's baser metals into gold—is always somewhere else, somewhere just beyond our grasp. "Every ship is a romantic object, except that we sail in. Embark, and the romance quits our vessel and hangs on every other sail in the horizon." Or, as he had put it in the earlier essay "Love": "each man sees his own life defaced and disfigured, as the life of man is not, to his imagination."

Sensible people, hearing these confessions of frustration and despair, counsel renunciation of the Self's imperial ambitions. But Emerson denies that any permanent renunciation is possible. For one thing, that glimpse of the whole we were granted as children survives in adult life as more than a memory. Just when we have, as we think, managed to adjust our desires to reality, the old vision reappears to tantalize us:

> How easily, if fate would suffer it, we might keep forever these beautiful limits, and adjust ourselves, once for all, to the perfect calculation of known cause and effect.... But ah! presently comes a day, or is it only a half-hour, with its angel-whispering,—which discomfits the conclusions of notions and years!

And this reminder, while it distresses us, calls to our attention something we cannot safely ignore. The desire that torments us is also the only "capital stock" we have to invest in the actions and relationships of life. The man who tried to conduct his business on the principles of common sense alone "would quickly be bankrupt. Power keeps quite another road than the turnpikes of choice and will; namely the subterranean and invisible tunnels and channels of life."

These meditations on power and ruthlessness are an important part of the essay "Experience." They constitute a sort of ground bass heard at intervals beneath the constantly varying melodies of the essay, and contribute not a little to the impression of toughness it makes on the reader's mind. Yet toughness is hardly the essay's most significant characteristic. What is strikingly new about "Experience" is the voice that is heard in its opening paragraph, a voice neither powerful nor ruthless, but instead full of bewilderment, exhaustion, and despair:

> Where do we find ourselves? In a series of which we do not know the extremes, and believe that it has none. We wake and find ourselves on a stair; there are stairs below us, which we seem to have ascended; there are stairs above us, many a one, which go upward and out of sight. But the Genius which according to the old belief stands at the door by which we enter, and gives us the lethe to drink, that we may tell no tales, mixed the cup too strongly, and we cannot shake off the lethargy now at noonday. Sleep lingers all our lifetime about our eyes, as night hovers all day in the boughs of the fir-tree. All things swim and glitter. Our life is not so much threatened as our

perception. Ghostlike we glide through nature, and should not know our place again.

When Dr. Beard, in his *American Nervousness*, wanted a phrase that would convey to a popular audience an accurate sense of the new disease he had identified and named *neurasthenia*, he instinctively chose a metaphor Emerson would have admired: "nervous bankruptcy."[4] In the peculiar lassitude of the prose here—so different from the militant assertiveness of "Circles" or "Self-Reliance"—Emerson has managed to create a stylistic correlative to the "Feeling of Profound Exhaustion" Dr. Beard found characteristic of the nervously bankrupt.[5] Insufficiency of vital force is in fact Emerson's chief complaint in this opening passage.

> Did our birth fall in some fit of indigence and frugality in nature, that she was so sparing of her fire and so liberal of her earth that it appears to us that we lack the affirmative principle, and though we have health and reason, yet we have no superfluity of spirit for new creation? We have enough to live and bring the year about, but not an ounce to impart or invest. Ah that our Genius were a little more of a genius! We are like the millers on the lower levels of a stream, when the factories above them have exhausted the water. We too fancy that the upper people have raised their dams.

No reader of Emerson's journals can be unfamiliar with the mood described here. Recurrent laments over want of stamina and of animal spirits, over feelings of exhaustion and despair, punctuate the earliest notebooks. "I have often found cause to complain that my thoughts have an ebb & flow," he noted in one of them. "The worst is, that the ebb is certain, long, & frequent, while the flow comes transiently & seldom." A few pages earlier, a pious composition intended as a meditation "Upon Men's Apathy to their Eternal interests" turns into a meditation upon apathy of a more personal sort—a meditation whose systematic hopelessness, coming from a youth of nineteen, almost raises a smile:

> In the pageant of life, Time & Necessity are the stern masters of ceremonies who admit no distinctions among the vast train of aspirants.... And though the appetite of youth for marvels & beauty is fain to draw deep & strong lines of contrast between one & another character we early learn to distrust them & to acquiesce in the unflattering & hopeless picture which Experience exhibits.

This grim lesson Emerson hastens to apply to his own disappointing life:

> We dreamed of great results from peculiar features of Character.
> We thought that the overflowing benevolence of our youth was
> pregnant with kind consequences to the world; that the agreeable
> qualities in the boy of courage, activity, intelligence, & good
> temper would prove in the man Virtues of extensive &
> remarkable practical effect.

The passage is revealing; it provides a glimpse of what Emerson's boyhood
ambition had really been—not to become a reclusive scholar and occasional
lecturer, but to be a public figure, an eloquent mover of men, like his hero
Daniel Webster. The disinterest of his elders in his visionary schemes of
regeneration had not dampened his personal ambitions; if anything, it had
increased them. "The momentary ardour of childhood found that manhood
& age were too cold to sympathise with it, & too hastily inferred that its own
merit was solitary & unrivalled & would by and by blaze up, & make an era
in Society." But this childhood ardor, like Wordsworth's "visionary gleam,"
eventually died away of its own accord:

> Alas. As it grew older it also grew colder & when it reached the
> period of manhood & of age it found that the waters of time, as
> they rolled had extinguished the fire that once glowed & there
> was no partial exemption for itself. The course of years rolls an
> unwelcome wisdom with them which forcibly teaches the vanity
> of human expectations.

And he concludes: "The dreams of my childhood are all fading away &
giving place to some very sober & very disgusting views of a quiet mediocrity
of talents & condition."

The intellectual revolution of the early 1830s—the discovery of the
God within—liberated Emerson from the hopelessness that had oppressed
his young manhood, but it could not do much for his stamina. He
circumvented the limitations of his constitution by carefully husbanding his
time and strength, and he learned to make the best of his alarming "*periods
of mentality*" ("one day I am a doctor, & the next I am a dunce") by means
of the unique method of composition he had already perfected by the mid-
thirties. He spent his mornings barricaded in his study, writing isolated
paragraphs in his journal when the spirit was upon him. When a longer
composition was needed—a sermon or a lecture—he quarried in these
journals for material and, as Chapman says, "threw together what seemed to

have a bearing on some subject, and gave it a title." Chapman adds, correctly, I think, that what keeps this method from resulting in an "incomprehensible chaos" is Emerson's single-mindedness:

> There was only one thought which could set him aflame, and that was the unfathomed might of man. This thought was his religion, his politics, his ethics, his philosophy. One moment of inspiration was in him own brother to the next moment of inspiration, although they might be separated by six weeks.[6]

What keeps this procedure from resulting in monotony for the reader, is first, the sheer power and felicity of Emerson's prose; next, the perpetual surprise of his observations (who else would have thought of comparing readers at the Boston Athenaeum to flies, aphids, and sucking infants?); and finally, his unflinching honesty, which will not let him rest until he has subjected his claim for the unfathomed might of man to every shred of negative evidence that can reasonably be urged against it. The combination of his single-mindedness and his insistence upon recognizing all the "opposite negations between which, as walls, his being is swung" is responsible for the curious fact about his work noticed long ago by Firkins. "Emerson's wish to get his whole philosophy into each essay tended toward sameness and promiscuity at once; it made the *essays similar* and the *paragraphs diverse*."[7] (It is also responsible for the fact that while his paragraphs are extraordinarily easy to remember word for word, they can be almost impossible to locate. Anything can be anyplace. The most time-consuming feature of being a student of Emerson is the necessity it places one under of repeatedly rereading half the collected *Works* and *Journals* in the maddening pursuit of some paragraph one can remember but not find.)

But his habits of composition, though they enabled him to produce a body of written work that would be remarkable enough for even a vigorous man, probably contributed to his sense of the unbridgeable gap between the life of the soul and the life of the senses, between the Reason and the Understanding. His ecstasies were carefully reserved for his study; the price he paid for them was an abnormally lowered vitality for the acts and perceptions of everyday life. He repeatedly complains of the "Lethean stream" that washes through him, of the "film or haze of unreality" that separates him from the world his senses perceive. How to transfer "nerve capital" (as a follower of Dr. Beard termed it[8]) from the column of the Reason to the column of the Understanding seemed to him life's chief insoluble problem. In "Montaigne" he writes:

The astonishment of life is the absence of any appearance of reconciliation between the theory and practice of life. Reason, the prized reality, the Law, is apprehended, now and then, for a serene and profound moment amidst the hubbub of cares and works which have no direct bearing on it; is then lost for months and years, and again found for an interval, to be lost again. If we compute it in time, we may, in fifty years, have half a dozen reasonable hours. But what are these cares and works the better? A method in the world we do not see, but this parallelism of great and little, which never discover the smallest tendency to converge.

Or, as he had once laconically observed: "Very little life in a lifetime."

Yet despite this discouraging arithmetic Emerson had always refused to abandon his insistence that the visionary moments constituted our *real* life, the one in which we felt most truly ourselves. This insistence is not quite as suicidal as it sounds, for the visionary moments, however brief they may be when measured by the clock, have a way of expanding while they are occurring into an eternal present that makes a mockery of duration. In a paragraph of "Circles" that looks forward to Thoreau's parable of the artist of Kouroo, Emerson had written:

It is the highest power of divine moments that they abolish our contritions also. I accuse myself of sloth and unprofitableness, day by day; but when these waves of God flow into me, I no longer reckon lost time. I no longer poorly compute my possible achievements by what remains to me of the month or the year; for these moments confer a sort of omnipresence and omnipotence, which asks nothing of duration, but sees that the energy of the mind is commensurate with the work to be done, without time.

With this proviso in mind it is easier to understand why Emerson could speculate in his journal that "in the memory of the disembodied soul the days or hours of pure Reason will shine with a steady light as the life of life & all the other days & weeks will appear but as hyphens which served to join these."

In "Experience" Emerson tries for the first time in his career to describe life as it looks from the standpoint of the hyphens rather than the heights, from the "waste sad time" (as Eliot calls it) separating the moments of vision rather than from the moments themselves. It is his attempt to confront the only form of suffering he recognized as genuinely tragic, because it was the only one for which his imagination could discover no answering compensation—the haze of unreality that sometimes suggested to him that we were "on the way back to Annihilation."

Emerson had originally planned to call the essay "Life." At first glance the difference between the two titles does not seem very great. Everything that happens in life can be described as an experience: a visionary moment as much as a bump on the head. Emerson himself uses the word this way in "The Transcendentalist" when he says that a transcendentalist's faith is based on a "certain brief experience" that surprises him in the midst of his everyday worries and pursuits.

Yet the word "experience" also had a technical meaning in empirical philosophy, where it refers to that portion of the world accessible to the senses, the world of time and space. This is the meaning it has in the works of Hume, whose skepticism had provoked the young Emerson into his first spiritual crisis during the decade of the 1820s. "Experience" is the weapon Hume uses to demolish belief in miracles and the argument for God's existence based on inferences from the evidence of design in the universe. If one accepted Hume's thesis—that "we have no knowledge but from Experience"—it was difficult to avoid his conclusion—that "we have no Experience of a Creator & therefore know of none." Hume could also use arguments from experience to shake belief in more fundamental assumptions: in the existence of matter, in the relationship of cause and effect, in the stability of personal identity. Emerson puzzled over these problems. In a high-spirited letter to his Aunt Mary written in 1823 he confessed that the doubts raised by this "Scotch Goliath" were as distressing to him as worries about the origin of evil or the freedom of the will. "Where," he asked rhetorically, "is the accomplished stripling who can cut off his most metaphysical head? Who is he that can stand up before him & prove the existence of the Universe, & of its Founder?" All the candidates in the "long & dull procession of Reasoners that have followed since" only proved, by their repeated attempts to confute Hume, that Hume had not been confuted.

Here, it is evident, Emerson is still accepting his teachers' argument that an attack on the existence of the material universe led inevitably to an attack on the existence of God. Whicher points out that "though Berkeley had denied the existence of matter independent of perception to confute sceptical materialism," to the Scottish Realists whose philosophical works dominated the Harvard scene in Emerson's youth, "the end product of the Ideal Theory was the scepticism of Hume."9

Emerson's discovery of "the God within" released him from the necessity of clinging to proofs of the existence of matter, since once the confirmation of the truths of religion had been made a purely intuitive affair, no longer dependent for its ratification on miracles perceivable by the senses, the "Ideal Theory" no longer seemed dangerous. The endless, fussy debates about whether we could trust the testimony of the Apostles who claimed to have witnessed the miracles of Jesus, about how the immutable laws of nature could have been temporarily suspended (e.g., whether Jesus made the water he walked on temporarily solid or himself temporarily weightless), about whether the gospels in which these events were recorded were genuine or spurious, neutral historical records or (as the German Higher Critics alleged) legendary or mythological narratives, could all be dispensed with in one liberating gesture. "Internal evidence outweighs all other to the inner man," Emerson wrote in 1830. "If the whole history of the New Testament had perished & its teachings remained—the spirituality of Paul, the grave, considerate, unerring advice of James would take the same rank with me that now they do." It is the truth of the doctrine that confirms the truth of the miracle, not the other way round. If it were not so, Emerson frankly confesses, he would probably "yield to Hume or any one that this, like all other miracle accounts, was probably false."

Hume's argument against the possibility of miracles had rested on the observation that our opinions about the reliability of testimony and about the probability of matters of fact are both drawn from experience. We usually believe the testimony of honorable witnesses, because we have found from experience that such men usually tell the truth. But we also form our opinions about the probability of matters of fact from our experience: whether it is likely to snow in July, whether a man can walk on water or rise from the dead. "The reason, why we place any credit in witnesses and historians, is not derived from any *connexion*, which we perceive *a priori*, between testimony and reality, but because we are accustomed to find a conformity between them. But when the fact attested is such a one as has seldom fallen under our observation, here is a contest of two opposite experiences; of which the one destroys the other, as far as its force goes, and the superior can only separate on the mind by the force, which remains."[10]

Emerson's mature position can best be characterized by saying that he accepts Hume's argument but reverses his conclusions. When the testimony involved is not the testimony of witnesses but the testimony of consciousness, the "superior force" clearly belongs to consciousness. Experience and consciousness are indeed in perpetual conflict: "life is made up of the intermixture and reaction of these two amicable powers, whose marriage appears beforehand monstrous, as each denies and tends to abolish the other." When an irreconcilable conflict occurs, it is consciousness, not experience, whose testimony we believe. Hence Emerson's delight in the "scientific" equivalent to this assertion: the law he attributed to the Swiss mathematician Euler and quoted in the "Idealism" chapter of *Nature*. "The sublime remark of Euler on his law of arches, 'This will be found contrary to all experience, yet it is true;' had already transferred nature into the mind, and left matter like an outcast corpse."

Idealism had always held a secret attraction for Emerson, which had survived unchanged even during the years when his teachers were telling him to regard it as dangerous. In a letter to Margaret Fuller in 1841 he writes: "I know but one solution to my nature & relations, which I find in the remembering the joy with which in my boyhood I caught the first hint of the Berkleian philosophy, and which I certainly never lost sight of afterwards." What Emerson means by the "Berkleian philosophy," as Whicher notes, is not Berkeley's particular system but

> simply the "noble doubt ... whether nature outwardly exists." The seductive reversal of his relations to the world, with which the imagination of every child is sometimes caught, transferring his recurrent sense of a dreaminess in his mode of life to outward nature, and releasing him in his imagination into a solitude peopled with illusions, was scepticism of a special kind—

but a kind that increasingly seemed not the murderer of faith but rather its midwife.[11] The man who believes that the mind alone is real, matter only a phenomenon, is easier to convince of spiritual realities than the empiricist who continually demands sensible proofs. "Idealism seems a preparation for a strictly moral life & so skepticism seems necessary for a universal holiness," Emerson noted in an early journal. Indeed, if what he asserts in "Montaigne" is correct—that "belief consists in accepting the affirmations of the soul; unbelief, in denying them"—it is the empiricist, not the idealist, who deserves the title of skeptic. With this in mind, the history of philosophy begins to look very different. The classical skeptics no longer look frightening—Emerson quotes with approval de Gérando's opinion that Sextus Empiricus' skepticism had been directed only at the external world, not at metaphysical truths. Even the Scotch Goliath begins to look less formidable. "Religion does that for the uncultivated which philosophy does for ~~Hume~~ Berkeley & Viasa; makes the mountains dance & smoke & disappear before the steadfast gaze of Reason." Emerson crossed out Hume's name (enlisting Hume as an ally of religion was presumably too radical an idea for Emerson at this point in his career, though the Emerson of "Circles" would have found it plausible), but that he thought of Hume in context at all is significant enough.

But Idealism as a doctrine was more than philosophically important to Emerson; it was emotionally important as well. *Nature* as originally planned was to have ended with the chapter "Idealism"; and in that chapter he suggests some of the chief attractions the doctrine possessed. When "piety or passion" lifts us into the realm of Ideas, "we become physically nimble and lightsome; we tread on air; life is no longer irksome, and we think it will never be so. No man fears age or misfortune or death in their serene company, for he is transported out of the region of change." "The best, the happiest moments of life are these delicious awakenings of the higher powers, and the reverential withdrawing of nature before its God."

No wonder Emerson seized eagerly upon every philosopher whose system tended toward idealism of one kind or another: Plato, Plotinus, Berkeley, Kant, Fichte, Schelling. Religious doctrines, too, he tends to judge by their approximations to idealism. In an early journal he notes with approval that idealism seems to be a primeval theory, and quotes from the Mahabharata (one of the sacred books of India) a sentence that neatly inverts the Peripatetic formula (*nihil in intellectu quod non ante fuerit in sensu*) upon which Locke had based his philosophy. "The senses are nothing but the soul's instrument of action, *no knowledge can come to the soul by their channel*" (emphasis added).

I have made this digression into Emerson's philosophical interests for a reason: the essay "Experience" cannot, I think, be fully understood without some grasp of the metaphorical ways in which he employs the technical vocabulary of epistemology to talk about things like grief, guilt, ruthlessness, and isolation. Stanley Cavell sees in Emerson the only thinker who can be said to have anticipated the Heidegger of *Being and Time* in an attempt "to formulate a kind of epistemology of moods":

> The idea is roughly that moods must be taken as having at least as sound a role in advising us of reality as sense-experience has; that, for example, coloring the world, attributing to it the qualities "mean" or "magnanimous," may be no less objective or subjective than coloring an apple, attributing to it the colors red and green. Or perhaps we should say: sense-experience is to objects what moods are to the world.[12]

What makes this difficult subject more complicated still is Emerson's own recognition that the various epistemological theories proposed by every philosopher from Plato to Kant might themselves be little more than metaphorical equivalents of moods or habitual ways of taking the world. "I fear the progress of Metaphysical philosophy may be found to consist in nothing else than the progressive introduction of apposite metaphors," Emerson had dryly remarked in an early journal. "Thus the Platonists congratulated themselves for ages upon their knowing that Mind was a dark chamber whereon ideas like shadows were painted. Men derided this as infantile when they afterwards learned that the Mind was a sheet of white paper whereon any & all characters might be written." The real difficulty in arriving at an epistemology of moods is that moods are likely to dictate beforehand the shape of one's epistemology. A soul in a state of exaltation will instinctively incline to the mystical idealism of the Mahabharata; a soul in a state of depression, to the skepticism of Hume. A healthy but nonreflective man might find the epistemology of the Scottish Realists sufficiently convincing; a more introspective man might not rest content until he had seen the relation between subject and object given transcendental ground in the philosophy of Kant.

Words like "experience" and "idealism" have different meanings in each of these systems, and different from any are the meanings they have acquired in popular use, where "idealism" is taken to mean any rosy or elevated estimate of human possibilities, and "experience" the process by which that estimate is lost. In "Experience" Emerson does not so much attempt to introduce order into this confusion as to exploit its ironies. If the essay, like life itself, is a "train of moods" or succession of "many-colored lenses which paint the world their own hue," each showing only what lies in its focus, then one of the chief ways of arriving at an epistemology of moods is by studying the shadings these words take on as the paragraphs pass by. From some moods within the essay, "experience" looks like a neutrally descriptive word; from others, a term of bitterness or contempt; from others still, the most savage of ironies. And the same thing holds true for "idealism," as one can see from the sentence (which may be the bitterest Emerson ever wrote) taken from the paragraphs of the essay that deal with the death of his son: "Grief too will make us idealists."

From the beginning of the essay the concept of experience is already involved in ironies. The opening image, which compares life to the climbing of an endless staircase, has reminded more than one critic of a Piranesi engraving, and Porte has pointed out that Emerson's references to "lethe" and "opium" recall a passage in DeQuincey's *Confessions of an English Opium-Eater*, where Piranesi's *Carceri d'Invenzione* is explicitly mentioned.[13] But DeQuincey was describing dreams induced by an actual drug; Emerson is describing the ordinary waking consciousness, life as it presents itself to the senses.

Hume, who thought that all knowledge came through experience, divided the contents of the mind into "IMPRESSIONS and IDEAS," the former derived from sensation (whether from external nature or the passions themselves), the latter the "faint images" of the former.[14] Since the two are different not in kind but only in degree, he pauses at the beginning of the *Treatise of Human Nature* to consider whether the two can ever be confused. He admits that in madness or fever or dreams ideas may become almost as lively as impressions, and that conversely there are some states in which "it sometimes happens, that our impressions are so faint and low, that we cannot distinguish them from our ideas."[15] What Emerson suggests in the opening paragraph of "Experience" is that the state Hume admitted as exceptional is in fact closer to being the norm: our impressions are most of the time as faint as our ideas, and a system of philosophy that separated one from the other according to the "degrees of force and liveliness, with which they strike upon the mind"[16] would very shortly lose the power to tell reality from phantasmagoria. The first irony we can record about experience is that it chiefly menaces the very philosophical system supposed to revere it. The exhaustion that attends it numbs the mind so that all the things we perceive "swim and glitter" like apparitions—a condition that, as Emerson accurately says, threatens not so much our life as our perception.

The second paragraph of the essay lodges a different complaint: the fact that experience and whatever wisdom can be derived from it are never coincident. Our life becomes meaningful only retroactively. "If any of us knew what we were doing, or where we are going, then when we think we best know! We do not know today whether we are busy or idle. In times when we have thought ourselves indolent, we have afterwards discovered that much was accomplished and much was begun in us." The most valuable experiences Wordsworth discovered in his childhood as he looked back on it were not the incidents a biographer would be likely to record but rather certain uncanny moments of heightened perception that occurred unexpectedly in the midst of ordinary childish sports—ice skating, robbing birds' nests, going for a night ride in a stolen boat—just as the most significant experience during the European tour he made as a young man turned out to be not the visions of sublime Alpine scenery but the vague feeling of depression that had succeeded the peasant's revelation that he and his companion had passed the highest point on their Alpine journey without recognizing it. Life and the meaning of life can never be apprehended simultaneously; like Pandarus in *Troilus and Criseyde* we can all justly complain "I hoppe alwey byhynde."[17]

Nor can any illumination ever prove final. "What a benefit if a rule could be given whereby the mind could at any moment *east* itself, & find the sun," Emerson had written in his journal. "But long after we have thought we were recovered & sane, light breaks in upon us & we find we have yet had no sane moment. Another morn rises on mid-noon." That final Miltonic allusion (along with its demonic counterpart, "under every deep a lower deep opens") may be regarded as a slightly more cheerful version of the staircase image that opens "Experience": it combines the suggestion of interminability with the suggestion that with each new layer of experience there is at least a widening of circumference or gain in wisdom. As Emerson says later on in the essay, "the years teach much that the days never know." Unfortunately, this wisdom clarifies only the past; each new situation finds us blundering like novices. "The individual is always mistaken." This melancholy but resigned conclusion resembles the opinion Yeats expresses in *Per Amica Silentia Lunae*, that since no disaster in life is exactly like another, there must always be "new bitterness, new disappointment";[18] it is perhaps even closer to the remark made by a contemporary Zen master, Shunryu Suzuki, to the effect that the life of a Zen master in pursuit of enlightenment "could be said to be so many years of *shoshaku jushaku*—'to succeed wrong with wrong,' or one continuous mistake."[19]

It is important to realize that at this point in the essay Emerson is *not* contrasting the wisdom that comes from experience with the higher wisdom that comes from consciousness. He is exploring a curious paradox that exists within experience itself. "All our days are so unprofitable while they pass, that 'tis wonderful where or when we ever got anything of this which we call wisdom, poetry, virtue. We never got it on any dated calendar day." The contrast between the pettiness of our daily lives and the accumulated wisdom that somehow results from them is so vast that even a resolute empiricist will be driven to mythology or fiction to account for it. "Some heavenly days must have been intercalated somewhere, like those that Hermes won with the dice of the Moon, that Osiris might be born."

Yet the cruelest feature of experience is the power it possesses of alienating *us* not only from our perceptions and our interpretations but even from our own sorrows:

What opium is instilled into all disaster! It shows formidable as we approach it, but there is at last no rough rasping friction, but the most slippery sliding surfaces; we fall soft on a thought; *Ate Dea* is gentle,—

"*Over men's heads walking aloft,*
With tenderfeet treading so soft."

People grieve and bemoan themselves, but it is not half so bad with them as they say. There are moods in which we court suffering, in the hope that here we shall find reality, sharp peaks and edges of truth. But it turns out to be only scene-painting and counterfeit. The only thing grief has taught me, is to know how shallow it is. That, like all the rest, plays about the surface, and never introduces me into the reality, for contact with which we would even pay the costly price of sons and lovers. Was it Boscovich who found out that bodies never come in contact? Well, souls never touch their objects. An innavigable sea washes with silent waves between us and the things we aim at and converse with. Grief too will make us idealists. In the death of my son, now more than two years ago, I seem to have lost a beautiful estate,—no more. I cannot get it nearer to me. If tomorrow I should be informed of the bankruptcy of my principle debtors, the loss of my property would be a great inconvenience to me, perhaps, for many years; but it would leave me as it found me,— neither better nor worse. So it is with this calamity; it docs not touch me; something which I fancied was a part of me, which could not be torn away without tearing me nor enlarged without enriching me, falls off and leaves no scar. It was caducous. I grieve that grief can teach me nothing, nor carry me one step into real nature. The Indian who was laid under a curse that the wind should not blow to him, nor fire burn him, is a type of us all. The dearest events are summer-rain and we the Para coats that shed every drop. Nothing is left us now but death. We look to that with a grim satisfaction, saying, There at least is a reality that will not dodge us.

I have quoted the whole of this magnificent passage because it is chiefly in its cumulative force that it achieves its great and disturbing power over us. I have never yet read a commentary on it that I thought did justice to the peculiar kind of shock it administers to the reader who is encountering the essay for the first time. The casual brutality of the sentence in which Emerson introduces the death of his son *as an illustration* is unmatched by anything I know of in literature, unless it is the parenthetical remark in which Virginia Woolf reports the death of Mrs. Ramsay in the "Time Passes" section of *To the Lighthouse*.

Not that the unreality or numbness Emerson reports is itself shocking. Many writers before and after Emerson have said as much. A similar experience forms the subject of Dickinson's chilling lyric, "After great pain, a formal feeling comes"; it is also analyzed in a passage of Sir Thomas Browne's *Hydrotaphia* from which Emerson had copied sentences into one of his early journals. "There is no antidote against the Opium of time," Browne reminds us, and then goes on to say:

> Darknesse and light divide the course of time, and oblivion shares with memory a great part even of our living beings; we slightly remember our felicities, and the smartest stroaks of affliction leave but short smart upon us. Sense endureth no extremities, and sorrows destroy us or themselves. To weep into stones are fables. Afflictions induce callosities, miseries are slippery, or fall like snow upon us, which notwithstanding is no unhappy stupidity. To be ignorant of evils to come, and forgetfull of evils past, is a mercifull provision in nature, whereby we digest the mixture of our few and evil dayes, and our delivered senses not relapsing into cutting remembrances, our sorrows are not kept raw by the edge of repetitions.[20]

The whole passage, even down to the details of its tactile imagery, is a striking anticipation of "Experience." Yet the differences are as noteworthy as the similarities. The slipperiness of misery, which Browne calls a "mercifull provision in nature," is for Emerson "the most unhandsome part of our condition." And this is so because Emerson, unlike Browne, sees in the unreality of grief only an intensification of our normal state of alienation or dislocation from the world our senses perceive. This distance—the "innavigable sea" that washes between us and the world—is the real torture. If grief could relieve it, if suffering could introduce us to the reality behind the glittering and evanescent phenomena, we would welcome it. For contact with that reality we would be *willing* to pay (as Emerson says in what is surely the most chilling of all his hyperboles) "even the costly price of sons and lovers."

But grief proves to be as shallow as everything else. In a letter written a week after the death of his son Emerson laments: "Alas! I chiefly grieve that I cannot grieve; that this fact takes no more deep hold than other facts, is as dreamlike as they; a lambent flame that will not burn playing on the surface of my river. Must every experience—those that promised to be dearest & most penetrative,—only kiss my cheek like the wind & pass away? I think of Ixion & Tantalus & Kehama." "Kehama" is an allusion to Robert Southey's long narrative poem *The Curse of Kehama*, in which a virtuous character named Ladurlad is laid under a curse by the wicked ruler Kehama, who, though himself a mere mortal, has learned to wrest such power from the gods that he is able to send a burning fire into Ladurlad's heart and brain, and at the same time order the elements to flee from him. As Ladurlad laments:

> The Winds of Heaven must never breathe on me;
>   The Rains and Dews must never fall on me;
> Water must mock my thirst and shrink from me;
>   The common earth must yield no fruit to me;
> Sleep, blessed Sleep! must never light on me;
>   And Death, who comes to all, must fly from me,
> And never, never set Ladurlad free.[21]

Ladurlad is the "Indian" mentioned in "Experience": in making him a "type of us all" Emerson gives us his grimmest assessment of the human condition: an endless, goalless pilgrimage, driven by an inner but unquenchable fire through a world that recedes perpetually before the pilgrim. The bitter lesson we learn from experience is the soul's imperviousness to experiences. The traumas are not traumatic. "The dearest events are summer-rain, and we the Para coats that shed every drop." If we look forward with a "grim satisfaction" to death, it is because it is the one event in life that we can be sure will not slip through our fingers. "There at least is a reality that will not dodge us."

Yet the central portion of the passage is the most explicitly self-lacerating. In observing that grief, like poetry or religion, convinces us of the insubstantiality of the phenomenal world, in offering as evidence for this assertion his own imperviousness to the death of his son, whose loss he likens, with deliberate vulgarity, to the loss of an estate, Emerson is indulging in a candor so "dreadful" (as Bishop puts it) that it has driven more than one critic to suppose that he either did not mean what he said or else was unaware of his meaning.[22]

Part of the problem comes from the difficulty of determining Emerson's tone in the passage. Bishop has pointed out Emerson's fondness for what he calls "tonal puns." He instances a sentence from *The Conduct of Life*: "Such as you are, the gods themselves could not help you." Bishop says: "One can hear a voice that says this insultingly and another voice, intimate and quiet, that says it encouragingly."[23] But he confesses that sentences like "*Ate Dea* is gentle" and "Grief too will make us idealists" and "I cannot get it nearer to me" leave him puzzled. Are they straightforward or ironical, desperate or resigned?[24] The answer, I think, is that we *can* imagine a voice that says all of these things with bitter irony, but that we can also imagine them being said in a voice as toneless and detached as that of a witness giving evidence in a war crimes trial, or that of the wasted and suffering discharged

soldier whom Wordsworth questions about his experiences in Book IV of
The Prelude:

> ... in all he said
> There was a strange half-absence, as of one
> Knowing too well the importance of his theme
> But feeling it no longer.[25]

Emerson is driven to offer his testimony by an inner necessity. I admire
Maurice Gonnaud's fine remark about this compulsion: "The greatness of an
essay like 'Experience' lies, I suggest, in our sense of the author's being
engaged in a pursuit of truth which has all the characters of faith except its
faculty of radiating happiness."[26]

What sharpens the sting of the revelations is Emerson's tacit
acknowledgment, through his phrasing and imagery, that fate itself has
retroactively conferred upon some brave assertions of the past the one kind
of irony it was beyond his power to intend. Thus "grief too will make us
idealists" both echoes and answers a journal entry of 1836 in which Emerson
was working out the concepts that later became part of the sixth chapter of
Nature: "Religion makes us idealists. Any strong passion does. The best, the
happiest moments of life are these delicious awakenings of the higher powers
& the reverential withdrawing of nature before its god." His remark that his
relationship to his son proved to be "caducous" recalls a happy declaration,
made after the departure of some friends in August of 1837, that he had faith
in the soul's powers of infinite regeneration: "these caducous relations are in
the soul like leaves ... & how often soever they are lopped off, yet still it
renews them ever." Even more chilling is the prophetic remark he made to
Jones Very during the latter's visit in 1838: "I told Jones Very that I had never
suffered, & that I could scarce bring myself to feel a concern for the safety &
life of my nearest friends that would satisfy them: that I saw clearly that if my
wife, my child, my mother, should be taken from me, I should still remain
whole with the same capacity of cheap enjoyment from all things." There is
a kind of self-contempt in this passage; Emerson had already survived so
many losses that he felt confident in predicting his response to more. But this
passage was written when little Waldo was barely two. In the intervening
years—years in which Emerson had delightedly recorded his small son's
doings and sayings in his otherwise austerely intellectual journal—he had
evidently come to hope that this relationship was somehow different, that it
was something that "could not be torn away without tearing me nor enlarged
without enriching me."

Alas. Though Elizabeth Hoar's brother Rockwood "was never more impressed with a human expression of agony than by that of Emerson leading the way into the room where little Waldo lay dead,"[27] Rusk tells us, Emerson discovered to his sorrow that the prophecy he had made in 1838 was true. In his young manhood he had been greatly stirred by the remark of a Methodist farmer he worked with one summer that men were always praying and that their prayers were always answered. "Experience" records Emerson's grim awareness that the price you pay for invulnerability is invulnerability.

The passages here recanted were all confined to Emerson's private journals—a fact that helps explain why the opening pages of "Experience," almost alone among Emerson's works, give the impression of being not heard but overheard. But these privately recorded passages are not the only ones to be so retracted. Nearly every critic of the essay has pointed out the connection between some detail of its imagery or argument and those of an earlier work that it systematically recants or retracts. Thus the opening question—"Where do we find ourselves?"—when compared to the boldness of *Nature*'s opening—"Let us inquire, to what end is nature?"—suggests the bewilderment that has overtaken this latter-day Oedipus as he turns from riddle solving to self-examination. The opening image of an endless staircase recalls the "mysterious ladder" of "Circles," but where the latter saw a new prospect of power from every rung, "Experience" sees only repetition and exhaustion. Idiosyncrasy or subjectivity, which in "Self-Reliance" was felt to be the source of one's chief value, now becomes part of the limitation of temperament, which shut us out from every truth our "colored and distorting lenses" cannot transmit. The horizon that in "Circles" was a promise of perpetual expansion has now become merely a metaphor for frustration: "Men seem to have learned of the horizon the art of perpetual retreating and reference." In *Nature* Emerson was a Transparent Eye-ball; in "Experience" he is shut in "a prison of glass which [he] cannot see." The "noble doubt" whether nature outwardly exists, the exhilarating suggestion that perhaps the whole of the outward universe is only a projection from the apocalypse of the mind, has become in "Experience" the Fall of Man.[28]

But if "Experience" is in one way a palinode, it is in another way a continuation, under grimmer conditions, of the faith Emerson had never relinquished. That faith first enters the essay only as a kind of recoil against the reductiveness of the argument in the section devoted to temperament. Life is a string of moods, each showing only what lies in its focus; temperament is the iron wire on which these beads are strung. "Men resist the conclusion in the morning, but adopt it as the evening wears on, that temper prevails over everything of time, place, and condition, and is inconsumable in the flames of religion."

Yet in the midst of this determinism Emerson suddenly pauses to note the "capital exception" every man makes to general or deterministic laws— that is, himself. Although every man believes every other to be "a fatal partialist," he never sees himself as anything other than a "universalist." (In a similar passage later on in the essay Emerson will observe that we make the same exception to moral laws, which is why no man can believe that "the crime in him is as black as in the felon.") In "Circles" Emerson had noted that "every man supposes himself not to be fully understood; and if there is any truth in him, if he rests at last on the divine soul, I see not how it can be otherwise. The last chamber, the last closet, he must feel was never opened; there is always a residuum unknown, unanalyzable. That is, every man believes he has a greater possibility." However much we may appear to one another as creatures limited by a given temperament, bound by the "links of the chain of physical necessity," the very fact that our consciousness rebels utterly at such a description of *ourselves* is the best evidence we have of the falsity of the doctrine. On its own level—the level of nature, of experience— temperament may be final, relativism inescapable.

> But it is impossible that the creative power should exclude itself. Into every intelligence there is a door which is never closed, through which the creator passes. The intellect, seeker of absolute truth, or the heart, lover of absolute good, intervenes for our succor, and at one whisper of these high powers we awake from our ineffectual struggles with this nightmare. We hurl it into its own hell, and cannot again contract ourselves to so base a state.

Yet this recovery, though it suggests the direction the essay will take, is by no means a final triumph over the lords of life. After Temperament there is Succession, by which Emerson means both the succession of "moods"— which he has already discussed—and the succession of "objects." The succession of moods is something we suffer; the succession of objects is something we choose. "We need change of objects." Our hunger for the whole keeps us restlessly searching through the world of experience in pursuit of a final consummation forever denied us. But if there are no final satisfactions, there are at least partial ones. In *The American Scholar* Emerson had compared inspiration to the "one central fire which flaming now out of the lips of Etna, lightens the capes of Sicily; and now out of the throat of Vesuvius, illuminates the towers and vineyards of Naples." The image he uses in "Experience" is considerably less apocalyptic, but the faith it expresses is the same: "Like a bird which alights nowhere, but hops perpetually from bough to bough, is the Power which abides in no man and no woman, but for a moment speaks from this one, and for another from that one."

The essay by this point seems to have established a pattern—a dip into despair, followed by a recoil of hope. But suddenly and unexpectedly Emerson turns on himself and his method: "what help from these fineries or pedantries? What help from thought? Life is not dialectics." This yawing back and forth between despair and hope is not, after all, how we spend most of our time. "Life is not intellectual or critical, but sturdy." Some way must be found to redeem the time, to treat it as something other than an emptiness separating moments of vision. "To fill the hour,—that is happiness; to fill the hour and leave no crevice for a repentance or an approval. We live amid surfaces, and the true art of life is to skate well on them." In these sentences we hear a different voice emerging, a voice that will become stronger in "Montaigne" and dominant in a book like *English Traits*. It is the voice of strong common sense, giving a view of the world Emerson had indeed expressed earlier, in things like the "Commodity" chapter of *Nature* and in essays like "Prudence" and "Compensation," but had never before offered as a serious *alternative* to the world of Reason. Now, for the first time, he proposes the "mid-world" as something other than a step on the way to vision.

Yet the mid-world offers no permanent anchorage either; moments of illumination will return whether we want them to or not, upsetting all our resolutions to keep "due metes and bounds." "Underneath the inharmonious and trivial particulars, is a musical perfection, the Ideal journeying always with us, the heaven without rent or seam." This region is something we do not make, but find, and when we find it all the old exhilaration returns. We respond with joy and amazement to the opening of "this august magnificence, old with the love and homage of innumerable ages, young with the life of life, the sunbright Mecca of the desert. And what a future it opens! I feel a new heart beating with the love of the new beauty. I am ready to die out of nature and be born again into this new yet unapproachable America I have found in the West."

For a vision of life that assessed man only from the platform of "experience" would leave out half his nature. "If I have described life as a flux of moods, I must now add that there is that in us which changes not and which ranks all sensations and states of mind." This something is the "central life" mentioned at the end of "Circles," the center that contains all possible circumferences. "The consciousness in each man is a sliding scale, which identifies him now with the First Cause, and now with the flesh of his body; life above life, in infinite degrees." Different religions have given this First

Cause different names—Muse, Holy Ghost, *nous*, love—but Emerson confesses that he likes best the one ventured by the Chinese sage Mencius: "vast-flowing vigor." Asked what he means by this, Mencius describes it as the power that can "fill up the vacancy between heaven and earth" and that "leaves no hunger." With this definition we have come as far as possible from the terminal exhaustion and depletion of the essay's opening paragraphs: "we have arrived as far as we can go. Suffice it for the joy of the universe that we have arrived not at a wall, but at interminable oceans. Our life seems not so much present as prospective; not for the affairs on which it is wasted, but as a hint of this vast-flowing vigor."

But if this is the end of the dialectic, it is not the end of the essay, which—like life itself—will not let us remain in any state of illumination for long. We are brought back to the mid-world in a paragraph that summarizes all that has come before:

> It is very unhappy, but too late to be helped, the discovery we have made that we exist. That discovery is called the Fall of Man. Ever afterwards we suspect our instruments. We have learned that we do not see directly but mediately, and that we have no means of correcting these colored and distorting lenses which we are, or of computing the amount of their errors. Perhaps these subject-lenses have a creative power; perhaps there are no objects. Once we lived in what we saw; now, the rapaciousness of this new power, which threatens to absorb all things, engages us. Nature, art, persons, letters, religions, objects, successively tumble in, and God is but one of its ideas.

As Michael Cowan notes, this investigation of Subjectiveness in some ways "represents a spiralling back to the lord of Illusion, but now seen from the viewpoint of the saved rather than the damned imagination."[29] What has made the difference is the discovery that there is an irreducible something in the soul that rebels fiercely at any attempt to reduce it to a mere "bundle of perceptions," and that is hence the best proof that any such definition is false. Knowing that the soul retains even in its grimmest moments "a door which is never closed, through which the creator passes" is the saving revelation that transforms the hell of Illusion into the purgatory of Subjectiveness. We are still unable to transcend the limitations of our vision, but now we seem not so much cut off from the real as the unconscious progenitors of it. Our "subject-lenses," unlike the object-lenses of a telescope or microscope, do not merely magnify reality, they determine its characteristics: "the chagrins which the bad heart gives off as bubbles, at once take form as ladies and gentlemen in the street, shopmen or barkeepers in hotels, and threaten or insult whatever is threatenable or insultable in us." This is a trivial example of a principle, anything but trivial, whose gradual triumph one can witness in the history of the race. Realism is the philosophical system of every primitive tribe, but as civilization advances, men come gradually to suspect that as it is the eye that makes the horizon, so it is the beholder who creates the things he perceives.

It is not to be denied that there is something melancholy about such self-awareness. In a lecture entitled "The Present Age," delivered in 1837, Emerson expresses the traditional Romantic envy of those luckier ages that lived in what they saw:

> Ours is distinguished from the Greek and Roman and Gothic ages, and all the periods of childhood and youth by being the age of the second thought. The golden age is gone and the silver is gone– the blessed eras of unconscious life, of intuition, of genius.... The ancients were self-united. We have found out the difference of outer and inner. They described. We reason. They acted. We philosophise.

The act of reflection severs us as with an "innavigable sea" from the "things we aim at and converse with," and at the same time plants in our minds the suspicion that these things, which *feel* so distant, may not be "out there" at all. On this point modern empiricism and idealism coincide. Hume wrote: "Let us fix our attention out of ourselves as much as possible: Let us chace our imagination to the heavens, or to the utmost limits of the universe; we can never really advance a step beyond ourselves, nor can conceive of any kind of existence, but those perceptions, which have appear'd in that narrow compass."[30] As Emerson remarked of a similar passage from the materialist Condillac, "what more could an idealist say?"

This imprisonment has some lamentable consequences, as Emerson is the first to acknowledge, for the kingdoms of mortal friendship and of love. "Marriage (in which is called the spiritual world) is impossible, because of the inequality between every subject and every object.... There will be the same gulf between every me and every thee as between the original and the picture." For the soul, though it incarnates itself in time as an ordinary mortal with ordinary limitations, is in fact "of a fatal and universal power, *admitting no co-life*" (emphasis added). To say this is to push one's philosophy considerably beyond antinomianism; it ought logically to lead to a state in which everything—theft, arson, murder—is permitted. Emerson does not attempt to refute this objection. Instead (in what is surely one of the more audacious gestures in American literature) he coolly embraces it. That crime occurs at all is the best evidence we have of our unshakable belief in the divinity of the self. "It is an instance of our faith in ourselves that men never speak of crime as lightly as they think.... Murder in the murderer is no such ruinous thought as poets and romancers will have it; it does not unsettle him or fright him from his ordinary notice of trifles; it is an act quite easy to be contemplated." Our reasons for abstaining from murder are (by a nice irony) purely empirical, derived from experience: "in its sequel [murder] turns out to be a horrible confounding of all relations." Emerson's own version of the categorical imperative derives from the same ontology. Just as the highest praise we can offer any artist is to think that he actually possessed the thought with which he has inspired us, so the highest tribute we can pay to a fellow human being is to assume that his exterior—which must remain to us merely a part of the phenomenal—conceals a Deity as central to itself as our own. "Let us treat the men and women well; treat them as if they were real; perhaps they are."

We have here reached the shadowy ground where philosophy and psychology merge. In the letter to Margaret Fuller quoted earlier Emerson had claimed that the Berkleian philosophy was the clue to his nature *and relations*. Idealism as a philosophical doctrine appealed to him partly because it offered a credible way of accounting for the loneliness and isolation to which he felt temperamentally condemned. In 1851, after a rambling talk with Thoreau in which both of them had "stated over again, to sadness, almost, the Eternal loneliness," Emerson exclaimed, "how insular & pathetically solitary, are all the people we know!" We are inclined to try to find excuses for our separation from others, but in more honest moments we admit the grimmer truth: "the Sea, vocation, poverty, are seeming fences, but Man is insular and cannot be touched. Every man is an infinitely repellent orb, and holds his individual being on that condition." Existence for each of us is a drama played out in a private theater that admits only one spectator:

> Men generally attempt early in life to make their brothers first, afterwards their wives, acquainted with what is going forward in their private theater, but they soon desist from the attempt on finding that they also have some farce or perhaps some ear- & heart-rending tragedy forward on their secret boards on which they are intent, and all parties acquiesce at last in a private box with the whole play performed before him Bolus.

The same haunting notion prompts the question that closes this section of

"Experience": "How long before our masquerade will end its noise of tambourines, laughter and shouting, and we will find it was a solitary performance?"

It is true, as Emerson says, that the muses of love and religion hate these developments. But our inescapable subjectivity has its own compensations. The "sharp peaks and edges of truth" we had hoped to find in reality we discover at last in the soul. God himself is "the native of these bleak rocks," an insight that "makes in morals the capital virtue of self-trust. We must hold hard to this poverty, however scandalous, and by more vigorous self-recoveries, after the sallies of action, possess our axis more firmly. The life of truth is cold and so far mournful; but it is not the slave of tears, contritions, and perturbations. It does not attempt another's work, nor adopt another's facts." As James Cox notes, "if 'Self-Reliance' was a ringing exhortation to trust the self, 'Experience' turns out to disclose that, after the last disillusion, there is nothing to rely on *but* the self.[31]

And the sunbright Mecca of the West? The New Jerusalem, the kingdom of man over nature? What has become of it? In a journal Emerson had once noted sadly that "it takes a great deal of elevation of thought to produce a very little elevation of life.... Gradually in long years we bend our living to our idea. But we serve seven years & twice seven for Rachel." In "Experience" Emerson admits that he has served his time—"I am not the novice I was fourteen, nor yet seven years ago"—and still must be content only with Leah. "Let who will ask, Where is the fruit? I find a private fruit sufficient." This private fruit is, as Yoder says, "consciousness without correspondent results"[32]—but I think it is not quite true to say that it is the only paradise offered us after the circuitous journey of "Experience." The view from Pisgah is as clear as it ever was.

In a letter to Margaret Fuller written to mark the second anniversary of his son's death Emerson declared himself no closer to reconciling himself to the calamity than when it was new, and compared himself to a poor Irishman who, when a court case went against him, said to the judge, "I am not satisfied." The senses have a right to perfection as well as the soul, and the soul will never rest content until these "ugly breaks" can be prevented. The attitude of defiance and the feeling of impotence recall a famous journal entry written a few months after his son's death. Speaking of Christ's sacrifice, he says:

> He did well. This great Defeat is hitherto the highest fact we
> have. But he that shall come shall do better. The mind requires a
> far higher exhibition of character, one which shall make itself

good to the senses as well as the soul. This was a great Defeat. We demand Victory.

If it is not clear how long we will have to wait for this victory, how wide is the distance between ourselves and the Promised Land, Emerson refuses to give up hope. "Patience and patience, we shall win at the last." Experience may counsel only despair, "but in the solitude to which every man is always returning" there is a "sanity" that gives a very different kind of advice. "Never mind the ridicule, never mind the defeat; up again, old heart!—it seems to say." The "romance" that fled from our ship at the beginning of "Experience" returns at the end to become the goal of our weary but still hopeful pilgrimage. The "true romance which the world exists to realize"— the point at which desire and fact, the pleasure principle and the reality principle, will coincide "will be the transformation of genius into practical power.

Yet the ending of "Experience," if it restates the old hope—or at least restates the impossibility of giving it up—hardly leaves us cheered. As Firkins says, "the victory is gained in the end, idealism is reestablished, but the world in which its authority is renewed looks to the common eye like a dismantled, almost a dispeopled, universe."[33] After such knowledge, what consolation?

Emerson develops two main answers to his question in the decade of the 1840s, one of them given in "The Poet," the other in "Montaigne." Both are attempts to find some sort of "paradise within" to compensate the individual for his loss of Eden and for his failure to reach the New Jerusalem. One is designed to satisfy the Reason, the other the Understanding. (The very fact that this distinction still remains is a sign that the consolations offered are clearly thought of as *second bests*.[34]) And both essays, in their imagery and structure, show that by now Emerson's four fables— contraction, dislocation, ossification, and reflection—have become a system of significances as useful to him as the Biblical stories had been to his ancestors: a series of types or analogies by which the chaotic impressions of experience could be ordered and understood.

NOTES

1. Firkins, *Ralph Waldo Emerson*, p. 112.

2. Alfred Lord Tennyson, "Ulysses," lines 18–21, in *The Poems of Tennyson*, ed. Christopher Ricks (New York: W. W. Norton & Co., 1972), p. 563.

3. "The Holy Grail," lines 438–439, from *Idylls of the King*, in *Poems of Tennyson*, p. 1674.

4. Beard, *American Nervousness*, p. 9.

5. George M. Beard, *A Practical Treatise on Nervous Exhaustion (Neurasthenia) Its Symptoms, Nature, Sequences, Treatment* (New York: William Wood & Co., 1880), p. 66.

6. Chapman, *Selected Writings*, p. 163.

7. Firkins, *Ralph Waldo Emerson*, p. 239.

8. Albert Abrams, *The Blues (Splanchnic Neurasthenia): Causes and Cures*, 2nd. ed., enlarged (New York: E. B. Treat & Co., 1905) p. 16.

9. Whicher, *Freedom and Fate*, p. 15.

10. David Hume, "Of Miracles," in *An Enquiry Concerning Human Understanding*, in: *Essays, Moral, Political, and Literary*, ed. T. H. Green and T. H. Grose, 2 vols. (London: Longmans, Green, & Co., 1875), I, 91–92.

11. Whicher, *Freedom and Fate*, p. 16.

12. Cavell, *The Senses of Walden*, p. 125.

13. Porte, *Representative Man*, p. 181, n. 10.

14. David Hume, *A Treatise of Human Nature, Being an Attempt to Introduce the Experimental Method of Reasoning into Moral Subjects*, ed. T. H. Green and T. H. Grose, 2 vols. (London: Longmans, Green, & Co., 1898), I, 311.

15. Ibid., I, 311–312.

16. Ibid., I, 311.

17. Chaucer, *Troilus and Criseyde*, Bk. 2, line 1107.

18. W. B. Yeats, *Per Amica Silentia Lunae* (London: Macmillan & Co., 1918), p. 41.

19. Shunryu Suzuki, *Zen Mind, Beginner's Mind*, ed. Trudy Dixon, with an introduction by Richard Baker (New York: John Weatherhill, 1970), p. 35.

20. *Hydrotaphia: Urne-Burial, or, A Brief Discourse of the Sepulchral Urnes Lately Found in Norfolk* (1658), in *Sir Thomas Browne: Selected Writings*, ed. Sir Geoffrey Keynes (Chicago: University of Chicago Press, 1968), pp. 150, 152. Among the sentences Emerson copied were "There is no antidote against the *Opium* of time," and "miseries are slippery, or fall like snow upon us, which notwithstanding is no unhappy stupidity." See *JMN*, III, 219–220.

21. *The Poetical Works of Robert Southey*, 10 vols. (London: Longman, Orme, Brown, Green, & Longmans, 1840), VIII, 21.

22. Bishop, *Emerson on the Soul*, p. 198.

23. Ibid., p. 139.

24. Ibid., pp. 196–197.

25. Wordsworth, *The Prelude*, 1850 version, Bk. 4, lines 442–445.

26. Gonnaud, *Emerson: Prophecy*, pp. 121–122.

27. Rusk, *Life*, p. 294.

28. See Bishop, *Emerson on the Soul*, pp. 193–194; Porte, *Representative Man*, p. 182; Whicher, *Freedom and Fate*, p. 121. For additional examples, see Yoder, *Orphic Poet*, pp. 45, 48.

29. Michael Cowan, *City of the West: Emerson, America, and Urban Metaphor* (New Haven, Conn.: Yale University Press, 1967), p. 120. Cowan's reading of "Experience" is excellent.

30. Hume, *Treatise of Human Nature*, p. 371.

31. Cox, *Emerson: Prophecy*, p. 80.

32. Yoder, *Orphic Poet*, p. 46.

33. Firkins, *Ralph Waldo Emerson*, p. 194.

34. Whicher points out that Emerson's later thought is "characteristically an affirmation of a *second best*." *Freedom and Fate*, p. 126.

HAROLD BLOOM

Emerson:
The American Religion

I start from a warning of Lichtenberg's.

> As soon as a man begins to see everything, he generally expresses
> himself obscurely—begins to speak with the tongues of angels.

But Lichtenberg also wrote, "The itch of a great prince gave us long
sleeves." The lengthened shadow of our American culture is Emerson's, and
Emerson indeed saw everything in everything, and spoke with the tongue of
a daemon. His truest achievement was to invent the American religion, and
my reverie intends a spiraling out from his center in order to track the
circumferences of that religion in a broad selection of those who emanated
out from him, directly and evasively, celebratory of or in negation to his
Gnosis. Starting from Emerson we came to where we are, and from that
impasse, which he prophesied, we will go by a path that most likely he
marked out also. The mind of Emerson is the mind of America, for worse
and for glory, and the central concern of that mind was the American
religion, which most memorably was named "self-reliance."

Of this religion, I begin by noting that it is *self*-reliance as opposed to
God-reliance, though Emerson thought the two were the same. I will
emphasize this proper interpretation by calling the doctrine "self-reliance,"

From *Agon: Towards a Theory of Revisionism*. © 1982 by Oxford University Press, Inc.

in distinction from Emerson's essay *Self-Reliance*. "Reliance" is not of the essence, but the Emersonian *self* is: "To talk of reliance is a poor external way of speaking. Speak rather of that which relies because it works and is." What "works and is" is the stranger god, or even alien god, within. Within? Deeper than the *psyche* is the *pneuma*, the spark, the uncreated self, distinct from the soul that God (or Demiurge) created. *Self*-reliance, in Emerson as in Meister Eckhart or in Valentinus the Gnostic, is the religion that celebrates and reveres what in the self is before the Creation, a whatness which from the perspective of religious orthodoxy can only be the primal Abyss.

In September 1866, when he was sixty-three, and burned out by his prophetic exultation during the Civil War, Emerson brooded in his journals on the return of the primal Abyss, which he had named Necessity, and which his descendant Stevens was to hail as "fatal Ananke the common god." Earlier in 1866, pondering Hegel, Emerson had set down, with a certain irony, his awareness of the European vision of the end of speculation:

> Hegel seems to say, Look, I have sat long gazing at the all but imperceptible transitions of thought to thought, until I have seen with eyes the true boundary.... I know that all observation will justify me, and to the future metaphysician I say, that he may measure the power of his perception by the degree of his accord with mine. This is the twilight of the gods, predicted in the Scandinavian mythology.

A few months later, this irony at another's apocalyptic egocentricity was transcended by a post-apocalyptic or Gnostic realization:

> There may be two or three or four steps, according to the genius of each, but for every seeing soul there are two absorbing facts,—*I and the Abyss*.

This grand outflaring of negative theology is a major text, however gnomic, of *the* American religion, Emersonianism, which this book aspires to identify, to describe, to celebrate, to join. I am not happy with the accounts of Emersonianism available to me. Of the religions native to the United States, Emersonianism or *our literary religion* remains the most diffuse and diffused, yet the only faith of spiritual significance, still of prophetic force for our future. An excursus upon the religions starting in America is necessary before I quest into the wavering interiors of the American religion proper. Sydney Ahlstrom in his definitive *A Religious History of the American People* (1972) recognizes "that Emerson is in fact the theologian of something we may almost term 'the American religion.'" Who were or could have been Emerson's rivals? Of religious geniuses our evening-land has been strangely unproductive, when our place in Western history is fully considered. We have had one great systematic theologian, in Jonathan Edwards, and something close to a second such figure in Horace Bushnell. But we have only the one seer, Emerson, and the essentially literary traditions that he fostered.

The founders of American heresies that have endured are quite plentiful, yet our major historians of American religion—Ahlstrom, W. W. Sweet, H.R. Niebuhr, M.E. Marty, S.E. Mead, C. E. Olmstead, among others—tend to agree that only a handful are of central importance. These would include Ellen Harmon White of the Seventh Day Adventists, Joseph Smith of the Mormons, Alexander Campbell of the Disciples of Christ, Mary Baker Eddy of Christian Science, and Charles Taze Russell of Jehovah's Witnesses. To read any or all of these is a difficult experience, for the founder's texts lack the power that the doctrines clearly are able to manifest. There is, thankfully, no Emersonian church, yet there are certain currents of Harmonial American religion that dubiously assert their descent from the visionary of *Nature* and the *Essays*. Aside from Mrs. Eddy, who seized on poor Bronson Alcott for an endorsement after the subtle Emerson had evaded her, the "health and harmony" Positive Thinkers notably include Ralph Waldo Trine, author of *In Tune with the Infinite* (1897), and his spiritual descendants Harry Emerson Fosdick and Norman Vincent Peale. We can add to this pseudo-Emersonian jumble the various Aquarian theosophies that continue to proliferate in America a decade after the sixties ebbed out. I cite all these sects and schisms because all of them have failed the true Emersonian test for the American religion, which I will state as my own dogma: *it cannot become the American religion until it first is canonized as American literature*. Though this explicit dogma is mine, it was the genius of Emerson implicitly to have established such a principle among us.

2

What in the nineteenth and twentieth centuries is religious writing? What can it be? Which of these passages, setting their polemics aside, is better described as religious writing?

> People say to me, that it is but a dream to suppose that Christianity should regain the organic power in human society which once it possessed. I cannot help that; I never said it could. I am not a politician; I am proposing no measures, but exposing

a fallacy, and resisting a pretence. Let Benthamism reign, if men dare no aspirations; but do not tell them to be romantic, and then solace them with glory; do not attempt by philosophy what was once done by religion. The ascendancy of Faith may be impracticable, but the reign of Knowledge is incomprehensible....

... He that has done nothing has known nothing. Vain is it to sit scheming and plausibly discoursing: up and be doing! If thy knowledge be real, put it forth from thee: grapple with real Nature; try thy theories there, and see how they hold out. Do one thing, for the first time in thy life do a thing; a new light will rise to thee on the doing of all things whatsoever....

I have taken these passages randomly enough; they lay near by. The distinguished first extract is both truly religious and wonderfully written, but the second is religious writing. Newman, in the first, from *The Tamworth Reading Room* (1841), knows both the truth and his own mind, and the relation between the two. Carlyle, in the second, from *Corn-Law Rhymes* (1832), knows only his own knowing, and sets that above both Newman's contraries, religion and philosophy. *Corn-Law Rhymes* became a precursor text for Emerson because he could recognize what had to be religious writing for the nineteenth century, and to that recognition, which alone would not have sufficed, Emerson added the American difference, which Carlyle could not ever understand. Subtle as this difference is, another intertextual juxtaposition can help reveal it:

"But it is with man's Soul as it was with Nature: the beginning of Creation is—Light. Till the eye have vision, the whole members are in bonds. Divine moment, when over the tempest-tossed Soul, as once over the wild-weltering Chaos, it is spoken: Let there be Light! Ever to the greatest that has felt such moment, is it not miraculous and God-announcing; even as, under simpler figures, to the simplest and least. The mad primeval Discord is hushed; the rudely-jumbled conflicting elements bind themselves into separate Firmaments: deep silent rock-foundations are built beneath; and the skyey vault with its everlasting Luminaries above: instead of a dark wasteful Chaos, we have a blooming, fertile, heaven-encompassed World."

"Nature is not fixed but fluid, Spirit alters, molds, makes it. The immobility or bruteness of nature is the absence of spirit; to pure spirit it is fluid, it is volatile, it is obedient. Every spirit builds itself a house, and beyond its house a world, and beyond its world a heaven. Know then that the world exists for you. For you is the phenomenon perfect. What we are, that only can we see.... Build therefore your own world. As fast as you conform your life to the pure idea in your mind, that will unfold its great proportions.... The kingdom of man over nature, which cometh not with observation,—a dominion such as now is beyond his dream of God,—he shall enter without more wonder than the blind man feels who is gradually, restored to perfect sight."

This juxtaposition is central, because the passages are. The first rhapsode is Carlyle's Teufelsdröckh uttering his Everlasting Yea in *Sartor Resartus*; the second is Emerson's Orphic poet chanting the conclusion of *Nature*. Carlyle's seeing soul triumphs over the Abyss, until he can say to himself: "Be no longer a Chaos, but a World, or even Worldkin. Produce! Produce!" The Abyss is bondage, the production is freedom, somehow still "in God's name!" Emerson, despite his supposed discipleship to Carlyle in *Nature*, has his seeing soul proclaim a world so metamorphic and beyond natural metamorphosis that its status is radically *prior* to that of the existent universe. For the earth is only part of the blind man's "dream of God." Carlyle's imagination remains orthodox, and rejects Chaos. Emerson's seeing, beyond observation, is more theosophical than Germanic Transcendental. The freedom to imagine "the pure idea in your mind" is the heretical absolute freedom of the Gnostic who identified his mind's purest idea with the original Abyss. American freedom, in the context of Emerson's American religion, indeed might be called "Abyss-radiance."

I return to the question of what, in the nineteenth century, makes writing *religious*. Having set Carlyle in the midst, between Newman and Emerson, I cite next the step in religious writing beyond even Emerson:

> ... we have an interval, and then our place knows us no more. Some spend this interval in listlessness, some in high passions, the wisest, at least among "the children of this world," in art and song. For our one chance lies in expanding that interval, in getting as many pulsations as possible into the given time.... ·

Pater, concluding *The Renaissance*, plays audaciously against Luke 16:8, where "the children of this world are in their generation wiser than the children of light." Literalizing the Gospel's irony, Pater insinuates that in his generation the children of this world are the only children of light. Light expands our fiction of duration, our interval or place in art, by a concealed allusion to the Blakean trope that also fascinated Yeats; the pulsation of an artery in which the poet's work is done. Pater sinuously murmurs his credo, which elsewhere in *The Renaissance* is truly intimated to be "a strange rival religion" opposed to warring orthodoxies, fit for "those who are neither for Jehovah nor for His enemies."

To name Emerson and Pater as truly "religious writers" is to call into question very nearly everything that phrase usually implies. More interestingly, this naming also questions that mode of displacement M. H. Abrams analyzes in his strong study *Natural Supernaturalism*: "not ... the deletion and replacement of religious ideas but rather the assimilation and reinterpretation of religious ideas." I believe that the following remarks of Abrams touch their limit precisely where Carlyle and Emerson part, on the American difference, and also where Carlyle and Ruskin part from Pater and what comes after. The story Abrams tells has been questioned by Hillis Miller, from a Nietzschean linguistic or Deconstructive perspective, so that Miller dissents from Abrams exactly where Nietzsche himself chose to attack Carlyle (which I cite below). But there is a more ancient perspective to turn against Abrams's patterns-of-displacement, an argument as to whether poetry did not inform religion before religion ever instructed poetry. And beyond this argument, there is the Gnostic critique of creation-theories both Hebraic and Platonic, a critique that relies always upon the awesome trope of the primal Abyss.

Abrams states his "displacement" thesis in a rhetoric of continuity:

> Much of what distinguishes writers I call "Romantic" derives from the fact that they undertook, whatever their religious creed or lack of creed, to save traditional concepts, schemes, and values which had been based on the relation of the Creator to his creature and creation, but to reformulate them within the prevailing two-term system of subject and object, ego and non-ego, the human mind or consciousness and its transactions with nature. Despite their displacement from a supernatural to a natural frame of reference, however, the ancient problems, terminology, and ways of thinking about human nature and history survived, as the implicit distinctions and categories through which even radically secular writers saw themselves and their world....

Such "displacement" is a rather benign process, as though the incarnation of the Poetic Character and the Incarnation proper could be assimilated to one another, or the former serve as the reinterpretation of the latter. But what if poetry as such is always a counter-theology, or Gentile Mythus, as Vico believed? Abrams, not unlike Matthew Arnold, reads religion as abiding in poetry, as though the poem were a saving remnant. But perhaps the saving remnant of *poetry* is the only force of what we call theology? And what can theology be except what Geoffrey Hartman anxiously terms it: "a vast, intricate domain of psychopoetic events," another litany of evasions? Poems are the original lies-against-time, as the Gnostics understood when they turned their dialectics to revisionary interpretations not only of the Bible and Plato, but of Homer as well. Gnosticism was the inaugural and most powerful of Deconstructions because it undid all genealogies, scrambled all hierarchies, allegorized every microcosm/macrocosm relation, and rejected every representation of divinity as non-referential.

Carlyle, though he gave Abrams both the scheme of displacement find the title-phrase of "natural supernaturalism," seems to me less and less self-deceived as he progressed onwards in life and work, which I think accounts for his always growing fury. Here I follow Nietzsche, in the twelfth "Skirmish" of *Twilight of the Idols* where he leaves us not much of the supposedly exemplary life of Carlyle:

> ... this unconscious and involuntary farce, this heroic-moralistic interpretation of dyspeptic states. Carlyle: a man of strong words and attitudes, a rhetor from *need*, constantly lured by the craving for a strong faith and the feeling of his incapacity for it (in this respect, a typical romantic!). The craving for a strong faith is no proof of a strong faith, but quite the contrary. If one has such a faith, then one can afford the beautiful luxury of skepticism; one is sure enough, firm enough, has ties enough for that. Carlyle drugs something in himself with the fortissimo of his veneration of men of strong faith and with his rage against the less simple minded: he *requires* noise. A constant passionate dishonesty against himself—that is his *proprium*; in this respect he is and remains interesting. Of course, in England he is admired precisely for his honesty. Well, that is English; and in view of the fact that the English are the people of consummate cant, it is even as it should be, and not only comprehensible. At bottom, Carlyle is an English atheist who makes it a point of honor not to be one.

It seems merely just to observe, following Nietzsche's formidable wit, that Carlyle contrived to be a religious writer without being a religious man.

His clear sense of the signs and characteristics of the times taught him that the authentic nineteenth-century writer had to be religious *qua* writer. The burden, as Carlyle knew, was not so much godlessness as belatedness, which compels a turn to Carlyle (and Emerson) on history.

3

Carlyle, with grim cheerfulness, tells us that history is an unreadable text, indeed a "complex manuscript, covered over with formless inextricably-entangled unknown characters,—nay, which is a Palimpsest, and bad once prophetic writing, still dimly legible there...." We can see emerging in this dark observation the basis for *The French Revolution*, and even for *Past and Present*. But that was Carlyle *On History* in 1830, just before the advent of Diogenes Teufelsdröckh, the author of *On History Again* in 1833, where the unreadable is read as Autobiography repressed by all Mankind: "a like unconscious talent of remembering and of forgetting again does the work here." The great instance of this hyperbolic or Sublime repression is surely Goethe, whose superb self-confidence breathes fiercely in his couplet cited by Carlyle as the first epigraph to *Sartor Resartus*:

> Mein Vermächtnis, wie herrlich weit und breit!
> Die Zeit ist mein Vermächtnis, mein Acker ist die Zeit.

Goethe's splendid, wide and broad inheritance is time itself, the seed-field that has the glory of having grown Goethe! But then, Goethe had no precursors in his own language, or none at least that could make him anxious. Carlyle trumpets his German inheritance: Goethe, Schiller, Fichte, Novalis, Kant, Schelling. His English inheritance was more troublesome to him, and the vehemence of his portrait of Coleridge reveals an unresolved relationship. This unacknowledged debt to Coleridge, with its too-conscious swerve away from Coleridge and into decisiveness and overt courage, pain accepted and work deified, may be the hidden basis for the paradoxes of Carlyle on time, at once resented with a Gnostic passion and worshipped as the seed-bed of a Goethean greatness made possible for the self. It is a liberation to know the American difference again when the reader turns from Carlyle's two essays on history to History, placed first of the *Essays* (1841) of Emerson:

> This human mind wrote history, and this must read it. The Sphinx must solve her own riddle. If the whole of history is in one man, it is all to be explained from individual experience....

... Property also holds of the soul, covers great spiritual facts, and instinctively we at first hold to it with swords and laws and wide and complex combinations. The obscure consciousness of this fact is the light of all our day, the claim of claims; the plea for education, for justice, for charity; the foundation of friendship and love and of the heroism and grandeur which belong to acts of self-reliance. It is remarkable that involuntarily we always read as superior beings.. ..

... The student is to read history actively and not passively; to esteem his own life the text, and books the commentary....

So much then for Carlyle on history; so much indeed for history. The text is not interpretable? But there is no text! There is only your own life, and the Wordsworthian light of all our day turns out to be: self-reliance. Emerson, in describing an 1847 quarrel with Carlyle in London, gave a vivid sense of his enforcing the American difference, somewhat at the expense of a friendship that was never the same again:

Carlyle ... had grown impatient of opposition, especially when talking of Cromwell. I differed from him ... in his estimate of Cromwell's character, and he rose like a great Norse giant from his chair—and, drawing a line with his finger, across the table, said, with terrible fierceness: "Then, sir, there is a line of separation between you and me as wide as that, and as deep as the pit."

Hardly a hyperbole, the reader will reflect, when he reads what two years later Carlyle printed as *The Nigger Question*. This remarkable performance doubtless was aimed against "Christian Philanthropy" and related hypocrisies, but the abominable greatness of the tract stems from its undeniable madness. The astonished reader discovers not fascism, but a terrible sexual hysteria rising up from poor Carlyle, as the repressed returns in the extraordinary trope of black pumpkin-eating:

... far over the sea, we have a few black persons rendered extremely "free" indeed.... Sitting yonder with their beautiful muzzles up to the ears in pumpkins, imbibing sweet pulps and juices; the grinder and incisor teeth ready for ever new work, and the pumpkins cheap as grass in those rich climates: while the sugar-crops rot round them uncut, because labour cannot be hired, so cheap are the pumpkins....

... and beautiful Blacks sitting there up to the ears in pumpkins, and doleful Whites sitting here without potatoes to eat....

... The fortunate Black man, very swiftly does he settle *his* account with supply and demand:—not so swiftly the less fortunate white man of those tropical locations. A bad case, his, just now. He himself cannot work; and his black neighbor, rich in pumpkin, is in no haste to help him. Sunk to the ears in pumpkin, imbibing saccharine juices, and much at his ease in the Creation, he can listen to the less fortunate white man's "demand" and take his own time in supplying it....

... An idle White gentleman is not pleasant to me: though I confess the real work for him is not easy to find, in these our epochs; and perhaps he is seeking, poor soul, and may find at last. But what say you to an idle Black gentleman, with his rum-bottle in his hand (for a little additional pumpkin you can have red-herrings and rum, in Demerara),—rum-bottle in his hand, no breeches on his body, pumpkin at discretion....

... Before the West Indies could grow a pumpkin for any Negro, how much European heroism had to spend itself in obscure battle; to sink, in mortal agony, before the jungles, the putrescences and waste savageries could become arable, and the Devils be in some measure chained there!

... A bit of the great Protector's own life lies there; beneath those pumpkins lies a bit of the life that was Oliver Cromwell's....

I have cited only a few passages out of this veritable procession of pumpkins, culminating in the vision of Carlyle's greatest hero pushing up the pumpkins so that unbreeched Blacks might exercise their potent teeth. Mere racism does not yield so pungent a phantasmagoria, and indeed I cannot credit it to Carlyle's, likely impotence either. This pumpkin litany is Carlyle's demi-Gnosticism at its worst, for here time is no fair seed-bed but rather devouring time, Kronos chewing us up as so many pumpkins, the time of "Getting Under Way" in *Sartor Resartus*:

... Me, however, as a Son of Time, unhappier than some others, was Time threatening to eat quite prematurely; for, strike as I might, there was no good Running, so obstructed was the path, so gyved were the feet....

Emerson, in truth, did not abide in his own heroic stance towards Time and History. The great declaration of his early intensity comes in the 1838 Journals: "A great man escapes out of the kingdom of time; he puts time under his feet." But the next decade featured ebb rather than influx of the Newness. What matter? The American, difference, however ill prepared to combat experience, had been stated, if not established. To come to that stating is to arrive fresh at Emerson's *Nature*, where the *clinamen* from Carlyle, and from Coleridge, is superbly turned.

4

Deconstructing any discourse by Ralph Waldo Emerson would be a hopeless enterprise, extravagantly demonstrating why Continental modes of interpretation are unlikely to add any lustres to the most American of writers. Where there are classic canons of construction, protrusions from the text can tempt an unravelling, but in a text like *Nature* (1836) all is protrusion. Emerson's first book is a blandly dissociative apocalypse, in which everything is a cheerful error, indeed a misreading, starting with the title, which says "Nature" but means "Man." The original epigraph, from Plotinus by way of the Cambridge Platonist Cudworth, itself deconstructs the title:

> Nature is but an image or imitation of wisdom, the last thing of the soul; nature being a thing which doth only do, but not know.

The attentive reader, puzzling a way now through Emerson's manifesto, will find it to be more the American Romantic equivalent to Blake's *The Marriage of Heaven and Hell* than to Coleridge's *Aids to Reflection* (which however it frequently echoes). At the Christological age of thirty-three (as was Blake in the *Marriage*), Emerson rises in the spirit to proclaim his own independent majority, but unlike Blake Emerson cheerfully and confidently proclaims his nation's annunciation also. Unfortunately, Emerson's vision precedes his style, and only scattered passages in *Nature* achieve the eloquence that became incessant from about a year later on almost to the end, prevailing long after the sage had much mind remaining. I will move here through the little book's centers of vision, abandoning the rest of it to time's revenges.

Prospects, and not retrospectives, is the Emersonian motto, as we can see by contrasting the title of the last chapter, "Prospects," to the opening sentences of the Introduction:

Our age is retrospective. It builds the sepulchres of the fathers. It writes biographies, histories, and criticism. The foregoing generations beheld God and nature face to face; we, through their eyes. Why should we not also enjoy an original relation to the universe?

The "fathers" are not British High Romantics, Boston Unitarians, New England Calvinist founders, but rather an enabling fiction, as Emerson well knows. They are Vico's giants, magic primitives, who invented all Gentile mythologies, all poetries of earth. Emerson joins them in the crucial trope of his first chapter, which remains the most notorious in his work:

Crossing a bare common, in snow puddles, at twilight, under a clouded sky, without having in my thoughts any occurrence of special good fortune, I have enjoyed a perfect exhilaration. I am glad to the brink of fear. In the woods, too, a man casts off his years, as the snake his slough, and at what period soever of life is always a child.... There I feel that nothing can befall me in life,—no disgrace, no calamity (leaving me my eyes), which nature cannot repair. Standing on the bare ground,—my head bathed by the blithe air and uplifted into infinite space,—all mean egotism vanishes. I become a transparent eyeball; I am nothing; I see all; the currents of the Universal Being circulate through me; I am part or parcel of God....

This is not a "Spiritual Newbirth, or Baphometic Fire-baptism," akin to those of Carlyle's Teufelsdröckh or Melville's Ahab, because Emerson's freedom rises out of the ordinary, and not out of crisis. But, despite a ruggedly commonplace genesis, there is little that is ordinary in the deliberately outrageous "I become a transparent eyeball." Kenneth Burke associates Emerson's imagery of transparence with the *crossing* or *bridging* action that is transcendence, and he finds the perfect paradigm for such figuration in the Virgilian underworld. The unburied dead, confronted by Charon's refusal to ferry them across Stygia, imploringly "stretched forth their hands through love of the farther shore." Emersonian transparency is such a stretching, a Sublime crossing of the gulf of solipsism, but *not* into a communion with others. As Emerson remarks: "The name of the nearest friend sounds then foreign and accidental: to be brothers, to be acquaintances, master or servant, is then a trifle and a disturbance." The farther shore has no persons upon it, because Emerson's farther shore or beyond is no part of nature, and has no room therefore for created beings. A second-century Gnostic would have understood Emerson's "I am nothing; I see all" as the mode of negation through which the knower again could stand in the Abyss, the place of original fullness, *before* the Creation.

A transparent eyeball is the emblem of the Primal Abyss regarding itself. What can an Abyss behold in an Abyss?

The answer, in our fallen or demiurgical perspective, can be dialectical, the endless ironic interplay of presence and absence, fullness and emptiness; in Gnostic vocabulary, Pleroma and Kenoma. But the Emerson of *Nature* was not yet willing to settle for such a deconstruction. Not upon an elevation, but taking his stance upon the bare American ground, Emerson demands Victory, to his senses as to his soul. The perfect exhilaration of a perpetual youth which comes to him is akin to what Hart Crane was to term an improved infancy. Against Wordsworth, Coleridge, Carlyle, the seer Emerson celebrates the American difference of *discontinuity*. "I am nothing" is a triumph of the Negative Way; "I see all" because I am that I am, discontinuously present not wherever but whenever I will to be present. "I am part or parcel of God," yet the god is not Jehovah but Orpheus, and Emerson momentarily is not merely the Orphic poet but the American Orpheus himself.

Poetic Orphism is a mixed and vexed matter, beyond disentanglement, and it is at the center of Emerson, even in the rhetorically immature *Nature*. I will digress upon it, and then rejoin *Nature* at its Orphic vortices.

5

The historian of Greek religion M. P. Nilsson shrewdly remarked that "Orphicism is a book religion, the first example of the kind in the history of Greek religion." Whatever it *may* have been historically, perhaps as early as the sixth century B.C.E., Orphism became the natural religion of Western poetry. Empedocles, an Emersonian favorite, shares Orphic characteristics with such various texts as certain Platonic myths, some odes of Pindar and fragments of poems recovered from South Italian Greek grave-sites. But later texts, mostly Neoplatonic, became the principal source for Emerson, who did not doubt their authenticity. W. K. C. Guthrie surmises a historical Orphism, devoted to Apollo, partly turned against Dionysos, and centered on a "belief in the latent divinity and immortality of the human soul" and on a necessity for constant purity; partly achieved through *ekstasis*.

Between the Hellenistic Neoplatonists and the seventeenth-century Cambridge variety, of whom Cudworth mattered most to Emerson, there had intervened the Florentine Renaissance mythologies, particularly Ficino's, which Christianized Orpheus. The baptized Orpheus lingers on in

Thomas Taylor, whose cloudy account may have been Emerson's most direct source for Orphism. But from *Nature* on, Emerson's Orpheus is simply Primal Man; who preceded the Creation, and very little occult lore actually gets into Emerson's quite autobiographical projection of himself as American Orpheus. His final Orphic reference, in the 1849 Journals, has about it the authority of a self-tested truth though its burden is extravagant, even for Emerson:

> ... Orpheus is no fable: you have only to sing, and the rocks will crystallize; sing, and the plant will organize; sing, and the animal will be born.

If Orpheus is fact in Emerson's life and work, this must be fact when seen in the light of an idea. The idea is the Central or Universal Man, the American More-than-Christ who is *to come*, the poet prefigured by Emerson himself as voice in the wilderness. In some sense he arrived as Walt Whitman, and some seventy years later as Hart Crane, but that is to run ahead of the story. In Emerson's mythopoeic and metamorphic conception, Central or Orphic Man is hardly to be distinguished from an Orphic view of language, and so breaks apart and is restituted just as language ebbs and flows:

> ... In what I call the cyclus of Orphic words, which I find in Bacon, in Cudworth, in Plutarch, in Plato, in that which the New Church would indicate when it speaks of the truths possessed by the primeval church broken up into fragments and floating hither and thither in the corrupt church, I perceive myself addressed thoroughly. They do teach the intellect and cause a gush of emotion; which we call the moral sublime; they pervade also the moral nature. Now the Universal Man when he comes, must so speak. He must recognize by addressing the whole nature.

Bacon's Orpheus was a Baconian philosopher-natural scientist; Cudworth's a Neoplatonic Christian; Plutarch's and Plato's, an image of spiritual purification. It is sly of Emerson to bring in the not very Orphic Swedenborgians of the New Church, but he really means his Central Man to be universal. The *sparagmos* of Orpheus is a prime emblem for the American; religion, whose motto I once ventured as: *Everything that can be broken should be broken*. Emerson's all-but-everything can be given in a brief, grim list:

February 8, 1831: death of his first wife, Ellen;

May 9, 1836: death of his brother, Charles;
January 27, 1842: death of his first son, Waldo.

These Orphic losses should have shattered the American Orpheus, for
all his life long these were the three persons he loved best. As losses they
mark the three phases in the strengthening of his self-reliant American
religion, an Orphism that would place him beyond further loss, at the high
price of coming to worship the goddess Ananke, dread but sublime
Necessity. But that worship came late to Emerson. He deferred it by a
metamorphic doctrine of Orpheus, best stated in his essay *History*:

> The power of music, the power of poetry, to unfit and as it
> were clap wings to solid nature, interprets the riddle of
> Orpheus....

This sentence is strangely flanked in the essay, though since Emerson's
unit of discourse tends more to be the sentence than the paragraph, the
strangeness is mitigated. Still, the preceding sentence is both occult and
puzzling:

> Man is the broken giant, and in all his weakness both his body
> and his mind are invigorated by habits of conversation with
> nature.

The Orphic riddle is the dialectic of strength and weakness *in Orpheus
himself*. Is he god or man? St. Augustine placed Orpheus at the head of poets
called theologians, and then added: "But these theologians were not
worshipped as gods, though in some fashion the kingdom of the godless is
wont to set Orpheus as head over the rites of the underworld." This is
admirably clear, but not sufficient to unriddle Orpheus. Jane Harrison
surmised that an actual man, Orpheus, came belatedly to the worship of
Dionysus and modified those rites, perhaps partly civilizing them. Guthrie
assimilated Orpheus to Apollo, while allowing the Dionysiac side also. E. R.
Dodds, most convincingly for my purposes, associates Orpheus with
Empedocles and ultimately with Thracian traditions of shamanism.
Describing Empedocles (and Orpheus), Dodds might be writing of
Emerson, granting only some temporal differences

> ... Empedocles represents not a new but a very old type of
> personality, the shaman who combines the still undifferentiated
> functions of magician and naturalist, poet and philosopher,

preacher, healer, and public counsellor. After him these functions
fell apart; philosophers henceforth were to be neither poets nor
magicians.... It was not a question of "synthesising" these wide
domains of practical and theoretical knowledge; in their quality as
Men of God they practised with confidence in all of them; the
"synthesis" was personal, not logical.

Emerson's Orpheus and Empedocles, like those of Dodds, were
mythical shamans, and perhaps Emerson as founder of the American religion
is best thought of as another mythical shaman. His Orphism was a
metamorphic religion of power whose prime purpose was divination, in what
can be called the Vichian sense of god-making. But why Orphism, when
other shamanisms were available? The native strain in Emerson rejected any
received religion. I am unable to accept a distinguished tradition in
scholarship that goes from Perry Miller to Sacvan Bercovitch, and that finds
Emerson to have been the heir, however involuntary, of the line that goes
from the Mathers to Jonathan Edwards. But I distrust also the received
scholarship that sees Emerson as the American disciple of Wordsworth,
Coleridge and Carlyle, and thus indirectly a weak descendant of German
High Transcendentalism, of Fichte and Schelling. And to fill out my litany
of rejections, I cannot find Emerson to be another Perennial Philosophy
Neoplatonist, mixing some Swedenborgianism into the froth of Cudworth
and Thomas Taylor. Since *Nature* is the text to which I will return, I cite as
commentary Stephen Whicher's *Freedom and Fate*, still the best book on
Emerson after a quarter-century:

> ... The lesson he would drive home is man's entire
> independence. The aim of this strain in his thought is not virtue,
> but freedom and mastery. It is radically anarchic, overthrowing all
> the authority of the past, all compromise or cooperation with
> others, in the name of the Power present and agent in the soul.
> Yet his true goal was not really a Stoic self-mastery, nor
> Christian holiness, but rather something more secular and harder
> to define—a quality he sometimes called *entirety*, or *self-union*....
> This self-sufficient unity or wholeness, transforming his
> relations with the world about him, is, as I read him, the central
> objective of the egoistic or transcendental Emerson, the prophet
> of Man created in the 1830's by his discovery of his own proper
> nature. This was what he meant by "sovereignty," or "majesty," or
> the striking phrase, several times repeated, "the erect position." ...

"This strain in his thought" I would identify as what, starting from Emerson, became the Native Strain in our literature. But why call Orphism a religion of "freedom and mastery," anarchic in overthrowing all the past and all contemporary otherness? The choice is Emerson's, as the final chapter of *Nature* shows, so that the question becomes: Why did Emerson identify his Primal, Central or Universal Man with Orpheus?

Hart Crane, Emerson's descendant through Whitman, provokes the same question at the formal close of *The Bridge*:

Now while thy petals spend the suns about us, hold
(O Thou whose radiance doth inherit me)
Atlantis,—hold thy floating singer late!

So to thine Everpresence, beyond time,
Like spears ensanguined of one tolling star
That bleeds infinity—the orphic strings,
Sidereal phalanxes, leap and converge:
—One Song, one Bridge of Fire!

The belated floating singer is still the metamorphic Orpheus of Ovid

... The poet's limbs were scattered in different places, but the waters of the Hebrus received his head and lyre. Wonderful to relate, as they floated down in midstream, the lyre uttered a plaintive melody and the lifeless tongue made a piteous murmur, while the river banks lamented in reply....

But beyond time, upon the transcendental bridge of fire that is his poem, Crane as American Orpheus vaults the problematics of loss even as Brooklyn Bridge vaultingly becomes the Orphic lyre bending, away from America as lost Atlantis, to whatever Crane can surmise beyond earth. If Coleridge could salute *The Prelude* as "an Orphic song indeed," then the American Crane could render the same salute to *The Bridge*. Emerson's Orphic songs, first in *Nature* and later in his essay *The Poet*, are Crane's ultimate paradigm, as he may not have known. To answer the question: Why an American Orpheus? I turn back now to *Nature*.

6

Between "Nature" proper, the little book's first chapter, with its epiphany of the transparent eyeball, and the final chapter "Prospects," with its two rhapsodies of the Orphic poet, intervene six rather inadequate chapters, all of which kindle at their close. I give here only these kindlings:

A man is fed, not that he may be fed, but that he may work.

But beauty in nature is not ultimate.

That which was unconscious truth, becomes, when interpreted and defined as an object, a part of the domain of knowledge—a new weapon in the magazine of power.

... the human form, of which all other organizations appear to be degradations....

... the soul holds itself off from a too trivial and microscopic study of the universal tablet. It respects the end too much to immerse itself in the means....

The world proceeds from the same spirit as the body of man. It is a remoter and inferior incarnation of God, a projection of God in the unconscious....

Perhaps Emerson might have kindled these kernels of his vision into something finer than the six chapters they crown. Their design is clear and impressive. Man's work moves beyond natural beauty through a power-making act of knowledge, which identifies the human form, beyond merely natural evidence, as the incarnation of God, an incarnation not yet elevated to full consciousness. That elevation is the enterprise of the Orphic poet, in the chapter "Prospects."

"... Man is the dwarf of himself. Once he was permeated and dissolved by spirit. He filled nature with his overflowing currents. Out from him sprang the sun and moon; from man the sun, from woman the moon. The laws of his mind, the periods of his actions externized themselves into day and night, into the year and the seasons. But, having made for himself this huge shell, his waters retired; he no longer fills the veins and veinlets; he is shrunk to a drop. He sees that the structure still fits him, but fits him colossaly. Say, rather, once it fitted him, now it corresponds to him from far and on high. He adores timidly his own work. Now is man the follower of the sun, and woman the follower of the moon. Yet sometimes he starts in his slumber, and wonders at himself and his house, and muses strangely at the resemblance betwixt him and it. He perceives that if his law is still paramount, if still he have elemental power, if his word is sterling yet in nature, it is not conscious power, it is not inferior but superior to his will. It is instinct." Thus my Orphic poet sang.

This "instinct" scarcely can be biological; like the Freudian drives of Eros and Thanatos it can only be mythological. Orphic, Gnostic or even Neoplatonic, it appears now in American colors and tropes. Call the Primal Man American, or even America (as Blake called him Albion, or Shelley, more misleadingly, Prometheus). America was a larger form than nature, filling nature with his emanative excess. Not Jehovah Elohim nor a Demiurge made the cosmos and time, but America, who thereupon shrunk to a drop. When this dwarf, once giant, starts in his sleep, then "gleams of a better light" come into experiential darkness. Very American is Emerson's catalog of those gleams of Reason:

> ... Such examples are, the traditions of miracles in the earliest antiquity of all nations; the history of Jesus Christ; the achievements of a principle, as in religious and political revolutions, and in the abolition of the slave-trade; the miracles of enthusiasm, as those reported of Swedenborg, Hohenlohe, and the Shakers; many obscure and yet contested facts, now arranged under the name of Animal Magnetism; prayer; eloquence; self-healing; and the wisdom of children.

A contemporary Carlyle might react to this list by querying: "But why has be left out flying saucers?" I myself would point to "eloquence" as the crucial item, fully equal and indeed superior in Emerson's view to "the history of Jesus Christ" or "prayer." Eloquence is the true Emersonian instance "of Reason's momentary grasp of the scepter; the exertions of a power which exists not in time or space, but an instantaneous in-streaming causing power." Eloquence is Influx, and Influx is a mode of divination, in the Vichian or double sense of god-making and of prophecy. Emerson, peculiarly American, definitive of what it is to be American, *uses* divination so as to transform all of nature into a transparent eyeball:

> ... The ruin or the blank, that we see when we look at nature, is in our own eye. The axis of vision is not coincident with the axis of things, and so they appear not transparent but opaque.

The reason why the world lacks unity, and lies broken and in
heaps, is because man is disunited with himself....

The American swerve here is from Milton, when in his invocation to
Book III of *Paradise Lost* he lamented that to his literal blindness nature
appeared a universal blank. But, more subtly, Emerson revises Coleridge's
previous swerve from Milton's lament, in the despairing cry of *Dejection: An
Ode*, where Coleridge sees literally but not figuratively: "And still I gaze—
and with how blank an eye." The American transumption of Emerson's
revisionary optics comes late, with the tragic self-recognition of the aged
Wallace Stevens in *The Auroras of Autumn*, when Stevens walks the
Emersonian-Whitmanian shores of America unable to convert his
movements into a freshly American figuration, a new variation upon the
tradition: "The man who is walking turns blankly on the sand."

What would it mean if the axis of vision and of things were to coincide?
What would a transparent world be, or yield? Wordsworth's *Tintern Abbey*
spoke of seeing into the life of things, while Blake urged a seeing *through*
rather than *with* the eye. Is Emerson as much reliant upon trope as these
British forerunners were, or do his optics prod us towards a pragmatic
difference? I suggest the latter, because Emerson as American seer is always
the shrewd Yankee, interested in what he called "commodity," and because
we ought never to forget that if he fathered Whitman and Thoreau and Frost
and (despite that son's evasions) Stevens, his pragmatic strain ensued in
William James, Peirce and even John Dewey.

The optics of transparency disturb only the aspect of this text that
marks it as a fiction of duration, while the topological residuum of the text
remains untroubled. Most tropes, as Emerson knew, have only a spatial
rather than a temporal dimension, metaphor proper and synecdoche and
metonymy among them. Irony and transumption or metalepsis, which
Emerson called the comic trick of language and Nietzsche the Eternal
Recurrence, are the temporal as well as spatial modes. The Emersonian
transparency or transcendence does not oppose itself to presence or spatial
immanence, but to the burden of time and of historical continuity. As the
quintessential American, Emerson did not need to transcend *space*, which
for him as for Whitman, Melville and Charles Olson was the central fact
about America. Transparency is therefore an agon with time, and not with
space, and opacity thus can be re-defined, in Emersonian terms, as being
fixed in time, being trapped in continuity. What Nietzsche called the will's
revenge against time's "it was" Emerson more cheerfully sees as a
transparency.

Pragmatically this did not mean, for Emerson, seeing things or people as though they were ectoplasm. It meant not seeing the fact except as an epiphany, as a manifestation of the God within the self-reliant seer:

> ... We make fables to hide the baldness of the fact and conform it, as we say, to the higher law of the mind. But when the fact is seen under the light of an idea, the gaudy fable fades and shrivels....

Why should Orpheus be incarnated again in America? Because he is the authentic prophet-god of discontinuity, of the breaking of tradition, and of re-inscribing tradition as a perpetual breaking, mending and then breaking again. The Orphic seer says of and to time: *It must be broken*. Even so, Emerson's own Orphic poet ends *Nature* by chanting a marvelous breaking:

> Nature is not fixed but fluid. Spirit alters, molds, makes it. The immobility or bruteness of nature is the absence of spirit; to pure spirit it is fluid, it is volatile, it is obedient. Every spirit builds itself a house, and beyond its house a world, and beyond its world a heaven. Know then that the world exists for you. For you is the phenomenon perfect. What we are, that only can we see. All that Adam had, all that Caesar could, you have and can do. Adam called his house, Rome; you perhaps call yours, a cobbler's trade; a hundred acres of ploughed land; or a scholar's garret. Yet line for line and point for point your dominion is as great as theirs, though without fine names. Build therefore your own world....

The metaphoric-mobile, fluid, volatile is precisely the Orphic stigma. I discussed this passage in section a, above, in terms of Abyss-radiance, but return to it now to venture a more radical interpretation. Pure spirit, or influx, is a remedial force not akin to what moved over the Abyss in merely demiurgical Creation, but rather itself the breath of the truly Primal Abyss. "Build therefore your own world" cannot mean that you are to emulate demiurgical creativity by stealing your material from the origin. Every man his own Demiurge hardly can be the motto for the Emersonian freedom. If seeing ranks above having, for Emerson, then knowing stands beyond seeing:

> The kingdom of man over nature, which cometh not with observation,—a dominion such as now is beyond his dream of God,—he shall enter without more wonder than the blind man feels who is gradually restored to perfect sight.

The crucial words are "now" and "gradually." If the dream of God were to be an Orphic and Gnostic dream of one's own occult self, then the reliance or religion would come now, and with great wonder. Emerson's curiously serene faith, as he closes *Nature*, is that gradually we will be restored to the perfect sight of our truly knowing self.

7

Emerson's theology of being an American, his vision of self-reliance, has nothing much in common with historical Gnosticism. In Gnosticism, this world is hell, and both man's body and man's soul are the work of the Demiurge who made this world. Only the *pneuma* or spark within the Gnostic elect is no part of the false and evil Creation. Emerson's monism, his hope for the American new Adam, and his Wordsworthian love of nature all mark him as a religious prophet whose God, however internalized, is very distinct from the alien God or Primal Abyss of Gnosticism.

I speak therefore not of Emerson's Gnosticism but of his Gnosis, of his way of knowing, which has nothing in common with philosophic epistemology. Though William James, Peirce and Dewey, and in another mode, Nietzsche, all are a part of Emerson's progeny, Emerson is not a philosopher, nor even a speculator with a philosophic theology. And though he stemmed from the mainstream Protestant tradition in America, Emerson is not a Christian, nor even a non-Christian theist in a philosophic sense. But I am not going to continue this litany of what our central man is not. Rather I will move directly to an account of Emerson's Gnosis, of that which he was and is, founder of *the* American religion, fountain of our literary and spiritual elite.

I will begin and end with my own favorite Emersonian sentence, from the first paragraph of the essay *Self-Reliance*:

> In every work of genius we recognize our own rejected thoughts; they come back to us with a certain alienated majesty.

Emerson says "rejected" where we might use the word "repressed," and his Gnosis begins with the reader's Sublime, a Freudian Negation in which thought comes back but we are still in flight from the emotional recognition that there is no author but ourselves. A strong reading indeed is the only text, the only revenge against time's "it was" that can endure. Self-estrangement produces the uncanniness of "majesty," and yet we do "recognize our own." Emerson's Gnosis rejects all history, including literary history, and dismisses all historians, including literary historians who want to tell the reader that what he recognizes in Emerson is Emerson's own thought rather than the reader's own Sublime.

A discourse upon Emerson's Gnosis, to be Emersonian rather than literary historical, itself must be Gnosis, or part of a Gnosis. It must speak of a knowing in which the knower himself is known, a reading in which he is read. It will not speak of epistemology, not even deconstructively of the epistemology of tropes, because it will read Emerson's tropes as figures of will, and not figures of knowledge, as images of voice and not images of writing.

"Why then do we prate of self-reliance?" is Emerson's rhetorical question, halfway through that essay. Falling back, with him, upon power as agent and upon a rich internal "way of speaking," I repeat his injunction: "Speak rather of that which relies because it works and is." "Works" as an Emersonian verb has Carlyle's tang to it. Prate not of happiness, but work, for the night cometh. But Emerson's *clinamen* away from Europe, away even from Coleridge and Carlyle, is to be heard in "that which relies because it works and is." In the American swerve, tradition is denied its last particle of authority, and the voice that is great within us rises up:

> Life only avails, not the having lived. Power ceases in the instant of repose; it resides in the moment of transition from a past to a new state, in the shooting of the gulf, in the darting of an aim....

There is no power in what already has been accomplished, and Emerson has not come to celebrate a new state, a gulf crossed, an aim hit. Power is an affair of crossings, of thresholds or transitional moments, evasions, substitutions, mental dilemmas resolved only by arbitrary acts of will. Power is in the traversing of the black holes of rhetoric, where the interpreter reads his own freedom to read. Or, we are read only by voicing, by the images for power we find that free us from the *already said*, from being one of the secondary men, traces of traces of traces.

I am suggesting that what a Gnosis of rhetoric, like Emerson's, prophetically wars against is every philosophy of rhetoric, and so now against the irony of irony and the randomness of all textuality. The Emersonian self, "that which relies because it works and is," is voice and not text, which is why it must splinter and destroy its own texts, subverting even the paragraph through the autonomy of sentences, the aggressivity of aphorisms. The sudden uncanniness of voice is Emerson's prime image for vocation, for the call that his Gnosis answers, as here in *Spiritual Laws*:

Each man has his own vocation. The talent is the call....

... It is the vice of our public speaking that it has not abandonment. Somewhere, not only every orator but every man should let out the length of all the reins; should find or make a frank and hearty expression of what force and meaning is in him....

Of this Emersonian spark or *pneuma*, this Gnostic true or antithetical self, as opposed to *psyche* or soul, we can observe that as an aggressive image of voice it will resist successfully all deconstruction. For this image is not a fiction *produced by* the original breaking-apart of the vessels of language but rather itself *tropes for* that primal breaking-apart. Emerson's image of voice is precisely a prophetic transumption of his son Nietzsche's image of truth as an army of figures of speech on the march, a march for which Heidegger gives us "language" or Derrida "writing" as a trope. The march keeps breaking up as voice keeps flowing in again, not as the image of presence but of Gnostic aboriginal absence, as here again in *Spiritual Laws* where the *thrownness* of all Gnosis returns in a forward falling:

... When the fruit is ripe, it falls. When the fruit is despatched, the leaf falls. The circuit of the waters is a mere falling. The walking of man and all animals is a falling forward. All our manual labor and works of strength, as prying, splitting, digging, rowing and so forth, are done by dint of continual falling, and the globe, earth, moon, comet, sun, star, fall forever and ever.

... Place yourself in the middle of the stream of power and wisdom which flows into you as life, place yourself in the full centre of that flood, then you are without effort impelled to truth, to right, and a perfect contentment....

I gloss these Emersonian passages by the formula: every fall is a *fall forward*, neither fortunate nor unfortunate, but *forward*, without effort, impelled to the American truth, which is that the stream of power and wisdom flowing in as life is eloquence. Emerson *is* the fountain of our will because he understood that, in America, in the evening-land, eloquence *had* to be enough. The image of voice is the image of influx, of the Newness, but always it knowingly is a broken image, or image of brokenness. Whitman, still Emerson's strongest ephebe, caught the inevitable tropes for this wounded image of American voice:

—and from this bush in the dooryard,
With delicate-color'd blossoms and heart-shaped leaves of rich green,
A sprig with its flower I break.

In the swamp in secluded recesses,
A shy and hidden bird is warbling a song.

Solitary the thrush,
The hermit withdrawn to himself, avoiding the settlements,
Sings by himself a song.

Song of the bleeding throat,
Death's outlet song of life, (for well dear brother I know,
If thou wast not granted to sing thou would'st surely die.)

The breaking of the tally, of the sprig of lilac, is one with the wounding of
the hermit thrush's throat, the breaking of voice, of the call, of prophetic
vocation. Because it is broken, castrated, it remains an image of voice and of life,
not the unbroken image of writing and of death. Whitman knows, even in
extremis, because his father Emerson knew, and both knowings are fallings
forward. What any philosophical knowing necessarily is or isn't I scarcely know,
but I can read Emerson because every knowing I do know is part of a
thrownness, a synecdoche for what Emerson wanted to call "victory" or
"freedom." Was it not Emerson's peculiar strength that what to me seems
catastrophe was to him—by the mad law of Compensation—converted to
victory? What made him free was his Gnosis, and I move now into its center, his
center, the image of voice that is self-reliance, at the high place of that rhapsody:

> ... It must be that when God speaketh he should communicate,
> not one thing, but all things; should fill the world with his voice;
> should scatter forth light, nature, time, souls, from the center of
> the present thought; and new date and new create the whole.
> Whenever a mind is simple and receives a divine wisdom, old
> Things pass away,—means, teachers, texts, temples fall; it lives
> now, and absorbs past and future into the present hour. All things
> are made sacred by relation to it,—one as much as another. All
> things are dissolved to their center by their cause....

Let us apply Whitman, since he was the strongest of the Emersonians.
In *Specimen Days* he wrote:

... The best part of Emersonianism is, it breeds the giant that destroys itself. Who wants to be any man's mere follower? lurks behind every page. No teacher ever taught, that has so provided for his pupil's setting up independently—no truer evolutionist.

Emerson also then is a teacher and a text that must pass away if you or I receive the Newness, a fresh influx of the image of voice. On Emerson's precept, no man's Gnosis can be another's, and Emerson's images of voice are fated to become yet more images of writing. Surely this is part of the lesson of the Middle or Skeptical Emerson, warning us against all idolatries, including my own deep temptation to idolize Emerson. Here is the admonition of his greatest essay, *Experience*:

> ... People forget that it is the eye which makes the horizon, and the rounding mind's eye which makes this or that man a type or representation of humanity, with the name of hero or saint. Jesus, the "providential man," is a good man on whom many people are agreed that these optical laws shall take effect....

Emerson, unlike Whitman, hoped to evade the American version of that "providential man." If no two disciples can agree upon Emerson's doctrine, and they cannot, we can grant the success of his evasion. Yet there is the center: evasion. Emersonianism, indeed like any Gnosis, moves back and forth between negation and extravagance, and always by way of evasion rather than by substitution. I will digress from Gnosis to Gnosticism, before shuttling back to Emerson's passage through *Experience* to *Fate*, middle and late essays no less modes of Gnosis than *Self-Reliance* is.

The way of evasion for the Gnostics meant freedom, and this was freedom from the god of this world, from time, from text, and from the soul and the body of the universe. Such freedom was both knowledge and salvation, since the knowledge of saving self involved was one with the knowledge of the alien true God and the Primal Abyss. How could so large a knowing be known? Only by an image or trope of the self that transgressed language through the most positive of negative moments. What Coleridge, in his orthodox nightmare, dreads as the Positive Negation of *Limbo* is known by the Gnostics as a being-there in the Pleroma, in the Place of Rest. Coleridge's negative moment loses the self without compensation. Emerson, in his 1838 Journal, slyly turning away from Coleridge, achieves a Gnostic Sublime, a negative moment that is all gain and no loss, the truly American moment of self-reliance:

In the highest moments, we are a vision. There is nothing that can be called gratitude nor properly joy. The soul is raised over passion. It seeth nothing so much as Identity. It is a Perceiving that Truth and Right ARE. Hence it becomes a perfect Peace out of the *knowing* that all things will go well. Vast spaces of nature the Atlantic Ocean, the South Sea; vast intervals of time years, centuries, are annihilated to it; this which I think and feel underlay that former state of life and circumstances, as it does underlie my present, and will always all circumstance, and what is called life and what is called death [my italics].

This passage is not so much an example of Gnostic rhetoric as it is part of a Gnosis of rhetoric, anti-epistemological without being vulnerable to the charge that it simply reverses an epistemological dilemma. In a transcendental hyperbole we mount beyond Coleridgean joy of the Secondary imagination because *we see nothing*. Instead, "we are a vision" and we know the identity between ourselves and our knowledge of ourselves. Space, time and mortality flee away, to be replaced by "the knowing." As always in Emerson, the knowing bruises a limit of language, and the impatient Seer transgresses in order to convey his "Perceiving that Truth and Right ARE," which compels the "ARE" to break through in capital letters. In its extravagance, this passage is nothing but tropological, yet its persuasive rhetoric achieves persuasion by the trick of affirming identity with a wholly discontinuous self, one which *knows* only the highest moments in which it *is* a vision. Emerson evades philosophy and chooses his Gnosis instead precisely because he is wary of the epistemological pitfalls that all trope risks. An image of voice is a fine tangle, well beyond logic, but it can testify only to the presence of things not seen, and its faith is wholly in the Optative Mood.

Yet if we move on from *Self-Reliance* first to *Experience* and then to *Fate*, we pass out of the Optative Mood and into the evidence of that world where men descend to meet, and where they cease to be a vision. But even in *Experience*, and then even more in *Fate*, we read not philosophy but Gnosis, a chastened knowing that is not chastened *as* knowing. Here is a single recovery from *Experience*:

... The partial action of each strong mind in one direction is a telescope for the objects on which it is pointed. But every other part of knowledge is to be pushed to the same extravagance, ere the soul attains her due sphericity....

... And we cannot say too little of our constitutional necessity of seeing things under private aspects, or saturated with our humors. And yet is the God the native of these bleak rocks. That need makes in morals the capital virtue of self-trust. We must hold hard to this poverty, however scandalous, and by more rigorous self-recoveries, after the sallies of action, possess our axis more firmly.

Rather than comment upon this in isolation, I juxtapose it first with a more scandalous poverty of *Fate*:

> ... A man speaking from insight affirms of himself what is true of the mind: seeing its immortality, he says, I am immortal; seeing its invincibility, he says, I am strong. It is not in us, but we are in it. It is of the maker, not of what is made....

The fragment of *Experience* makes imaginative need, epistemological lack, itself into potential Gnosis, the potentia of power. But the resting-point of *Fate* is a more drastic Gnosis, for there the mind and the self have dissociated, in order to win the compensation of the self as spark of the uncreated. And in a coda to this discourse I now abandon Emerson for the giant of Emersonianism, for the question that is a giant himself. What does Emersonianism teach us about an American Gnosis, and what is it which makes that Gnosis still available to us?

The primary teaching of any Gnosis is to deny that human existence is a historical existence. Emerson's American Gnosis denies our belatedness by urging us not to listen to tradition. If you listen hard to tradition, as Walter Benjamin said Kafka did, then you do not see, and Emersonianism wants you to *see*. See what? That is the wrong question, for Gnosis directs *how* to see, meaning to *see earliest*, as though no one had ever seen before you. Gnosis directs also in stance, in taking up a place from which to see earliest, which is one with the place of belated poetry, which is to say, American poetry in particular.

In poetry, a "place" is *where* something is *known*, while a figure or trope is *when* something is willed or desired. In belated poetry, as in any other Gnosis, the place where knowing is located is always a name, but one that comes by negation; an unnaming yields this name. But to un-name in a poem, you first mime and then over-mime and finally super-mime the name you displace. Emerson and Gnosticism alike seek the terrible burden of a super-mimesis. The American poet must overthrow even Shakespeare, a doomed enterprise that shadows *Moby-Dick*, despite our generous overpraise of the crippling of Melville's greatness by *King Lear*. Whitman must be the new Adam, the new Moses, and the new Christ, impossible aspirations that astonishingly he did not disappoint wholly. An imaginative literature that stems from a Gnosis, rather than a philosophy, is both enhanced and ruined by its super-mimetic teleologies. In every work of genius—in the Bible, Shakespeare, Spenser, Milton, Wordsworth—just there Hawthorne, Melville, Whitman, Thoreau, Dickinson, Henry James learned to recognize their own rejected thoughts. Frost, Stevens, Hart Crane, Faulkner and so many more later encountered their rejected thoughts coming back to them with a certain alienated majesty, when they read their American nineteenth-century precursors. Plato entered the agon with Homer to be the mind of Greece, but here in America we had no Homer. The mind of America perhaps was Emersonian even before Emerson. After him, the literary, indeed the religious mind of America has had no choice, as he cannot be rejected or even deconstructed. He *is* our rhetoric as he is our Gnosis, and I take it that, his sly evasion of both Hegel and Hume deprived us of our philosophy. Since he will not conclude haunting us, I evade concluding here, except for a single hint. He was an interior orator, and not an instructor; a vitalizer and not an historian. We will never know our own knowing, through or despite him, until we learn the lesson our profession refuses. I end therefore by quoting against us an eloquence from the essay *History*, which the seer rightly chose to lead off his essays:

> ... Those men who cannot answer by a superior wisdom these facts or questions of time, serve them. Facts encumber them, tyrannize over them, and make the men of routine, the men of *sense*, in whom a literal obedience to facts has extinguished every spark of that light by which man is truly man....

That, in one dark epiphany, *is* Emerson's Gnosis.

SHARON CAMERON

Representing Grief:
Emerson's "Experience"

I

"Where do we find ourselves?" Emerson's "Experience" begins,[1] implicitly answering a question raised seven years earlier in and about "The American Scholar": "Let us inquire what light new days and events have thrown on his character, and his hopes?" (53). This time the question implies its own answer. The place Emerson finds himself is one where no light is ("night hovers all day in the boughs of the fir tree"). And it is more oppressive than that because he can't see where he is and he can't see his way out. What he attests to is stupor:

> We wake and find ourselves on a stair; there are stairs below us, which we seem to have ascended; there are stairs above us, many a one, which go upward and out of sight. But the Genius which, according to the old belief, stands at the door by which we enter, and gives us the lethe to drink, that we may tell no tales, mixed the cup too strongly, and we cannot shake off the lethargy now at noonday. Sleep lingers all our lifetime about our eyes, as night hovers all day in the boughs of the fir-tree. All things swim and glitter. Our life is not so much threatened as our perception. (471)

From *Representations* 15 (Summer 1986). © 1986 by the Regents of the University of California.

Perhaps the most striking part of the testament is the disavowal of the very feeling that pervades these pages. For feeling survives the complaints of its being canceled. Emerson is conceding with one part of himself what he is disputing with another.

If vertigo for Emerson is occasioned by being in a mid-world from which vision is occluded, for the reader vertigo is occasioned by assertions that only half successfully cancel each other:

> The only thing grief has taught me, is to know how shallow it is.... Grief too will make us idealists. In the death of my son, now more than two years ago, I seem to have lost a beautiful estate— no more. I cannot get it nearer to me.... This calamity ... does not touch me: some thing which I fancied was part of me, which could not be torn away without tearing me, nor enlarged without enriching me, falls off from me, and leaves no scar. It was caducous. I grieve that grief can teach me nothing. (472–73)

These insistent denials of feeling—on the occasion of which each time feeling suffers a resurgence—are curious. For the Emerson of the essay's beginning *cannot* get grief nearer him. He cannot acknowledge grief any way but this. Still, what is interesting about the acknowledgment is its absolute adequacy. The acknowledgment, in fact, culminates in perhaps the essay's most frequently cited passage:

> I take this evanescence and lubricity of all objects, which lets them slip through our fingers then when we clutch hardest, to be the most unhandsome part of our condition. (473)

True to the double pattern of assertion thus far, the grammatical reference for "this evanescence" is not only the life of the child but also the evasiveness of the grief occasioned by the child's death. This puts us in no danger of mistaking the reference. Why then does Emerson mistake it, seeming to mourn the loss of his affect more than the loss of his son? Partly because he has asserted "opium is instilled in all disaster." Hence disaster can be voiced only if the voice is then denied. What, though, is the connection between the articulation of grief and the inability to experience grief ("I cannot get it nearer me") and a second, more critical dissociation between the meditation on grief at Waldo's death in these relentless first few pages and the enumeration of daily losses and incompletions with which the rest of the essay is concerned?

All critics of Emerson have commented on the contradictory feature of the essays—namely on the fact that Emerson fails to take account of his own discrepant statements. O. W. Firkins explains unaddressed discrepancies in Emerson's essays by suggesting that disparate phenomena do not need to be admitted because Emerson perceives their ultimate unity:

> The whole fascination of life for him lay in the disclosure of identity in variety, that is, in the concurrence, *the running together*, of several distinct images or ideas....
>
> No man ever breathed ... who found more pleasure than Emerson in the disclosure of hidden likeness.[2]

Firkins thus maintains that Emerson treats differences as likenesses because that is what they will become. In an opposite spirit, R. A. Yoder argues that in Emerson's essays disparate phenomena must be understood as instantiating the dialectical trinity of thesis/antithesis/synthesis. While Firkins implicitly suggests that Emerson need not admit differences because, properly seen, they must be construed as features of a nuanced but single entity, and while Yoder claims differences are ultimately recognized, other critics—Stephen Whicher, Barbara Packer, Eric Cheyfitz—argue that discrepant statements cannot be registered as such because Emerson can never separate the half of the antithesis to be repudiated from the half of the antithesis to be embraced.[3] I want in my own discussion to examine the two suppositions: "not able to" (Packer, Cheyfitz, Whicher) and "not necessary to" (Firkins and Yoder). Why in one instance is acknowledgment prohibited, and why in the other instance is acknowledgment found gratuitous? My interest in these questions is neither structural nor rhetorical. I rather wish to investigate the way in which dissociation reflects a self's relation to its own divergent claims.

Why are there frequently two voices in an Emerson essay? Why two voices that seem deaf to each other's words?[4] In an essay like "Experience" are claims voiced, repudiated, and differently iterated so that the self that can say words and the self that can hear them may be brought into relation and implicitly reconciled with each other? If so, is the idea of "integration," and the appropriateness of a psychoanalytic context which that word suggests, validated by the essay? What disables the psychoanalytic and philosophical explanations that the idea of dissociation and schism inevitably invite? In "Experience"—which, I shall argue, bears a special relation to the problem of discrepancy in Emerson's essays—an admission of grief is soon contested, first by the denial of grief and second by the disappearance of the subject of grief from the essay's subsequent pages. It is true that the two parts of "Experience" are not explicitly discrepant or contradictory. They are implicitly so, for—to specify the contradiction in terms that restate the problem—the initial pages of the essay claim that grief over Waldo's death does not register, while the body of the essay shows the ranges of that register. Why should Emerson not acknowledge the relation between the loss of the child and the perception of daily losses when one generates the other?

In the discussion that follows, addressing these questions, I contest the critical categories in which "Experience," in particular, and Emerson's essays in general, have been spoken of. So doing, I propose another set of terms, for "synthesis" and "contradiction" are not useful to describe Emerson's "Experience." These terms are inadequate partly because "Experience" is different from Emerson's other essays (in it, for example, dissociation is considered as well as enacted). But they are also inadequate in a deeper sense. Specifically, to speak of the split between experience and idealism (which is the superficial form contradiction takes in "Experience") is to appropriate the essay by a logic it resists. My discussion will suggest that what is at stake in the essay is not a question of logic but rather a question of the elegiac. In "Experience," I shall argue, the elegiac has a logic of its own—not one of working through (not one of synthesis) and not one of explicit conflict. It may seem along the way as if I am describing, or as if Emerson is portraying, a condition of "melancholia." Instead, I argue, he is creating a powerful and systematic representation of grief. I shall get hold of the terms of this representation by coming at it several times and from different angles. In section II, I delineate the dissociated elements that "order" the essay. Because I relinquish explanations of synthesis or contradiction, it may look as if the essay's subjects have an arbitrary hierarchy, or as if I have introduced the arbitrariness by a poststructuralist critique of conventional ways of reading Emerson that could as well apply to a representation of any subject as to a representation of grief. To the extent that concerns in "Experience" are all governed by Emerson's relation to the dead child, this arbitrariness is illusory—a claim I elaborate in section III, when I examine passages that establish grief as the essay's determining focus. Finally, in IV, I consider the problem of an adequate vocabulary for Emerson's essay. For although it is the task of "Experience" to extricate grief from the numbness to whose spell consciousness has consigned it in the essay's first few pages and to represent, if not to see, what it looks like, it is not immediately clear how we are to understand the dynamic represented.

II

It is almost inconceivable that after the initial pages of Emerson's "Experience," in which the mind is apparently successful in its attempt to render itself unconscious of the grief occasioned by the death of Emerson's five-year-old son, the essay, with no transition, should abandon this subject, abstractly turning its attention to the annoyance of daily vagaries. One explanation for the disjunctiveness of the shift is that the man who insists upon an imperviousness to grief ("this calamity ... does not touch me") is so devastated by the subject from which he claims himself exempt that he can say no more about it. And in fact it is the case at the beginning of "Experience" that "all things swim and glitter" because dissociation replaces tears and because the man who writes these words knows that tears are the particular experience from which dissociation will protect him.

Emerson had said, "Our life is not so much threatened as our perception." In the context of the initial pages, the nature of the threat seems to be the inability to see at all, the stupor of dissociation. In the context of the body of the essay, the nature of the threat is that all ways of seeing are informed by Waldo's death. No vision is exempt from being dissolved by a grief that is causally unrelated to it. All things swim and glitter because everything is transient, either a loss in its own right or subject to loss—and these ordinary losses are governed by the extraordinary one with the bare statement of which the essay begins. Although it may seem, then, that Waldo's death is set forth and set aside, in fact the essay is a testament to the pervasiveness of a loss so inclusive that it is suddenly inseparable from experience itself.

What the initial pages of "Experience" hope for and despair of is a testament to grief's reality—its felt manifestations.

> There are moods in which we court suffering, in the hope that here, at least, we shall find reality, sharp peaks and edges of truth. But it turns out to be scene-painting and counterfeit. The only thing grief has taught me, is to know how shallow it is. That, like all the rest, plays about the surface, and never introduces me into the reality, for contact with which, we would even pay the costly price of sons and lovers. (472–73)

"Contact" with grief—its absolute inseparability from every conceivable aspect of experience—is just what is being courted in the essay's initial pages and just what is achieved in the pages that follow. Thus, "Where do we find ourselves?" elicits, on balance, an answer whose shock we are not initially in a position to appreciate:

> In a series of which we do not know the extremes, and believe that it has none. (471)

What is extreme is the predication of a series—of consequences, of things touched by Waldo's death here emblematized by the particular range of subjects considered in the essay—that has no regress (Emerson, after the first three pages, never directly returns to talk of Waldo's death), and that has no terminus either. Moreover, the connection between the grief over Waldo's death and the grief that characterizes the daily losses and incompletions is all the more terrible because it goes without saying. It goes without saying, and any understanding of the relation between the first few pages and the rest of the essay depends upon its being assumed.

In fact, although the essay's initial pages describe the feeling of grief as a deficient one ("The only thing grief has taught me, is to know how shallow it is"), the body of the essay revises that assessment, calling into question Emerson's expectation (and ours) of what grief is. For ideas of depth, integration, internalization, perhaps acknowledgment, too (ideas anathema to the notion of grief and experience as both are here defined), suppose a contact with experience equivalent to its mastery. Grief—"which like all the rest, plays about the surface, and never introduces me into reality"—withholds contact with a reality that does not equivocate with experience, because unlike death, to which Emerson compares it, grief does not end experience. What is being redefined, then, is the idea about our relation to experience—about whether that relation is one of surface or depth.

At one level the connection between the two parts of the essay could not be simpler: Emerson's response to Waldo's death informs his responses to all other experiences. The two are related as cause and effect. But Emerson also implicitly proposes that we construe the connection in equative as well as causal terms. Grief and experience are equivalent because the characteristics of grief are identical to the characteristics of experience, as each is separately defined. Specifically, they are equal to each other because dissociation defines both. With respect to grief, the manifestation of dissociation is stupor, the inability to feel. Four years after the death of his wife Ellen in 1831, Emerson writes in his journals:

> I loved Ellen, & love her with an affection that would ask nothing but its indulgence to make me blessed. Yet when she was taken from me, the air was still sweet, the sun was not taken down from my firmament.[5]

On 4 February 1842, a week after the death of his child, in a letter to Caroline Sturgis:

Alas! I chiefly grieve that I cannot grieve; that this fact takes no more deep hold than other facts, is as dreamlike as they; a lambent flame that will not burn playing on the surface of my river. Must every experience—those that promised to be dearest & most penetrative,—only kiss my cheek like the wind & pass away? I think of Ixion & Tantalus & Kehama.[6]

These figures borrowed from Greek mythology, in the case of Ixion and Tantalus, and in the case of Kehama from Robert Southey's *The Curse of Kehama*, are crossbred so that what the emergent figure suffers is to perceive in perpetuity the existence of a feeling he is deprived of experiencing—like Tantalus, condemned to stand always in water up to his chin, with fruit-laden branches above his head and both water and fruit receding from his reach at each attempt to eat or drink.

The passage from "Experience," drawing on the despair if not the actual words of these earlier notations, specifies its hopelessness in comparable—not identical—terms. For one way to talk about the relation between journal, letter, and essay is in terms of reverberation. Voices not in dialogue pick up each other in oblique ways:

The Indian who was laid under a curse, that the wind should not blow on him, nor water flow to him, nor fire burn him, is a type of us all. The dearest events are summer-rain and we the Para coats that shed every drop. (473)

It is in the context of such invulnerability that Emerson a few lines earlier in the essay had remarked:

Grief too will make us idealists.

Emerson is not only saying: because grief tells us we are deprived of what we love, we must therefore reflect on what we no longer experience. He is also saying: because grief tells us nothing, because we are in its presence without feeling our relation to it, we must imagine even it. We must hypothesize the sorrow, and the source of the sorrow, we are unable to feel. It is, of course, true that the opposite could be argued: since grief is an affect, Emerson is positing a feeling he cannot take back as quickly as I suggest. Yet it is not that Emerson retracts or takes grief back. It is rather that he seems never to acknowledge the consequences of having allowed it direct expression. When Emerson offers up prospectively (to gain "contact with grief") "the costly price of sons and lovers" that he has already paid, it is to illustrate what it feels like to be deprived of proper affect. What it feels like is to imagine you are in a position to relinquish (are therefore still in possession of) what you have already lost. And the disparity between the man's offer and his ignorance of its illegitimacy is all the more shocking when we remember that the sacrifice being contemplated is of a wife and a child. If we recoil from the brutality of this assault, what we recoil from is the fact that to the man who voices these words they do not seem brutal because they do not seem real. There could be no more harrowing testimony to the terror of idealism than this example of a self forced prospectively to imagine the loss it retrospectively refuses to feel.

Dissociation is also apparent in Emerson's itemization of the essay's subjects (in the poem that precedes the essay and, yet again, in a paragraph that is placed toward its close) as these designations seem divorced from, and seem only arbitrarily to apply to, discrete portions of the essay. In fact, although Emerson provides us with a gloss of the essay's subjects, he simultaneously calls attention to the gloss's inadequacy:

> Illusion, Temperament, Succession, Surface, Surprise, Reality, Subjectiveness,—these are threads on the loom of time, these are the lords of life. I dare not assume to give their order, but I name them as I find them in my way. (490–91)

It is not, moreover, clear where the arbitrariness indicated above comes from, whether the lack of order is in the threads or in Emerson's ability to specify the order of the threads. As the language of the passage implies, the distinction blurs in the making.

In fact the second part of the essay demonstrates the unsuccessful attempt to understand phenomena, much as the first part of the essay demonstrated an unsuccessful attempt to feel them. If the sentence whose import dominates the essay's initial pages is "Grief too will make us idealists," the sentence whose meaning dominates the remainder of the essay is "Life has no memory" (484). The stupefaction is so extreme that we see in the sentence's verbal displacement the self attribute to life its own disputed amnesia. What it would dissociate itself from is not the incoherence of the tragic (on which the initial pages turned their back) but rather the confusion of the everyday. For despite the mind's efforts to wrestle phenomena into comprehensible shape, to ascribe meanings to experience in which it can believe, our thoughts lose their grip. We betray our convictions, or they betray us.

In "Experience" the particular form this betrayal takes is that our ambivalence leads us to advocate antithetical beliefs, and, as if that ambivalence were not bad enough, we cancel the distinction between the opposite beliefs ostensibly being contested. Thus Emerson asserts that our lives are fixed because the succession of moods is limited by temperament. But he then disavows this claim, suggesting that to believe in such limitations is to "house with the insane" (476). Yet both assessments amount to the same thing because although hope tells us our moods and life must change, Emerson's exemplification of that change ("I have had good lessons from pictures, which I have since seen without emotion or remark" [476]) is purely pejorative. Change is possible/Change is not/If change is possible we stand only to lose by it. Because at best these formulations are only contradictory, Emerson dismisses the turns of this particular thought and dismisses the efficacy of thought in general:

> But what help from these fineries or pedantries? What help from thought? Life is not dialectics. (478)

Since there is no help from thought, Emerson will rise above his ruminations to consider actions and surfaces. Once he does so, terms like "betrayal" and "the plaint of tragedy" (477), which were initially suggested by the death of the child, seem empty and abstract:

> The whole frame of things preaches indifferency. Do not craze yourself with thinking, but go about your business anywhere. Life is not intellectual or critical, but sturdy.... To fill the hour,—that is happiness; to fill the hour, and leave no crevice for a repentance or an approval. We live amid surfaces, and the true art of life is to skate well on them. (478)

The praise of the transitory in which "we must set up the strong present tense," since life "is a flitting state, a tent for the night" (481), culminates in the assertion:

> We thrive by casualties. Our chief experiences have been casual. (483)

The association of the casual with the casualty (an association in which the latter is inevitably particularized as Waldo's death)—like the earlier comparison of Waldo's death with the loss of an estate—is shocking, for in each case phenomena psychically divorced from each other (the property and the child, the casual and the casualty) are made categorically comparable. The vulgarity of alluding to these losses as if they were comparable is meant to replicate the vulgarity of experience's obliviousness to any niceties of human perception. The man who must sacrifice not simply his child but also his belief that the sacrifice has special meaning replicates the failure of discrimination by which he sees himself victimized. The vengeance of experience lies in the way it gives and takes away as if its losses were equivalent. The vengeance of response lies in its adherence to this fiction. Vengeance is involved because losses are not equal. In positing their equivalence, Emerson preserves the sanctity of his feeling, preserves by keeping hidden or unconscious (that is, dissociated) his sorrow for the child, as if hidden the feeling escapes the words that debase it, and, as I have noted earlier about this same passage, escapes acknowledgment of its actuality, and, perhaps, therefore too its fact. Emerson brings together the loss of the child and the loss of the estate, then, to preserve on one level a crucial disparity between the feeling and the words which degrade it that has crucially been violated on another—the disparity between a trivial and a consequential loss. He, alternately, undermines our supposition that the casual and the casualty are only etymologically related. In that enigmatic "We thrive by casualties. Our chief events have been casual," he suggests that the accidental is the incidental on which meaning has been conferred. Events assume meaning (that is, connection) in the present, then, at tremendous cost. For our relation to meaning, at least with the recollection of Waldo in mind, is in the form of fatality.

Of course things can mean, retrospectively ("The years teach much which the days never know" [483]), but then they have no relation to us. Wisdom, divorced from any memory of how we came to possess it, is likewise divorced from any actual experience of it. The bottom line of this separation is absolute subjectivity—unconsciousness that separates existence from our thoughts about it; thoughts from action; action from agency; temporal units from each other.

> That which proceeds in succession might be remembered, but that which is coexistent, or ejaculated from a deeper cause, as yet far from being conscious, knows not its own tendency. (484)

Throughout the essay the complaint seems to be that you can endure loss but not suffer it; you can gain wisdom but not experience the gain because at any given moment you are oblivious to what you are experiencing. As a consequence, events have significance as fatalities, or they have no significance at all. You can know and you can have, but you cannot know what you have, because you cannot connect the two, for connection— between experience and its register in feeling (in the first part of the essay)

or experience and the understanding of it (in the second part of the essay)—
is just what seems impossible.

The word "experience" itself, associated with empiricism and therefore
with one half of the conventional philosophical dichotomy of which
"idealism" is the complement, has been painstakingly dislodged from the
neatness of this dialectic and redefined as a mere middle, standing between
what we desire and what we get, what we recall and what we expect. No
longer part of a known opposition, experience stands between such
oppositions, but—as Emerson will note, altering the spatial understanding—
connected to them obliquely. Insofar as "experience" seems to designate the
self's relation to its present, it redefines identity by disengaging the self from
both past and future. But the self's relation to the present is similarly defined
by disengagement, for if "experience" indicates those phenomena that
happen to the self, it also, definitionally, implies that such phenomena are
alien to the self. Thus the idea of a self is first made to forfeit its connection
to a past and a future (it is made temporally discontinuous), and then made
to reconceive its connection to a present as a relation, not an identity (it is
made spatially discontinuous). "You will not remember... and you will not
expect" (483), the imperative issued by the negative conditions that govern,
respectively, the inability to feel or understand, is really a dictate that
disallows connection between the serial and the significant, the casual and
the casualty.

The present may be the privileged moment that best survives the
charges made against it, for, to recapitulate a thematic of the essay, if loss is
always figured as the loss of the present moment, the redress of that loss will
always be figured as the immediacy of the present. Indeed it could be argued
that insofar as the essay thematizes a solution to the dissociation it describes,
it does so by valorizing the idea of a present over which discontinuity fails to
hold sway. If one were describing the progression of the essay, adhering to
the logic of this thematic, the description would read as follows. First
Emerson laments the absence of contact with the child. Or rather, as the
child is incidental to his lament, the man grieves numbness, grieves the loss
of contact with feelings occasioned by the child's death. Then he revalues the
importance of such contact, finding it undesirable. In conclusion, he
proposes a substitution for contact. Namely, while at the essay's beginning
Emerson mourns the lack of binding—of temporal moments to each other,
of spatial connections—at the conclusion he celebrates the force of
unbinding; he celebrates the primacy of the present moment, dissociated
from all other moments. He rejoices in the power of the self to outdistance
its need for connections. He finds wholeness gratuitous.

The trouble with this thematic, or with this interpretation of the thematic, is that it supposes the loss of affect rather than the loss of the son to be the primary object mourned. The thematic implies that what was mourned at the essay's beginning was not the child but rather the man's feeling. (Hence, without much adjustment, if feeling is lost it can also be recuperated.) That assessment seems to me to mistake the subject of many of the essay's passages, much as the man in the essay could be said to exemplify the problem of mistaking the subject of his own words. I shall discuss these passages whose power comes from the fact that they challenge the thematic, that they are antagonistic to it, providing a crucial countermovement against it. Specifically, they suggest that mastery is not in a real present, not in any moment, but rather in a psychic state or space. If the temporal terms urged by the thematic suggest a cure to the curse of experiences that are ever present and never present—and specifically suggest a cure to the loss of the man's affect—the spatial terms of the essay suggest that what is at stake is not the recuperation of affect but rather the recuperation of the child.

For despite the charges made in the essay, it does not present us with a theory of tragedy, and it does not present us with a facile accommodation to loss. It rather presents us with a theory of "power;" which is importantly related to the way in which Emerson comes to terms with the death of his son.[7] This theory posits itself between the conditions staked out in the essay's first half (you must suffer grief without feeling it) and those staked out in the second half (you must live life without understanding it), staked out, in other words, between the casualty and the casual, between the cataclysmic and the everyday.

At the essay's beginning obliquity is impotence:

Nature doesn't like to be observed.... Direct strokes she never gave us power to make; all our blows glance, all our hits are accidents. Our relations to each other are oblique and casual. (473)

By the middle of the essay obliquity is power:

A man is like a bit of Labrador spar, which has no lustre as you turn it in your hand, until you come to a particular angle; then it shows deep and beautiful colors. There is no adaptation or universal applicability in men, but each has his special talent, and the mastery of successful men consists in adroitly keeping themselves where and when that turn shall be oftenest to be practiced. (477)

Having discussed the ways in which the essay's unfolding concerns can be considered, in the remaining two sections I shall focus on the essay's beginning and end, as well as on the subject of grief that connects the two. So doing, I wish to expose the "turn" Emerson "practices" in "Experience," for it is through that turn that the dissociation attached to death is converted to the dissociation that facilitates power. I shall have more to say specifically about the question of power at the end of my discussion. First, however, I wish to address the conversion I have described. As this conversion depends on understanding Emerson's equivocal expression of grief (and his ultimately unequivocal relation to it), I shall press hard on certain passages, some of them introduced earlier in my discussion.

III

The centrality of Waldo's death for Emerson is attested to in journal entries contemporaneous with the event. That centrality is reiterated in the following extraordinary passage of 8 July 1857, also from the journals:

> This morning I had the remains of my mother & of my son Waldo removed from the tomb of Mrs. Ripley to my lot in "Sleepy Hollow." The sun shone brightly on the coffins, of which Waldo's was well preserved—now fifteen years. I ventured to look into the coffin. (*JMN* 14:154)

In that flatly declarative last sentence Emerson records his sense of the risk associated with looking for the child, or of looking at the child's remains, or of looking into the space where the child is or was. If the journal entry shies away from specifying what is looked for and what is seen, the essay, "Experience," does not.

"Experience" is an elegy, an essay whose primary task is its work of mourning, and, in light of that poorly concealed fact, it is surprising that critics have consistently spoken of the child as only one of several causes equal in their provocation of listlessness and despair. In those few discussions in which Waldo's death is acknowledged to have special status, it is still not seen as it crucially must be: the occasion that generates in a nontrivial way all other losses that succeed it. For Waldo's death is not just one of a number of phenomena equally precipitated and having parity with each other. Raising itself above the evasively identified "series of which we do not know the extremes, and believe that it has none" of the essay's second sentence, and enunciating itself outside of Emerson's itemization of the essay's ostensible subjects ("Illusion," "Temperament," "Succession," "Surprise," "Reality,"

"Subjectiveness") from whose abstraction it is definitionally exempt, the grief occasioned by the death of the child is the essay's first cause; it begets the other subjects, the consideration of which—Emerson's and ours—depends on our understanding their relation to Waldo's death. Mourning does its work in that the loss and grief initially attached to a single experience ultimately pervades the perception of all experience so that there is no boundary to grief, nothing that is not susceptible to it.

Freud in "Mourning and Melancholia" characterizes such grief as accompanied by "loss of interest in the outside world—insofar as it does not recall [the dead one] ... the ... turning away from any activity that is not connected with thoughts of him."[8] And although Emerson does not explicitly enumerate connections between the loss of the child and the perception of daily losses (of power, of wholeness, of will, of possession), he implicitly insists we recognize the connection in a central remark:

> It is very unhappy, but too late to be helped, the discovery we
> have made, that we exist. That discovery is called the Fall of Man.
> Ever afterwards, we suspect our instruments. We have learned
> that we do not see directly, but mediately ... perhaps there are no
> objects. (487)

We are invited to take this declaration two ways. One emphasizes subjectivity ("we do not see directly, but mediately"). The other emphasizes loss—the death of the child calling into question the reality of all other phenomena ("perhaps there are no objects"), with separation (the man from the child) preceding the subjectivity with which the paragraph seems exclusively concerned.

The discovery "that something which I fancied was part of me, which could not be torn away without tearing me, nor enlarged without enriching me, falls off from me and leaves no scar. It was caducous"—this discovery, or this account of the discovery, anatomizes in visceral terms the severed connection it claims cannot be felt. Emerson describes a vision of loss that registers on the body—mutilating, scarring, rending. And nothing about the negations in that same sentence, which manifestly contradict the vision of mutilation, in fact contradict it at all. It is a case of displacement because although Emerson claims he is mourning the loss of feeling, in fact what he is mourning is the lack of feeling's effects. Loss does not touch him not because he does not feel it but rather—he says—because the feeling has no palpable consequences. Here "consequences" seem imagined not only as a bodily manifestation but also as that particular bodily manifestation that affects the body of the mourner. Loss does not injure the mourner's bodily integrity, although the primitiveness of supposing it could establishes the fantasy connection between the man and the child whose absence is lamented. The mind anatomizes the loss as a severed connection with part of itself. And the graphic terms of the wish that it could be so (for if it were so there would be a correspondence between the feeling in the body and its representation by the body, its exaction *from* the body—an eye for an eye, a pound of flesh) remains unsavaged by death's actual effects.

Another way to regard the displacement I have described might be to say that because Emerson is here focusing on the discrepancy between the feeling of bodily violation and the fact of bodily intactness, he has displaced his attention from the loss of the child to the absence of the corporeal violation he would have the loss register. Thus there is some sense in which grief "does not touch" him. And that is not only the content of the complaint (that he has no contact with it, no bodily relation to it) but also its point (that grief does not touch him, that it has no effect on him). Emerson cannot "experience" the child's death. Cannot and does not wish to. Because to mourn the child in the only way mourning can be done is also to relinquish him. Thus from one point of view the deficiency of reality—or our deficient relation to it—protects not only the self (from the same fate as the dead child) but also the self's relation to the dead child.

Though in the mind the death of the child is equivalent to the death of the self—at least to its mutilation—the world belies the corporeality (hence the completeness) of that equivalence: "Marriage (in what is called the spiritual world) is impossible, because of the inequality between every subject and every object" (487–88). A passage from the essay's first three pages italicizes the point:

> Nothing is left us now but death. We look to that with a grim satisfaction, saying, there at last is reality that will not dodge us. (473)

Satisfaction so conceived illustrates a particularly brutal version of the conclusion to which Emerson comes: the only way for him to have access to the child's death is to experience his own. Yet if experience gives the lie to conception because the death of the child is not equivalent to the death of the man, and because insofar as it affects the man it affects the man's mind or his heart (not rending or scarring his body), if in these ways death is less than the mind imagined, in its uncompromising equivalence with every other aspect of experience, that same loss is more than the mind imagined—it is displaced from the specific catastrophe to the general understanding.

If "effects" are being measured, we see that there is no more apocalyptic one than that in which the death of the son leads to this conclusion: "the discovery we have made, that we exist," a discovery contextualized unambiguously as follows: "That discovery is called the Fall of Man." Thus what was different from what the mind imagined becomes more than what the mind imagined, Emerson turning away from the death of the son whom he struggles not to mourn, converting grief to analysis, experience to reflection, loss of the son to perception of death. Although the subject of Waldo's death may appear to be abandoned after the third page of the essay, then, it is the moving force without which the philosophic split between experience and idealism can only be trivial. Death removes things from the immediate to the abstract. It always marks the limits of the experienced. Indeed the essay demonstrates a kind of enactive stylistics. What is never said is that it is the son who can no longer be experienced. Instead of lingering on the enormity of that fact, Emerson deflects his attention to experience itself, specifically to that "evanescence and lubricity of all objects, which lets them slip through our fingers then when we grasp the hardest." Once we understand the deflection we see it is pointless to ask, "Why does Emerson never allude to the son again?" To take up the son's death as a displacement—to deflect the discussion of the son into experiences that "second" the son's loss, that reiterate or duplicate it—is to talk about the son the only way he can be talked about: at the remove to which death has placed him.

Our complaint about Emerson's dismissal of the subject of Waldo's death (for it is as a dismissal or abandonment that we first experience the displacement I have been describing) is akin to Emerson's own disappointment that grief does not do to the body what it does to the mind, and to a corollary disappointment, noted in a passage I cited earlier which observes that grief is superficial. Grief is superficial because it has no depth and because it is not penetrative. That grief is not penetrative means that the self cannot be pierced through by it. If the self could be pierced through by grief, the self would be equivalent to grief, hence not required to feel it. If we consider the two notions—of depth and penetration—we see that "depth" (or its absence) has to do with outsides, "penetration" has to do with insides. The conjunction of the two (and of the self's inadequate relation to each) implied by the essay treats the self as a double surface.

Such a way of figuring it still leaves the self separate from what it contemplates. It is this separateness Emerson attempts to rectify when he complains that grief is "shallow ... like all the rest, plays about the surface, and never introduces me into ... reality." In the context of the hope implied by the sentence (that grief could be equal to all that is external to it), "introduces" is an interesting verb for, negotiating the difference between self and reality, it suggests not incidentally, that the two could come together. Another of the metaphors differently extended by this hope implies the self could attain reality as a palpable achievement:

> There are moods in which we court suffering, in the hope that here, at least, we shall find reality, sharp peaks and edges of truth. (472)

The theatricality of the spatializations is repudiated when Emerson recognizes them as such: "But it turns out to be scene-painting and counterfeit." Although grief affects us, it is neither one with experience nor with our own experience. Our relation to it is skittish, inconsequential. As Emerson moves from equating grief with "sharp peaks and edges" to associating it with "depth" and then with "surface," we see the spatializations per se—of height, depth, and in the last resort of surface—ultimately dismissed as illusory. The images that presuppose access to grief belie the dissociation that characterizes it in fact:

> Was it Boscovich who found out that bodies never come in contact? Well, souls never touch their objects. An innavigable sea washes with silent waves between us and the things we aim at and converse with.... In the death of my son, now more than two years ago, I seem to have lost a beautiful estate,—no more. I cannot get it nearer to me. (472)

In Emerson's essay grief becomes a trope for experience because the self's relation to experience, like its relation to grief, is oblique, angled, contingent, dissociated. Thus the point I want to insist on with respect to the obliquity and dissociation in "Experience" is that these features of discourse are inevitable. Once the self understands its relation to experience, what it understands is that something has been removed. Death is the source of that understanding, teaching us our relation to every other event.

As I have noted, then, after the essay's first three pages, we see that what appears to be a displacement from the subject of Waldo's death is no displacement at all. It is rather a reiteration of the child's death, which ostensibly has been displaced, for the only way the dead son can be recalled is in a delegatory way. We see how this reiteration works in the passage from the letter cited earlier from 1842, when a week after Waldo's death Emerson writes:

> Alas! I chiefly grieve that I cannot grieve; that this fact takes no more deep hold than other facts, is as dreamlike as they; a

> lambent flame that will not burn the surface of my river. Must
> every experience—those that promised to be dearest & most
> penetrative,—only kiss my cheek like the wind & pass away?

The image above is not here a trope for the passing of all experience. It is rather a metaphor for the son reincarnated as a trope. So too in Emerson's essay: although grief is a trope for experience, it is always the particular experience, the death of the son, that is being simultaneously evoked and evaded. In the passage just cited, the child is evoked because the image of the wind kissing the man's cheek recalls the child even as it acknowledges his absence in the substitution of personification for person. In the passage from the essay which corresponds to that in the letter, contradictory imperatives similarly characterize a discourse in which grief is expressed and disavowed by the same words.

When writing of "the Indian who was laid under a curse, that the wind should not blow on him, nor the water flow to him, nor fire burn him" who is "a type of us all," Emerson laments his own imperviousness to grief, his inability to register it. Yet although he mourns that "the dearest events are summer-rain and we the Para coats that shed every drop"—although the man claims he is deficient of feeling—the trope rather suggests feeling so extensive that it overwhelms the bounds of the personal, becoming absorbed by the universe in an externalization: the shedding of the rain expressing the man's grief for him. In addition, the passage insists on a confusion between mourning and the thing mourned. Drops as rain (emblematizing the child who is lost) become drops as tears (emblematizing grief at that loss). Thus the expression of loss is made inseparable from its source, and equally inseparable from the man who asserts obliviousness to it. For even as grief is externalized as rain, the man also owns up to its source in himself. Thus one way of reading "and we the Para coats that shed every drop" is to see the phrase as connoting the evanescence of grief when the self repels and exteriorizes what it will not feel. An opposite way of reading the same sentence—bitter either way we understand it—is to note it depicting grief so inseparable from the self that identity is defined by the man's emphasized claim to it: "The dearest events are summer-rain and we the Para coats that shed every drop." In the implicitly italicized pronoun of that sentence, Emerson is reiterating the idea of his bodily connection to the son whose body, in some similarly mysterious way, came from his own—a connection that in the sentences "It falls off from me and leaves no scar. It was caducous," he had contested. Underscoring the ambiguity of rain and tears, grief that is delegated and grief that is owned, the essay remains unclear as to whether "the dearest events," which the man says he cannot feel/which the man says he does feel, signify the child or the child's death—"events" being a word that is purposively evasive. The point to be made about this ambiguity is that it is a representative one. The child cannot now be experienced apart from his death, and, as the essay in its entirety is at pains to inform us, it is just in his death that he cannot be experienced at all.

If contradiction is at the heart of the passages I have described, this is in keeping with the strategy of the essay, which never concedes ultimately (the absence of grief) what it concedes initially (the absence of grief); hence the triumph of its ending. Grief is never given in to and therefore is never given up. To this end—the savoring of grief; the reenactment of the man's relation to it—there is a repetitiveness to the instances and examples of it in the essay, as if each one were employed to replicate the conflict whose doubleness I have described. Once we see that the figure of the son appears everywhere in the essay, we no longer wish to ask: why is the subject introduced so as to be dismissed? We rather wish to ask an opposite question: why does the man's grief need to be repeated, mirrored in all aspects of experience as if there were no end to it? The point of this repetition in psychological terms is to continue to place in apposition the contradictory impulses—the refusal to mourn/the imperative to mourn—that I have been describing. For if it is the case that the child must be relinquished, this is how he is to be relinquished, by what Freud calls a "struggle." Because—paraphrasing Freud—although the testing of reality shows that the loved object no longer exists, people never willingly abandon a libido-position:

> [This struggle] is now carried through ... under great expense of time and cathectic energy, while all the time the existence of the loved object is continued in the mind.... Why this process of carrying out the behest of reality, bit by bit, which is in the nature of a compromise, should be extraordinarily painful is not at all easy to explain in terms of mental economics. It is worth noting that this pain seems natural to us. (*Standard Edition*, 14:245)

Repetition in "Experience" dramatizes the partiality of experience—the "bit by bit" to which Freud refers. Also its fleetingness. The man can mourn the same indirect relation to experience and to grief ten times because each time—every single time—what he says is both fleeting and partial. Thus the parts of the essay and the expressions of grief that they represent are not disparate and they are not integrated. They are continuous, but as a series of continuous displacements.

IV

One could describe the problem of contradiction that characterizes Emerson's essays as one of dissociation created by his disinclination to comment on the relation between contradictory assertions—his unwillingness first to admit them and second to instruct us on how we are to proceed in light of them. "Experience," I have claimed, bears a special relation to the problem of dissociation. It does so for several reasons, which I am now prepared to elaborate.

First, of all of Emerson's essays it is the only one to thematize dissociation, conceiving it initially in terms of death and ultimately in terms of power. Therefore, to the extent that it addresses itself to the source (death) and the consequence (power) of dissociation—the central concern in all of Emerson's essays—it has something to tell us about the questions that arise in them. Here I should reiterate that in "Experience" the dissociation precipitated by death and that connected to power are not in fact the same. I shall shortly amplify this point.

Second, "Experience" bears a special relation to the question of dissociation because, in the split between the essay's first three pages and its body, it exemplifies the most severe instance of dissociation in Emerson's oeuvre—a severity whose consequences have determined critics' inability coherently to locate the dominant subject in the essay. As I have noted, if they do see the death of the child as central, they have viewed it as the first of a number of phenomena to which Emerson has an equally contingent relation rather than understanding its generative connection to all else that follows. As a consequence, to the extent that they have observed that the essay is dominated by the problem of discrepancy or contradiction or dissociation they have done so in terms that invoke the dichotomy between idealism and experience without simultaneously understanding that the very ability to conceptualize division in these abstract terms is in "Experience" presented implicitly as a consequence of the child's death.

Third, "Experience" bears a special relation to the question of dissociation in Emerson's essays because, as its title suggests, its status is different from that of the rest of Emerson's essays. Though the title itself is an abstraction, the essay refers to things as experienced, not as abstracted.[9] To explain my distinction: although the essay does not have a different kind of disorder from Emerson's other essays, it has a different relation to its own disorder. One way of understanding this difference is to observe that "Experience" does not contest the reality it describes. It does not have a confrontational relation to the experience of which it renders an account. In characterizing the early essays (like "The Divinity School Address," "Self-

Reliance," *Nature*) as confrontational, I mean to suggest that they challenge experience, offering alternatives to it: the primacy of soul in "The Divinity School Address" and of the involuntary in "Self-Reliance." In characterizing the late essays (like "Fate") as differently confrontational, I mean to suggest that although these essays appear to accept the terms of experience, because they do so in a formal dialectic that concludes in a synthesis, the synthesis mitigates or dissolves the acceptance to which Emerson—in an essay like "Fate"—initially concedes. (Needless to say, these generalizations ideally ought to be substantiated by readings of the essays in question.) Distinguishing itself from the strategies of early and late essays, "Experience" neither stands in opposition to experience nor synthesizes the oppositions in experience that it recognizes and makes explicit. Rather, it situates itself in the midst of the issues it is considering, taking no "position" on its announced topic. An analogy may help to elucidate the way in which I wish to characterize "Experience" as different from the essays that precede and follow it. In "Fate" Emerson will recognize the beautiful as the contingent, codifying that recognition in the directive: "Let us build altars to the Beautiful Necessity" (967). "Beautiful Necessity" is a trope for the oxymoronic recognition in whose grip Emerson finds himself in "Experience" before he has learned to stand outside of the perception and, coolly, to find a figure for it.

Moreover—to explore my analogy—if we investigate the source of power in the two essays ("Fate" and "Experience") we see how it differs. The power of "Fate" lies in the antagonism between its concluding image—altars built to Beautiful Necessity—and the rest of the essay. The idea of a sacrifice, and the particular terms of its valorization here, occur *after* the argument (fate includes all and therefore fate includes free will) has been successfully conducted. The image clinches the argument by changing its terms. Establishing a distance between the conclusion and the dialectic that precedes it, Emerson suggests that what is at stake is neither fate nor freedom, but rather the simpler question of whether the world is to be conceived as incoherent or meaningful:

> If we thought men were free in the sense, that, in a single exception one fantastical will could prevail over the law of things, it were all one as if a child's hand could pull down the sun. If, in the least particular, one could derange the order of nature,—who would accept the gift of life? (967)

It is a question with no contest, and its brilliance lies in its dismissive relation to everything that has preceded it, as much as announcing: forget previous arguments and previous ways of positioning the argument, however logically persuasive; this is the real issue.

In "Fate" we see where the essay becomes empowered—in the juxtaposition of the image of "Beautiful Necessity" to the previous exposition. Yet if in "Fate" power comes in the adjacence of the image to the argument, in "Experience" the obliquity of power saturates the essay; power comes from the inability to nail it down anywhere. Power pervades the essay in the multiple instances of dissociation, as these succeed each other in a series "of which we do not know the extremes, and believe that it has none." Although some change occurs between the stupor of the essay's beginning and the determined energy of its final pages, this change does not take place prospectively in the essay's last sentence, though that is where Emerson alludes to a potential "transformation of genius into practical power," and though that is where the critics, following Emerson's signpost, have located it—albeit with bewilderment at what would be its precipitous expression, were it really to emerge for the first time in that sentence.

Although I want to insist on our inability to say where the essay's transformation takes place, the change can be described by pointing to the man's altered relation to his own grief as this is expressed at the essay's beginning and end. At the essay's beginning, the man disavows grief—disavows and preserves it in the ways that, as I have suggested, specifically have to do with the idea that loss makes the body of the mourner deficient. At the conclusion of the essay, grief has become a gratitude, specifically expressed at the intactness of the man's body. In fact grief is entirely absent from the passage cited below, which, as a consequence, may look disconnected from earlier passages considered, though, as I shall explain, a figurative subtext relates them:

> When I receive a new gift, I do not macerate my body to make the account square, for, if I should die, I could not make the account square. The benefit overran the merit the first day, and has overran the merit ever since. The merit itself, so-called, I reckon part of the receiving. (491)

Granted, the word "macerate," which describes the wasting away of flesh by fasting, presents a different image of bodily loss than that in the earlier passages (which depict loss as a scarring of the body, or as a tearing of the body, or simply as an expenditure of the body—as in tears or other vital fluids). Yet to the extent that all of these passages are concerned with getting and spending, with things given and taken away, with what is and can be lost—and with loss as something that affects the body—I believe we are required to see these passages as related. Specifically, we are required to ask: what has happened between the initial passages and the later ones—between passages that do not admit to loss (but which describe its toll on the body) and passages that talk openly about getting and losing (and which show the body intact)?

Before I address this question, I want to call attention to two other pertinent points that suggest a connection between the passage cited above and the earlier passages that address the child's death explicitly. One is the monetary imagery that governs the description of the child's death analogized initially to "the bankruptcy of my principle debtors ... the loss of my property" (473); in the passage above such imagery seems reinvoked to describe compensation: "the making of my account square." The second point of connection between this passage and earlier ones is that since the death considered in the essay has pertained to the child not the man, and since, moreover, death has been actual not prospective, the subjunctive "if I should die," at this point in the essay, is affectively indistinguishable from the retrospective "since he has died" of the essay's opening pages, and this substitution matters because the conclusion that follows is a conclusion about the child's death.

In the spectacularly understated end of the essay, the subject of death is not absent from consideration; rather it is reiterated. But, as the initial pages of the essay put grief at a remove because the man had no access to it, the concluding pages of the essay put grief at a remove because there is no reason for it. In these pages grief is not inaccessible—grief is gratuitous. Gifts are not taken away; rather they are received. The body is not macerated; it is nourished at great cost; the subject considered is not the death of the child but rather the death of the self. As a consequence of the double displacements I have described, loss is nowhere conceded in Emerson's "Experience"—not at the beginning where grief is deemed inaccessible; not at the end where it is deemed gratuitous. Yet it marks every page less the first three—if in no other way than in the sacrifice of the subject stated in direct terms. In fact while the inability to mourn becomes a refusal to mourn, as we have seen, this conversion distracts attention from the essay's most salient fact—that the child who is banished from most of its pages nevertheless affects those, pages as an incompletely displaced presence.

Several observations may clarify the transformation I have described. In psychoanalytic terms the man is able to move from images of bodily loss to ones of bodily wholeness because he has internalized the child— introjected him—and, so doing, he has simultaneously conceded the child's absence from the world. This explanation—on which one understanding of the end of the essay crucially depends—is simultaneously challenged by aspects of the essay that contest the idea of "integration" implicit in it, for the essay invites kinds of explanations that it then repels as inadequate. In asserting that the Freudian explanation might be inadequate—because the work of mourning needs to be repeated; because there are no conclusions to the repetitions in the essay (hence the child never returns to the essay's consideration); because insofar as the lost object is introjected, that introjected object is inaccessible to the man (hence the evasiveness of the subject of Emerson's essay, "Experience")—I want immediately to acknowledge that my own understanding of the process of mourning in the essay depends on a Freudian model. Moreover, one could argue that the psychoanalytic model seems inadequate because Emerson subverts a real working through of grief. But it could also be argued that the model seems inadequate because, insofar as Emerson does give us a picture of mourning that is accomplished, we see that the way in which it is accomplished is not, as Freud suggests, in terms of integration, introjection, completion, or accessibility.

In this connection, Jacques Derrida's account of Nicolas Abraham and Maria Torok's distinction between incorporation and introjection is of interest to me, for they resist the idea that mourning is a process that can be completed, and—directly relevant to the question of the dead child's "place" in Emerson's essay—they therefore also call into question the problem of how spatially to represent the introjected object.[10] I am specifically interested in their notion that introjection is a process that takes place secretly—that the object introjected is kept in a secret place—and I am interested in Derrida's elaboration of this theory: that the consequence of secrecy is a cryptic text. The theoretical understanding of introjection as a phenomenon that occurs in such a way as to leave the introjected object both unavailable and invisible to the self in which it is encrypted offers a means to picture the way in which Waldo dominates the essay from which he has disappeared.[11]

If we assume for a moment, though, the usefulness of the psychoanalytic perspective, we see that it is impossible to say where the internalization has occurred. The introjection has been completed in the "bit by bit" that Freud describes as the process of mourning. The primary transformation, Emerson's claim notwithstanding, is not of genius into practical power. It is rather of the loss of the child into the loss of the man's affect and then, again, of the loss of the man's affect into the recuperation of that affect. Thus it would seem that mourning eschewed at the beginning of the essay becomes mourning that is completed at the end of the essay—but for the fact that the subject of the child never returns to these pages. To put this another way: the thematic of the essay may imply power for those present moments over which dissociation and, therefore, death do not preside. But this thematic is blocked by a countermovement in the essay (emblematized by the child's incompletely banished presence) that predicates power not in any actual moment, not in a time, but rather in a fantasized psychic space.

Two pages before the conclusion of the essay Emerson writes:

Life wears to me a visionary face. Hardest, roughest action is visionary also. (491)

This assertion resumes the meditation begun by the sentence "Grief too will make us idealists" (473), as if it had not been broken off some eighteen pages earlier. Grief will make us idealists because grief will make the man imagine the child who can no longer be experienced. But if action as well as grief is in need of being imagined, then the distinctions between thought and action, the imagined and the experienced, the child and the recollection of the child—between all those oppositions the essay has worked to preserve—are inconsequential. To put this another way: in the fact that the second sentence appears to echo the first and also to contradict the exclusivity of its claims—hence to amplify them—it seems that action and the visionary now exist on the same plane. But as this is an essay entitled "Experience," the plane on which they exist is outside the essay.

   Although there is a local meaning, then, to "Hardest, roughest action is visionary also" (namely that if "hankering after an overt or practical effect" is "apostasy" we must envision the effect we are denied from experiencing), in the context of the issues that govern the whole meditation, the sentence "Hardest, roughest action is visionary also" has a broader, subversive meaning. What it subverts is the distinction between idealism and experience on which the discriminations in the essay consistently depend. It does this not so as to unite the two inside the essay (the essay has repeatedly demonstrated the impossibility of such a union) but rather to unite them in some hypothetical outside. If the child, who must now be imagined, exists at a remove, and if action (the most palpable characteristic of experience) exists at that same remove, then although both have been evacuated from the observations made by the essay (from what it purports to be able to talk about) in the parity of the essay's treatment of them—ousting each, as it does, from what it insists can be experienced—they are somewhere related. Although spatializing the issue this way personifies and gothicizes it, repeated metaphors of spatialization (apparent, for example, in the paragraph that describes grief in terms of depth, surface, peaks, edges) have invited just this kind of analysis. They have done so for a reason.

Dissociation in "Experience," and differently in Emerson's other essays, always seems resorted to so as to sustain at a remove what cannot be sustained in immediacy. In other essays this adjacency exists for the purpose of relegating qualifications to the margins when these conflict with the essay's polemical thrust. In "Self-Reliance," for example, the idea of the tyranny of the unconscious is exorcised to a sideline where it can contest but not come in contact with the essay's dominant voice, which wishes to stipulate conflict between the self and the social world undisturbed by the complications of any division in the former.[12] The legislative and repressive task assigned to obliquity in Emerson's essays is therefore, not surprisingly, the source of power. Obliquity sweeps aside objections, makes them tangential, disabling their ability to interfere with the essay's claims. In essays that characteristically desire into existence the prospective and the hypothetical, this legislative strategy is absolutely central. Power is not so much a consequence of obliquity per se, then, as it is a consequence of the driving force that marginalizes objections to primary claims without ever emasculating those claims. The metaphor is intended, for Emerson's primary claims are always at risk of having their potency threatened. If power, in general, is rapacious and anarchic ("Power keeps quite another road than the turnpikes of will and choice" [482]), man can only resist the force that itself resists control. Thus the tension of Emerson's essays is a consequence of keeping ideas that challenge central premises, however imperfectly, at a remove.

In "Experience" power is no less characterized by the tension I have described, but it is differently sourced. The essay introduces grief over the child's death only to usher it out of the text to some liminal place (for the essay's beginning suggests that grief is not only marginalized but will also frame what follows), some statutory nowhere where, undisturbed by the resolutions the essay records, Emerson preserves the loss he will not directly address. In "Experience," obliquity exists not to prevent what is dismissed to the periphery from disturbing what is said on the page; obliquity rather exists to preserve what is dismissed from anything that might threaten it—specifically, it exists to empower the grief that the essay has marginalized.[13]

Thus, although Emerson in "Experience" disavows spatializations that depend on ideas of integration, he relies on spatializations that depend on ideas of proximity. The essay inverts the central and the peripheral, the margin and the page, as well as the relative values implicitly attributed to each, and the triumph of its ending depends upon the inversion. "It does not touch me," Emerson says of grief at the beginning of the essay, but the lament turns to defiance at the end of the essay, where grief is the subject that cannot be touched. If the conversion I am describing savages the idea of reconciliation—to the child's death, to everything death represents—this is in keeping with the rest of the essay, which, like some science-fiction manifesto, insists definitionally on the isolated, the alien, the rootless, the excluded:

> We fancy that we are strangers, and not so intimately domesticated in the planet as the wild man, and the wild beast and bird. But the exclusion reaches them also.... Fox and woodchuck, hawk and snipe, and bittern, when nearly seen, have no more root in the deep world than man, and are just such superficial tenants of the globe. Then the new molecular philosophy shows astronomical interspaces betwixt atom and atom; shows the world is all outside; it has no inside. (480–81)

In assertions like these, of which "Experience" is elemented, the idea of a depth psychology which conceptualizes mourning as a "task carried through" seems all but phantasmal.

NOTES

1. Ralph Waldo Emerson, *Essays & Lectures*, ed. Joel Porte, The Library of America (New York, 1983), 471. Subsequent references to Emerson's essays are from this edition and are cited in parentheses in the text.

2. O.W. Firkins, *Ralph Waldo Emerson* (New York, 1915), 237, 341. In its entirety this book provides bracing discussions of Emerson's essays.

3. Stephen Whicher, *Freedom and Fate: An Inner Life of Ralph Waldo Emerson* (Philadelphia, 1953), designates the antithesis in terms of freedom and fate. Eric Cheyfitz, *The Transparent: Sexual Politics in the Language of Emerson* (Baltimore, 1981), situates antithetical assertions in a psychoanalytic context, illuminating the conflict between male and female, specifically with reference to *Nature*. Julie Ellison, in *Emerson's Romantic Style* (Princeton, 1984), discusses antithetical features of the essays by activating the Bloomian machinery of authority and its counters. In "Emerson's Dialectic," *Criticism* 11 (Fall 1969): 313–28, R. A. Yoder describes the dialectic moves in a number of Emerson's essays. Barbara Packer's *Emerson's Fall: A New Interpretation of the Major Essays* (New York, 1982) offers a comprehensive treatment of the unresolved dialectic established between and within essays. For one of the most compelling accounts of Emerson's language at odds with itself—considered in the context of his resistance to stabilizing moments of culture—see Richard Poirier's "The Question of Genius," *Raritan* 5, no. 4 (Spring 1986): 77–104.

4. I should immediately note that my use of "voice" is a metaphor, for Emerson's essay is written. It is discourse. But it is discourse in which assertions function as voices at odds with each other. This is the case not only in "Experience" but also in other essays. In "Self-Reliance," for example, contradictory assertions are adjacent to the essay's central argument, which is clear: where the world thinks one thing and the self thinks another, the self is to follow its own inclinations. But while Emerson is quick to admonish "insist on yourself," the terms in which the self is described reinstate the very restrictions—dictated

by dependence on others and by the will contesting forces stronger than it—that we supposed had been vanquished. Specifically, while some descriptions in the essay characterize the self by the volatility of its "intuition" and "inconsistency," other descriptions in the essay characterize the self as an acrostic, which "read it forward, backward, or across, it still spells the same thing" (266). While some quotations suggest the self is to follow what Emerson calls its "whim," other quotations elaborate the prohibitions against doing so because "perception is not whimsical, but fatal" (269), having consequences not simply for the self but for succeeding generations: "If I see a trait, my children will see it after me" (269). From the vantage of some quotations in "Self-Reliance," you must change your way of thinking and believe in self-trust. From the vantage of other quotations in "Self-Reliance," you cannot change your way of thinking (or your changes of thinking are not up to you) because perception is fatal, not whimsical. A slightly different instance of the dissociation I have been describing is exemplified by "Circles," where contradiction is manifested between a self who knows that "people wish to be settled" and a self who knows that "only insofar as they are unsettled is there any hope for them" (413). Although the assertions could be regarded as two halves of a single utterance (the first half articulating what men desire, the second half articulating what it behooves them to desire), the consistent double terms that characterize the essay suggest that Emerson is emphasizing adversary stances rather than the bipartite structure of a single proposition. Thus the beginning of the following sentence exemplifies ebullience at change, but the conclusion of that same sentence emphasizes terror at the sacrifice change necessitates:

> The very hopes of man, the thoughts of his heart, the religion of nations, the manner and morals of mankind, are all at the mercy of a new generalization. (407)

The man who two pages prior to this exclamation had steadily counseled "fear not the new generalization" (405) is not the man who here sees himself explicitly at its "mercy."
In essays like "Self-Reliance" and "Circles," contradictions notwithstanding, one could argue that the emphasis is clear. In "Compensation," however, it is less easy to determine the relation between contradictory voices. The positive reading of "Compensation" might be paraphrased as follows: there are no incompletions in the world; the idea of the fragmentary is a delusion—a reading substantiated by a quotation like the following one: "We can no more halve things ... than we can get an inside that shall have no outside" (291). But an equally plausible reading of "Compensation" might be paraphrased alternatively: wholeness or compensation is not in fact a reassurance that all will be given; it is rather a reassurance that all will be taken away—a reading substantiated by the following quotation: "The vulgar proverb, 'I will get it from his purse or from his skin,' is sound philosophy" (294).

   Within each of these essays it makes sense that Emerson's attitude should shift. What is unaccountable about the shifts is that they remain unremarked upon. One might say of these shifts that they are unconceded—in that they are unrecognized—at any rate, they are unnoted, treated as if they were nonexistent, as if the discrepant statements between which the essay vacillates occupy such different registers as never to have to come into contact at all. What is unaccountable is that in "Circles," "Self-Reliance," and "Compensation" Emerson treats contradictory statements as if they were complementary statements.

   5. *The Journals and Miscellaneous Notebooks of Ralph Waldo Emerson*, ed. William H. Gilman, et al., 16 vols. (Cambridge, Mass., 1960), 5:19–20. Subsequent references are cited in parentheses and abbreviated as *JMN*.

6. *The Letters of Ralph Waldo Emerson, 1842–1847*, vol. 3, ed. Ralph L. Rusk (New York, 1939), 9. See also the several letters written in the days preceding this one, especially that to Elizabeth Palmer Peabody on 28 January 1842:

> In the death of my boy ... has departed all that is glad & festal & almost all that is social even, for me, from this world. My second child is also sick, but I cannot in a lifetime incur another such loss. (8)

The letter in which Emerson "grieve[s] that I cannot grieve" can be seen as a retort to this one, and the discrepant responses in the letters as anticipating or duplicating those of the essay.

7. The concern with "power" in Emerson's late essays—especially in *The Conduct of Life*—replaces the concern with the "present" and the "possible" in *Essays, First Series*. The shift is anticipated in the concluding sentence of "Experience," where we are told "the true romance which the world expects to realize, will be the transformation of genius into practical power" (492). If you do not believe in possibility, or if you believe the present has no possibility that you can exploit, you had better have power—a substitution made explicit in another sentence from "Experience": "Once we lived in what we saw; now, the rapaciousness of this new power engages us" (487). Other sentences in "Experience" explain the difficulty of the engagement: "Power which abides in no man and no woman, but for a moment speaks from this one, and for another moment from that one" (477); "Power keeps quite another road than the turnpikes of choice and will, namely, the subterranean and invisible tunnels and channels of life" (482); "Life itself is a mixture of power and form, and will not bear the least excess of either" (478); "The most attractive class of people are those who are powerful obliquely, and not by direct stroke; men of genius, but not yet accredited: one gets the cheer of their light, without paying too great a tax" (483); "[Our friends] stand on the brink of the ocean of thought and power, but they never take the single step that would bring them there" (477). Power is most potent, most itself, "the single step" away that, at once, best defines it and marks its inaccessibility.

8. *The Standard Edition of the Complete Psychological Works of Sigmund Freud*, trans. James Strachey, vol. 14 (London, 1957), 244. Subsequent references to this edition.

9. Perhaps the title of Emerson's essay is an allusion to Montaigne's "De l'expérience" In any case Emerson's essay, as I am describing it—in its refusal to abstract from experience, in the oblique connection between one part of the exposition and another, in the consequent imperative that the reader decipher a coherent if hidden plot—seems as clearly related to Montaigne's other essays as to other essays of Emerson's own.

10. Jacques Derrida, "Fors" *The Georgia Review* 31 (1977): 64–116. Nicolas Abraham and Maria Torok's *Crytonymie: Le Verbier de l'Homme aux loups* (Paris, 1976) and Abraham's *L'Ecorce et le noyau* (Paris, 1978) are largely untranslated. See, however, Abraham's "The Shell and the Kernel," which supplies its title to the latter volume, translated in *Diacritics* 9 (1979): 4–28.

11. My notion of the dead child's evasive relation to "Experience" is illuminated by Abraham and Torok's definition of introjection as that phenomenon which absorbs into the ego a lost object or corpse that it then preserves in a fantasmatic crypt or hermetically concealed place—a space that can't be gotten at. And it is related to Derrida's extension of this idea: that the fantasmatic space of the crypt is also a linguistic space. But in this reading of "Experience," my notion differs from theirs with respect to the question of how the introjected object is to be spatialized and with reference to its accessibility. Derrida, following Abraham and Torok, asserts that an incorporated object is always readable,

whereas an introjected object never is. In "Experience," however; the antithesis of "always" with "never" misstates the case. Because the lost object remains partially or liminally visible (it is the subject of the preface, but is absent from the body of the essay), "Experience" openly invites the kind of reading I am offering, while simultaneously refusing to confirm it. Thus my idea of the marginality of the subject is not only a spatial one. Or rather, the spatialization calls attention to the fact that the magical power attached to the dead child is generated by the tension between what is visible and invisible; between the prospect of introjection conceived in terms of integration (held out by the essay's beginning) and the frustration of that prospect in the body of the essay, which only incompletely and indirectly assimilates both the subject and the loss. I shall argue that power comes from this marginality.

12. In "Self-Reliance" the self disencumbered of cursory constraints, with the idea of the cursory radically reconceived, remains fundamentally bound by its sympathies and aversions—by all that involuntarily comes to define it. Thus the two assertions "Nothing is at last sacred but the integrity of your own mind" and "I would write on the lintels of the door-post, *Whim*," may be ideally compatible, but they are experientially at odds. The degree to which this conflict remains unacknowledged as well as unexamined is the degree to which it cannot be considered perfunctory.

13. There would be another way to understand the relation between power and marginalization. It depends upon the convention (familiar to Emerson from such works as Ben Jonson's "On My First Son" and Wordsworth's "The Thorn") in which dead children are enabling because, in terms of the oedipal drama, they don't penetrate/castrate, as the man who wards off "experiences most penetrative" fears they might. If you kill them off, however, it's not just that you avoid the negative of castration, you are also bequeathed the positive penance of grief. In the case of "Experience," of course, grief is not wholly positive because it is not wholly felt. That escalates its value. Because grief is imperfect and glancing, you have to repeat it to keep converting your losses. Yet the oedipal drama I have scripted is only a metaphor. It is not penetration the man fears and it is not the child the man kills. Rather, these are a screen for the avoidance of all conflict—an avoidance that is, in fact, a move of empowerment. Power depends upon the evasion of conflict, upon denaturing the psychological terms the essay provokes the reader into contemplating.

DAVID BROMWICH

From Wordsworth to Emerson

My title says a little more than it means. I will not really be telling how to get from Wordsworth to Emerson, or describing the forces that intervened to create some sort of continuity between them. Instead, I want to point to something in Wordsworth and something in Emerson, and to show by description why they belong together. I have in mind a thought which impresses both writers with its difficulty—a thought which resists the intelligence but which both choose to treat as a communicable truth. It has to do with the soul and the complex ideas by which the soul may be defended. Words like *hope* and *trust* sometimes give a name to such ideas, and I will be alluding to other names presently. Let me now suggest only the general grounds of argument. Emerson was as happy to declare, as Wordsworth was reluctant to admit, the thought they shared about self-trust, or our ability to "keep / Heights which the soul is competent to gain." In elaborating this contrast between them, I mean to offer an illustrative anecdote concerning the growth, in the nineteenth century, of an individualism which was noncontractual and nonpossessive.

There has been a debate about the Immortality Ode among modern critics of Wordsworth in which most readers feel they have to take a side. In the terms given by that debate, the poem is about growing old, or about growing up. Either way, it has a motive related to the poet's sense that he

From *Romantic Revolutions: Criticism and Theory*. © 1990 by David Bromwich.

stands at a transition between two kinds of activity. These belong, first, to the imagination, which alone suffices for the creation of poems; and, second, to the "philosophic mind" by which a poet may be accommodated to the proper sympathies of human life. Wordsworth's position on the good of such sympathies is ambiguous. Because they come from unchosen attachments, they can seem to compel us like the force of custom, "Heavy as frost, and deep almost as life." On the other hand, the acts (including acts of love) that we perform from sympathy are just such as we might have performed freely had our minds been unconstrained by an habitual self-regard. In this way the philosophic mind appears to be allied with the poet's imagination after all.

The puzzle remains why Wordsworth should have been so equivocal—compared to other writers of his time—about the sympathies he might expect to share with his readers. He says in the Preface to *Lyrical Ballads* that the poet must give pleasure and that, "Except this one restriction, there is no object standing between the Poet and the image of things."[1] It is odd to think of pleasure, in a sense that allies it with communication, as *limiting* the poet's own sight of the image of things. Maybe the suggestion that the reader's pleasure can hold back the poet's seeing goes some way to explain Wordsworth's uncertainty about how far common sympathies may hinder imagination.

Of course in the debate I mentioned, questions like these are referred to the antithesis between childhood (which is linked with poetic powers) and the philosophic mind (which is linked with "the soothing thoughts that spring / Out of human suffering"). But I do not want to guess at Wordsworth's supposed feelings about his own fate as a poet because I do not think the motive of the poem can be found anywhere in this area. The motive is not Wordsworth's failure or success in cheering himself up but rather a feeling close to guilt. It is a guilt, however, respecting what might as well have been a source of pride: namely, the poet's knowledge that there are certain thoughts all his own, which he, having lived his life and felt the sentiments associated with it, can understand and cherish as no one else can do. What Wordsworth would like to say in this poem is something Emerson does say in "Self Reliance": "Absolve you to yourself, and you shall have the suffrage of the world."[2] But the ideas of obligation in which Wordsworth believed made him reject that as an impossible gesture. What the ode ends up saying is something more like, "Absolve you to the world, and you shall have the suffrage of yourself." The world, however, believes in the suffrage of no power but itself, and it cannot ever wholly absolve him.

From Burke and other moralists, Wordsworth inherited an idea of morality as formed by common interests and tending to subordinate the individual to the community. On this view personal liberty and social order stand in an uneasy tension with each other. The choices of conscience are not beyond challenge, and they are hard to generalize from, being themselves only the internalization of worldly reason and prejudice. It is by coming to know the passions, affections, and sentiments we share with others that we recognize our relationship of mutual attachment to others in a society; by such attachment, in turn, that we are able to see the good of the duties we impose on ourselves as obligations; and by this whole picturing of our selves within the scene of other people's thoughts, feelings, and condition of life that we start to be moral beings and so are humanized. From the beginning of his career, Wordsworth talked in this way about morality; and against this background in another ode, he defined a personal imperative of duty. But in one respect the morality I have described—anti-rationalist, and noncontractual, though it was—spoke in a language that was not his. It seemed to allow no reckoning with the thoughts that made his imagination unlike anyone else's.

For the thoughts that define one's personal character always have to come, says Wordsworth, from an aspect of oneself (a faculty, perhaps) that relates to another aspect of oneself (an instinct, perhaps). These thoughts come to light through the imagination's action upon a deposit so elusive that to catch the sense of it Wordsworth mixes metaphors and calls it a *spot* of *time*. The thoughts in question, that is to say, are discovered by a thinking and writing later self, in a search across moments from an earlier life that can now be looked on as a scene of indefinite striving or possibility. It is for this reason that throughout *The Prelude* Wordsworth describes childhood, in the personal sphere, with the same figures of speech he reserves for the French Revolution in the political sphere. I think Hazlitt was right therefore when he assumed that the phrase, "What though the radiance which was once so bright / Be now for ever taken from my sight," referred at once to youth itself and to the youth of the revolution. But, if that is so, one may conclude that the observance of homecoming in this poem has likewise a double reference. Wordsworth is turning back from the French Enlightenment morality of nature to the still-abiding English morality of sentiments and affections; and, at the same time, from the liberty of an unchartered life to the necessary constraints of a community. Certainly the poem has a good deal of the pathos one associates with an ambivalent return: "We will grieve not, rather find / Strength in what remains behind."

But that only alters the question a little. To whom, or what, does Wordsworth feel answerable for the rightness of his return? Or again (though it is much the same question), to what causes does he lay the unhappiness of his departure? These difficulties the ode does not solve; nor can it, given the nature of the man who wrote it. For Wordsworth's former self-betrayal, like his present self-expiation, is twofold. By wandering to a site of radical enlightenment and reformation, he had turned against England, the place that nursed him, the home (in the largest sense) of all the childhood rovings that first gave him an idea of freedom. And yet by giving up France and its radiance now, and taking on himself the bonds of a native life, he surrenders the very freedom that has been for him a condition of self-knowledge, and that has made him conscious of his separable membership in a community. The last lines of the ode emerge in so unbroken a cadence that one can fail to notice how strangely they recur to the note of ambivalence.

> Thanks to the human heart by which we live,
> Thanks to its tenderness, its joys, and fears,
> To me the meanest flower that blows can give
> Thoughts that do often lie too deep for tears.

We live by the human heart; but the thoughts come to *me*. The shared joys and fears of this conclusion recall the wedding, the funeral, and other ceremonial occasions that have appeared rather grimly in the more conventional part of the poem. Amid all this grand evocation of public observances is one who stands alone aware of thoughts the meanest flower can give; just as, earlier in the poem, with children culling flowers on every side, only the child Wordsworth could feel "The Pansy at my feet / Doth the same tale repeat."

Plainly something in the poem, including one part of Wordsworth, wants us to be able to say that these solitary thoughts are the same as those "soothing thoughts that spring / Out of human suffering." In that case they would truly belong to Wordsworth's new and comparatively selfless existence. But the poem only half conceals an allusion to the fact that his thoughts are of a different kind. They can often be, it says, "too deep for tears," which means that they come with no affections of the usual sort. So a principle of self, and even of self-reliance, has tacitly been declared at the end of a poem that aimed from the first at an other-regarding dedication of the poet's imaginings. The result must appear difficult, almost opaque, if placed beside the poem's moral directives elsewhere. A person gazing earnestly at the meanest flower will look anomalous compared to someone contemplating a picturesque landscape of fountains, meadows, hills, and groves. But for Wordsworth it is enough to know that his choice is intelligible to him. I take the end of the ode to suggest that any venture of Wordsworth's life, however it affects the community he lives in, will be justified only in the light of a personal principle from which finally there is no appeal—not even to responses like tears, which others can be imagined to share. Leigh Hunt thought that tears were "the tributes, more or less worthy, of self-pity to self-love. Whenever we shed tears, we take pity on ourselves; and we feel ... that we deserve to have the pity taken."[3] I think this helps in reading the last line of the ode. Wordsworth's conviction about his own thoughts has deepened beyond the want even of an appeal to *self*-sympathy. He no longer expects others to pass in sad review the events of his life (as if those events added up to a tale worthy of their pity). And he tells us that he himself is unable to see his life in this way.

I have concentrated thus far on the end of the ode both because it is decisive and because it is memorable. But, in looking back on the poem, one may come to feel that its frequent turnings, the very traits that make it an ode, were the result of an effort to control and render outstanding what is always inward in the poet's thoughts. I can give two examples of this, the first structural and general, the second figural and particular. The poem, we know, was written in two parts, the first four sections at one time and then the last seven; and it does feel as if it had been written that way. The whole first part is imagined by Wordsworth with a persistent intensity of grief for himself: it is "I," writing about me and the things that are mine. "Two years at least," according to the Fenwick Note, elapsed between the last line of the fourth section ("Where is it now, the glory and the dream?") and the first line of the fifth ("Our birth is but a sleep and a forgetting"), and if we ask what has come into the poem in that time, the answer is the "we" that steals upon us quietly and that dominates the rest of the ode.

This is, if I may put it so, the first Arnoldian consolation in English poetry. It works its way by various ruses in the next several sections: first Wordsworth tries out the myth of preexistence, then he supposes the child a foster-child nursed by mother earth (so he has already lost something; there never was a time when he had not lost it); then, in a curious and unassimilable satirical bit, he dandles and pokes the child some more, and pushes him back among his proper companions, regarding him now as a conscious, imitative being ("A six years' Darling of pigmy size!"). In this perspective the address to the child as "Mighty Prophet! Seer blest!" which strikes many readers as hyperbolic, may have seemed to Wordsworth a compensation for the liberty he took with the child in the preceding sections.

So much for the structural effort of control—the movement from I to We, from an inward and incommunicable subject to an outward and common one—and Wordsworth's feeling that this is both a necessary passage and a focus of new anxieties. For the figural representation of that effort, I turn to the ninth section, in which, as I read it, nothing at last is controlled. The hope that nature, being the source of a shared sentiment, will therefore be translatable to other people, seems here as precarious as ever. Wordsworth has spoken of "Delight and liberty, the simple creed / Of Childhood," but now he adds:

>   Not for these I raise
>   The song of thanks and praise;
>   But for those obstinate questionings
>   Of sense and outward things,
>   Fallings from us, vanishings;
>   Blank misgivings of a Creature
>   Moving about in worlds not realised,
>   High instincts before which our mortal Nature
>   Did tremble like a guilty Thing surprised:
>   But for those first affections,
>   Those shadowy recollections,
>   Which, be they what they may,
>   Are yet the fountain light of all our day,
>   Are yet a master light of all our seeing;
>   Uphold us, cherish, and have power to make
>   Our noisy years seem moments in the being
>   Of the eternal Silence....

Note that, in this analysis of thought, Wordsworth gives three distinct moments, with corresponding kinds of moral agency, which seem to stand for three different phases of consciousness. In the creed of childhood liberty, the child possesses himself without knowing that he does. Grown up and joined to our mortal nature, he will be unable to imagine such freedom except in grown-up terms, as a prompter of fear and guilt. But Wordsworth is interested in neither of these moments, neither of the extremes. He chooses rather to celebrate the child-consciousness at the moment of farewell, when the boy is just starting to know the "blank misgivings" (blank, because why should he feel them?) that signify his passage into the moral life of society. His instincts even at this moment are high, for he is sure, without having to be conscious, of his difference from other people and the rightness of that difference.

Yet the common moral life deals not so much with high instincts as with middling hopes and fears and prudential arrangements, and, once committed to these, the child will participate in our mortal nature. He is, however, thereby diminished only with respect to his own instincts, which he has disappointed. What is cryptic about the whole passage is that it speaks as if the loss related mostly to perception; the "fallings from us, vanishings" are fallings and vanishings from sight; and we know (among other sources, again, from the Fenwick Note) that perception formed a large part of Wordsworth's thinking about the idealisms of childhood. However, on the interpretation I have sketched, the great lines of the ninth section were not written by a man reflecting on the character of his perceptions. In all of these metaphors, the tenor belongs to morality and not metaphysics—but morality in the reverse of Wordsworth's usual self-distrustful sense. The child himself was a principle all his own before he could ever reflect on the fact, but his individual character, his soul, becomes definite to him only as he begins to see it passing; and he sees that happen vividly whenever he is imposed on by other people's claims.

Such, then, is the moment Wordsworth selects for thanks and praise: the moment when, having fallen part way from our selves, we discover that we exist, and look for certain traces of past seeing to uphold and cherish. But that is not quite right either. By resorting to normal ideas of cause, effect, and agency to explain Wordsworth's conception, I have distorted it. According to the grammar of the lines, we do not uphold and cherish anything; rather, it is those recollections, instincts, misgivings, in their very falling from us, that uphold and cherish us: they compose whatever we are, and we are nothing else, even if the consequent sense of ourselves has come from nothing but impressions caught in flight. Wordsworth's practice of self-recovery does not reach beyond this fact which resists all further discussion. The knowledge we have of our own identity is the representation, by a conscious self, of something fugitive in the life of a creature not yet individuated, with whom we share some memories and a name.

Emerson read the ode early and pondered it often, and was, in fact, among the first to have called it an Ode on Immortality. I want to begin this inquiry into his relationship to the poem by asking what he meant by a difficult sentence in the first paragraph of "Self Reliance": "In every work of genius we recognize our own rejected thoughts; they come back to us with a certain alienated majesty." What kind of thoughts did Emerson mean? One feels that he was trying to describe, and trying not to illustrate, a scene of the uncanny return of something repressed in ourselves—just the kind of scene Wordsworth did commonly illustrate, as in the boat-stealing episode of *The Prelude*. I do not tell myself (Emerson would thus be saying), till I discover it unbidden in some external thing, how thoroughly a principle of self-trust governed even the things I could care for. That principle has made the world over, in keeping with my character and moods; so that I suppose for me to respond to them, they must always have been mine.

In the light of this clue I think it is worth recalling the history of the composition of "Self-Reliance." Emerson occasionally mentions Wordsworth in his lectures of the 1830s, though some of his praise is rather equivocal.[4] Then in January 1839 at the Masonic Temple in Boston, he delivers a lecture on genius, with a draft of some remarks he will work in to "Self-Reliance":

> To believe your own thought,—that is genius.... In every work of genius, you recognize your own rejected thoughts. Here as in science the true chemist collects what every body else throws away. Our own thoughts come back to us in unexpected majesty. We are admonished to hold fast our trust in instincts another time. What self-reliance is shown in every poetic description! Trifles so simple and fugitive that no man remembers the poet seizes and by force of them hurls you instantly into the presence of his joys.[5]

Fugitive and *instincts* have come back to him from the ode. And a little further on, he generalizes: "The reason of this trust is indeed very deep for the soul is sight, and all facts are hers; facts are her words with which she speaketh her sense and well she knoweth what facts speak to the imagination and the soul."[6] However, between the two passages above Emerson needed to quote some poetry; he chose the lines about skating that later went into *The Prelude*, beginning "So through the darkness and the cold we flew," and ending "Till all was tranquil as a summer sea." It is one of the earliest quotations I know by any critic of materials from Wordsworth's autobiographical poem; though the passage was available to others where Emerson found it, in the four-volume edition published in Boston in 1824.

He quoted well from a new source, but he was thinking about the ode, of which "Self-Reliance" gives an original reading. If for us now, his individualism is generally accounted more radical than Wordsworth's, that is because he made himself be the sort of reader Wordsworth could not afford to be. Across the divide of those vanishings, and writing wholly from the side of our mortal nature, Wordsworth had come to have too many misgivings. The particular use of Emerson therefore, for someone interested in English Romanticism, is that he recovers a revolutionary idea of Wordsworth's aims. But, as in Wordsworth after 1797 or so, it is a revolution without a social medium in which to operate. The beautiful sublimation that Wordsworth had performed, by speaking of the French Revolution in a parable about childhood, Emerson continues by speaking of American democracy in a parable about the self. And on a single point of terminology, the two authors do converge. The individual power which they aim to preserve they call neither the child nor the self but the soul.

Yet in the sentence of "Self-Reliance" that I began with, much of Emerson's thought turns on his use of a rarer word, "alienated." It can have a religious sense of course, and maybe that is the primary one here: having alienated myself from the god who is my self, I find that my face is turned toward him again in every meaningful look I give or receive. But there is also a social sense of the word (the alienation of property) which stays near the surface with almost the force of a pun. I have alienated myself from my own estate; but wherever I cast my eye I find it still before me. That would be sufficiently Wordsworthian; and it fits in with the following sentence from "Self Reliance," about the power we can call upon if we have once been strong in the past: "That is it which throws thunder into Chatham's voice, and dignity into Washington's port, and America into Adam's eye." So the two metaphors that alienation can imply—the religious one about sight and the social one about property—are suggested together in Adam's gaze at his lands. It is important that the lands be inherited as naturally as an instinct, and not earned as the reward of labor or service. For Emerson will also want to say: "Prayer that craves a particular commodity, anything less than all good, is vicious."

I shall return later to Wordsworth's and Emerson's ideas of property. Besides, there is a connection between the immortality Ode and "Self-Reliance" which ought to concern us more. I mean the path by which Wordsworth moves from his intimations to the glimpse of the "immortal sea which brought us hither"; by which Emerson is able to pass from the accusing philanthropists who muddle his thoughts to the conception of an aboriginal Self. Both proceed by means of an inverted genealogy. Wordsworth says, "The Child is Father of the Man." Emerson says, "Is the acorn better than the oak which is its fulness and completion? Is the parent better than the child into whom he has cast his ripened being? Whence this worship of the past?" Which is very strange, until one realizes it is playing against the Wordsworth, and even then it is not much less strange. Wordsworth's little allegory itself is grotesque if one tries to picture it rather than reason about it. But once we scale it down from allegory to mere exaggeration, it seems to say that the child is both wiser, in his closeness to the source of things, and at the same time more capable than the father, in having not yet had to acquiesce in the ways of custom and habit. Because he establishes the character the man will have to obey, the child is father to him. On the other hand—what *could* Emerson have meant? One expects the acorn will be compared to the oak as the child to the parent, but he works it the other way around, and says the oak is the child "into whom [the parent] has cast his ripened being." So the child there stands above the parent by being the realized thing that is livelier to the imagination than the potential thing. The child, in his characteristic independence, outranks the parent in his thoughtless conformity, as the fully developed entity does the inchoate or elementary.

One cannot help being struck as well by a difference in the function of the metaphors. The child, as Wordsworth sees him, can actually come before, precede, influence the man *in the continuity of a single life*, and in that sense be his own father. But there is no sense in which the child Emerson imagines (with the integral strength Emerson imputes to such a creature) will admit that the parent came before, preceded, or influenced him in any but the trivial manner in which an acorn comes before an oak. The reason Emerson can do without this admission is that he is not in fact talking about the continuity of a single life. Why look to virtuous actions, he asks, when you have before you the man who is himself the embodied virtue? Start thinking about acts and you scatter your forces. On this view the composition of a life by particular choices of conduct toward others looks like a chimerical aspiration. Even the possibility of knowing days "bound each to each by natural piety" may come to seem an invention of institutional morality which one could very well do without. I am alluding here to Wordsworth's use of the phrase *natural piety* in the epigraph to the ode: as far as I know, *The Prelude* is the first work of moral reflection in which virtue is made to depend on a conscious attempt to compose a life of such naturally linked actions.

Emerson would have found this way of thinking antipathetic, for to judge particular acts somehow implies judging them from outside; which is done by rules, or at least by conventions of judgment; which, in turn, bring to mind the kind of scrutiny that can make society "a conspiracy against the manhood" of each of its members. But there may be another clue to his reaction in the word piety. It shares a root with *expiation*, about which Emerson has this to say: "I do not wish to expiate, but to live. My life is for itself and not for a spectacle." To the extent that Wordsworth does regard his life as a spectacle, his thinking seems to be in line with ordinary republican sentiments about how one has to live with respect to others. One acts, that is, under a consciousness of fortune and men's eyes. By contrast, Emerson has already so far sacrificed consistency, and with it even the aim of being the hero of his own life, that he is hardly susceptible to much anxiety about the story others may make of it. Indeed the very idea of story is non-Emersonian. He says, still in "Self-Reliance," that "all history resolves itself very easily into the biography of a few stout and earnest persons," and he might as fairly have added that biography itself is only the insight of believing persons into "a great responsible Thinker and Actor working wherever a man works." We sympathize with such a man and want to imagine his life in just the degree that we find our own thoughts come back in his with a certain alienated majesty.[7]

I said earlier that Emerson, like Wordsworth, appeals from an idea of the self to an idea of the soul. Here is the passage from "Self-Reliance" in which he declares his faith:

> The magnetism which all original action exerts is explained when we inquire the reason of self-trust. Who is the Trustee? What is the aboriginal Self, on which a universal reliance may be grounded? What is the nature and power of that science-baffling star, without parallax, without calculable elements, which shoots a ray of beauty even into trivial and impure actions, if the least mark of independence appear? The inquiry leads us to that source, at once the essence of genius, of virtue, and of life, which we call Spontaneity or Instinct. We denote this primary wisdom as Intuition, whilst all later teachings are tuitions. In that deep force, the last fact behind which analysis cannot go, all things find their common origin. For the sense of being which in calm hours rises, we know not how, in the soul, is not diverse from things, from space, from light, from time, from man, but one with them and proceeds obviously from the same source whence their life and being also proceed. We first share the life by which things exist and afterwards see them as appearances in nature and forget that we have shared their cause. Here is the fountain of action and of thought. Here are the lungs of that inspiration which giveth man wisdom and which cannot be denied without impiety and atheism. We lie in the lap of immense intelligence, which makes us receivers of its truth and organs of its activity. When we discern justice, when we discern truth, we do nothing of ourselves, but allow a passage to its beams. If we ask whence this comes, if we seek to pry into the soul that causes, all philosophy is at fault. Its presence or its absence is all we can affirm. Every man discriminates between the voluntary acts of his mind and his involuntary perceptions, and knows that to his involuntary perceptions a perfect faith is due. He may err in the expression of them, but he knows that these things are so, like day and night, not to be disputed. My wilful actions and acquisitions are but roving; the idlest reverie, the faintest native emotion, command my curiosity and respect. Thoughtless people contradict as

readily the statement of perceptions as of opinions, or rather much more readily; for they do not distinguish between perception and notion. They fancy that I choose to see this or that thing. But perception is not whimsical, but fatal. If I see a trait, my children will see it after me, and in course of time all mankind,—although it may chance that no one has seen it before me. For my perception is as much a fact as the sun.

When Emerson writes "We lie in the lap of immense intelligence," I think he means that our nurse or foster-mother (the same one who "fills her lap with pleasures all her own") is *not* the earth. We do not belong to someone who can speak for nature and human nature, and by doing so wean us from ourselves, and make us forget the glory from which we came. Rather that intelligence is simply ourselves. So that the receding of its power from us is a tendency of life to which we need not submit. Emerson, of course, can make his claim the more plausibly because he conceives of the soul as somehow beyond the reach of our experiential self: it is "that science-baffling star, without parallax, without calculable elements ... the last fact behind which analysis cannot go."

Seeking a clue to his intentions here, let us recall that in the paragraph quoted above, as in some other celebrated passages, Emerson speaks of the soul's force in a metaphor borrowed from electromagnetism. The soul makes a current of being, and can do so merely by having brought two things into relation, like a coil of wire with a magnet. This explains his confidence about the fatality of perception once a given character and the physical universe have been brought into contact with each other. For the power that is generated as a result may appear to be both timeless and oddly undifferentiated. True, one of Emerson's aims is to concentrate all energy in the present: it seems to be part of his larger project of disencumbering the self, and America, of a grave and incapacitating reverence for the past. But though the entire figure concerning magnetism has this form, it is intended above all as a metaphor about process, and the power in question can hardly be constant or static. We come to know it, indeed, only in moments of passage from one state to another—that is to say, in fallings from us which are also fallings toward something deeper in ourselves. As Emerson remarks a little further on, in a striking revision of the ninth section of the ode: "Life only avails, not the having lived. Power ceases in the instant of repose; it resides in the moment of transition from a past to a new state, in the shooting of the gulf, in the darting to an aim. This one fact the world hates; that the soul *becomes*...."

Wordsworth had placed the moment of repose in the past, though it is a question whether he really thought it belonged there: he seems to have wanted to defend himself from the knowledge that it might still lie in the future. When, in the "Ode to Duty," he writes "I long for a repose that ever is the same," it is a longing against both imagination and freedom.

Emerson for his part believed that individual power tends to harden soon enough into just such a repose; but he wants us to believe that the opposite is always possible; and his departure from Wordsworth is connected with his own violent hatred of memory. To the conspicuous faith of the ode, that our memories leave the deposit from which our profoundest thoughts derive, Emerson replies in "Self-Reliance": "Why should you keep your head over your shoulder? Why drag about this corpse of your memory, lest you contradict somewhat you have stated in this or that public place? Suppose you should contradict yourself; what then?" We are once again at the point where natural piety, consistency of opinion, and a respect for duties laid upon oneself as actor in the spectacle of social morality, come to seem names for the same thing. Wordsworth, however reluctantly, is responsive to their call, and Emerson is not.

Every other divergence I have noticed between Wordsworth's and Emerson's reading of the self plainly follows from their opposite prejudices about memory. But I want to close by remarking a slightly different, almost physical, correlative of the self which both writers treat allusively and which may bring out a permanent difference in the social backgrounds from which English and American Romanticism took shape. The self-trust of an individual in the writing of both Wordsworth and Emerson has something to do with the secure possession of property. Wordsworth uses a complex word for the motive by which property and the self are linked: the word is *hope*. Thus we are told of the hero of "Michael" that the news of his forfeit of lands

> for a moment took
> More hope out of his life than he supposed
> That any old man ever could have lost.

Hope, in this Wordsworthian grammar, has to be represented as a partitive substance, like land or earnings. But hope for Michael is the imaginative measure of that practical thing, property. To put it another way, a strong self like Michael finds in property the sanction of his individual way of life. The model both for the poet, who dwells in effort and expectation and desire, and the citizen who lives an exemplary life of natural piety, is the return to a given spot of earth by a Cumbrian freeholder. It was of such people that Wordsworth observed in his letter of 1801 to Charles James Fox: "Their little tract of land serves as a kind of permanent rallying point for their domestic feelings.[8]

On the face of things Emerson, notwithstanding his popular reputation, has a much more disdainful view of property, and in "Self-Reliance" preeminently. He says near the end of the essay that "the reliance on Property, including the reliance on governments which protect it, is the want of self-reliance." (It is pertinent that he also says, "Fear and hope are beneath [the soul]. There is somewhat low even in hope.") And yet, Emerson is always close to a figurative language that keeps in view associations of property; as, for example, in the long passage above, with its rhetorical question, "Who is the Trustee?" He seems, in short, to have been interested in property as a material instance of a principle which the soul prefers to keep ideal. Though not, therefore, connected as cause and effect, secure property and self-reliance know each other as versions of autonomy, and are perhaps justly suspicious of each other's claims. But Emerson writes of a society in which this kind of sanction could be taken more for granted than in England. Little of the available land in America had yet been either claimed or enclosed. It is in fact the apparent detachment of the self from property that makes Emerson so elusive a guide to readers who expect a writer like him to be involved in the work of social criticism, whereas Wordsworth, though his politics at any time of his life are difficult to characterize, has been steadily serviceable to radical as well as reactionary communitarians.

Maybe Emerson's unsatisfactoriness here, his intention not to satisfy interests like these, marks a more general refusal of the spectacle of expiation. It may also seem to mark the point at which we have to start reading him against no writer earlier than himself. I have been arguing only that the peculiar quality of his detachment was a possible development from Wordsworth. He said of Wordsworth in *English Traits* that "alone in his time, he treated the human mind well, and with an absolute trust. The Ode on Immortality is the high-water mark which the human intellect has reached in this age. New means were employed, and new realms added to the empire of the muse, by his courage." This is conventional language but for Emerson its meaning was not conventional. The high-water mark had to be very high indeed to reach us, as far inland as we were in conformity and habitual practices. And, for Wordsworth, whose deference to the bonds of custom was great in exact proportion to his self-doubt, to show the thoughts of the soul must have seemed an even stranger undertaking than it has been for his successors, who have had his own example to invigorate them. All I have tried to explain in this essay is what Emerson rightly called Wordsworth's courage.

Notes

1. "Preface to *Lyrical Ballads*," in *Selected Poems and Prefaces*, ed. Jack Stillinger (Boston, 1965), p. 454. All quotations of Wordsworth's poems are from this edition.

2. "Self-Reliance," in *Selections from Ralph Waldo Emerson*, ed. Stephen E. Whicher (Boston, 1957), p. 149. All quotations of "Self-Reliance" are from this edition.

3. Leigh Hunt, *Imagination and Fancy* (London, 1883), p. 302.

4. He more than once refers to Wordsworth's poetic talents as "feeble." I take it he meant by this to deny Wordsworth the power of a rich inventiveness while granting him a power much stranger and less parochially literary.

5. *The Early Lectures of Ralph Waldo Emerson*, ed. Robert E. Spiller and Wallace E. Williams (Cambridge, Mass., 1972), 3:77. The overt echoes of the ode in "Self-Reliance," of which I have little to say here, may be useful to list for the reader who hoped for a different kind of commentary. They seem to me these: "[A boy] cumbers himself never about consequences, about interests.... But the man is as it were clapped into jail by his consciousness." "[Man] dares not say 'I think', 'I am', but quotes some saint or sage. He is ashamed before the blade of grass or the blowing rose."

6. Ibid., 3:78.

7. Carlyle wanted the majesty to return, unalienated, in the life of a hero, who would make a great figure for a race, and not merely for individual readers. The choice has broad consequences for his thinking about history. It cannot be for him (what Emerson says it is) "an impertinence and an injury if it be any thing more than a cheerful apologue or parable of my being and becoming." The Carlyle parable is gloomy because it always belongs to a whole people, over the heads of the individuals who recall it.

8. *Early Letters of William and Dorothy Wordsworth* (1787–1805), ed. Ernest De Selincourt (Oxford, 1935), p. 262.

DAVID M. ROBINSON

"Here or Nowhere":
Essays: Second Series

THE AMPHIBIOUS SELF

"We are amphibious creatures, weaponed for two elements, having two
sets of faculties, the particular and the catholic." (*CW*, 3:135)

"E xperience" signals a break in Emerson's development, and there
seems to be a general perception that the "late" Emerson can be dated
roughly from that essay. But how his transformation occurred, and how we
are to value it, are more difficult questions. "Acquiescence," Stephen E.
Whicher's loaded term, has dictated the assessment, and I suspect the
teaching, of Emerson since the 1950s, with a resulting stress on the
importance of the work of the late 1830s. In this model, "Experience"
exploded the romantic ethos of the earlier work and forced Emerson to
retreat into chastened final commentary on "fate." But this explanation has
obscured a full sense of Emerson's enormous creative achievement in the late
1840s and 1850s.[70] The break "Experience" signals is better understood as
the movement toward an ethical pragmatism, a growing insistence that the
ideal must be experienced in and through the world of fact, time, and social
relations. "Experience," especially in its conclusion, suggests that direction,
but it is best understood through the texture of the entire volume of *Essays:*

From *Emerson and the Conduct of Life: Pragmatism and Ethical Purpose in the Later Work.* © 1993
by Cambridge University Press.

Second Series, from which only "The Poet" and "Experience" have achieved much stature in the Emerson canon. "Experience" was certainly the most compelling expression of Emerson's pragmatic reaction to the polarities of experience, but the significance of its conclusion is amplified by other essays in the volume. The thematic nucleus of the book can be located in an 1842 conversation with his Swedenborgian friend Sampson Reed: "In town I also talked with Sampson Reed, of Swedenborg & the rest. 'It is not so in your experience, but it is so in the other world.'—'Other world?' I reply, 'there is no other world; here or nowhere is the whole fact; all the Universe over, there is but one thing,—this old double, Creator-creature, mind-matter, right-wrong'" (*JMN*, 8:182–3). In countering Reed's dualism, Emerson hit on a fundamental principle of *Essays: Second Series*, and arguably of his entire later work. He incorporated the conversation into "Nominalist and Realist," a lesser-known essay with a close thematic connection to "Experience."[71] In "Experience" the condition of the "double consciousness," in which potential is constantly weighed against a disappointing reality, was represented as the lack of coherence between inner and outer experience, the realization that "an innavigable sea washes with silent waves between us and the things we aim at and converse with." This dilemma is restated in "Nominalist and Realist" as the dichotomy between our faith in humanity and our sense of the failings of individuals. To focus too exclusively on a totalized concept of the human robs us of the specificity, and ultimately the reality, of persons. But to see only persons is to lose any larger sense of human possibility in the moil of individual limitations. The cumbersome title of the essay is rooted in Emerson's long-held concept of the "universal man," an idealization of the higher moral possibilities of human nature. He therefore found the medieval debate over the metaphysical status of universal concepts applicable to the relation between individual personalities and generic concepts of the human race, and a point from which he could work toward a reconciliation between the universal and the individual. The same issue, of course, would be central to his next book, *Representative Men*, and these texts indicate the ways that Emerson was revising his conception of the universal.

Although Emerson defends the "reality" of universals, holding to the necessity of theoretical generalizing about human possibility, his position is not without its problems, as the following remarks suggest: "In the famous dispute with the Nominalists, the Realists had a good deal of reason. General ideas are essences. They are our gods: they round and ennoble the most partial and sordid way of living. Our proclivity to details cannot quite degrade our life, and divest it of poetry" (*CW*, 3:136). The "general ideas" defended by the realists are an important reminder that a sense of worth can be preserved when discrete human actions fail to offer any support for that faith. "A man is only a relative and representative nature ... a hint of the truth," suggestive to us of general principles but never embodying the truth completely (*CW*, 3:133).[72] These questions were directly rooted in Emerson's personal situation in the middle 1840s, a time when he was attempting to beat back the demands from his friends for commitment to political projects of various sorts, while he simultaneously approached on his own terms the most appropriate methods of achieving the "practical power" he had advocated in "Experience." In one sense, "Nominalist and Realist" is a complicated attempt to answer this double bind, warning against the potential loss of judgment that too narrow a sense of political commitment can bring, while also insisting that particular facts are the only measure of general truths.

The opposition of the individual and the universal perspectives accounts for the gap between our projections and reality, because "our exaggeration of all fine characters arises from the fact, that we identify each in turn with the soul" (*CW*, 3:134). The soul is the universal; character, as we see it, is particular. To be a social creature is thus to be "amphibious," capable of surviving in two worlds, and "having two sets of faculties, the particular and the catholic" (*CW*, 3:135). If the pull of the over-soul dictates that we see humanity in its broadest, and most optimistic, light, the intransigent reality of individuals keeps our feet firmly planted on the ground. Or, to put this more concretely, Emerson was hoping to preserve his general faith in social progress even as he witnessed the sometimes inept or incongruous ways that his transcendentalist and abolitionist friends tried to effect it. The reformers often seemed to him to be duplicating the ills they were attempting to eradicate. Thus it is with an attitude of bemused tolerance that he speaks of the boredom of human sameness, reminding us that we must look beyond the individual at times to maintain any sense of commitment to human causes: "I wish to speak with all respect of persons, but sometimes I must pinch myself to keep awake, and preserve the due decorum. They melt so fast into each other, that they are like grass and trees, and it needs an effort to treat them as individuals" (*CW*, 3:138–9). Yet it is individuals and their particular lives that finally constitute the texture of social life, and the only sphere of moral action. "Nature will not be Buddhist," Emerson noted; "she resents generalizing, and insults the philosopher in every moment with a million fresh particulars." Such "insults" remind us that the universal is grounded in the particular and that the individual must be apprehended before any generalization is possible:[73] "It is all idle talking: as much as a man is a whole, so is he also a part; and it were partial not to see it." Human perception is itself partial because it must periodically adjust its focus from the particular to the general. Although the change is essential, it must be remembered that one method of focus comes at the cost of the other, excluding a crucial aspect of the total reality we hope to understand. "You have not got rid of parts by denying them, but are the more partial. You are one thing, but nature is *one thing and the other thing*, in the same moment" (*CW*, 3:139).

This fundamental dilemma prevents any definitive—and static—conception of the human estate, but as the essay develops, Emerson's emphasis leans toward the particular. Because of the inevitable partiality of our own perception, we can apprehend the whole only through what he calls the "succession" of particulars. "Succession" had been one of his "lords of life" in "Experience," and he had struggled with the "secret of illusoriness" caused by the perpetual "succession of moods or objects" (*CW*, 3:32). In "Nominalist and Realist," Emerson identifies succession as the necessity that gives value to the intellectual capacity to abstract unified meaning from disparate particulars, a guarantee that "the whole tune shall be played." As disparate colors on a wheel can, by the speed of rotation, be blended into one, so can we extract unity from the myriad parts of nature. Succession reveals the individual as part of a larger framework of an inclusive unity, the proof that "Nature keeps herself whole" (*CW*, 3:142). This wholeness is not experiential but idealized through reflection, as memory combines the discrete experiences of moments over time.

This discipline of abstracting the succession of parts into a discernible whole, the capacity to "see the parts wisely" (*CW*, 3:143), is based on the necessity of viewing discrete particulars as best we can, but refusing to view them only as particulars. It is a process by which we engraft our ever-present desire for universality onto particular moments of insight. Emerson found his metaphor for such seeing close to home, in the autumn fields around Concord: "We fancy men are individuals; so are pumpkins; but every pumpkin in the field, goes through every point of pumpkin history" (*CW*, 3:144). The shared pattern of development, visible only in a particular pumpkin, confirms its place in a universal scheme. We may see only the pumpkin, but we must see it as an instance of universal law.

It is one thing to see a pumpkin as an instance of a law, but quite another to see one's friends that way. Emerson saves what may be the biographical key to the essay for a concluding meditation on human relations, one of the moments in which he struggled most openly with the difficulties of mutual human understanding. The discussion of his conversation with "a pair of philosophers" also reveals in a veiled and indirect way his ambivalence over the pragmatics of reform. Joseph Slater identifies these "philosophers" as Charles Lane and Bronson Alcott (*CW*, 3:226), who had discussed their plans for utopian reform at Fruitlands with Emerson in

April 1843. Emerson had been frankly skeptical of the Brook Farm experiment; he was, despite his sympathy and support for Alcott, close to derision about the plans for Fruitlands.[74] And, from what we can gather of Emerson's account, transcribed in large part directly from his journal into the text of "Nominalist and Realist," the conversation had been edgy: "I endeavoured to show my good men that I loved every thing by turns & nothing long; that I loved the Centre, but doated on the superficies, that I loved Man, but men seemed to me mice & rats, that I revered saints but woke up glad that the dear old Devil kept his state in Boston, that I was glad of men of every gift & nobility, but would not live in their arms" (*JMN*, 8:386; see also *CW*, 3:145). We can safely assume that Lane and Alcott had pressed Emerson for a commitment to their communal experiment, and that he had rebuffed them with this explanation of his perpetually shifting outlook. That he felt some guilt about the incident is evident from both the journal entry and the context of the essay, in which he used the conversation to illustrate his sense of the failure of constancy in human relations: "If we could have any security against moods! If the profoundest prophet could be holden to his words, and the hearer who is ready to sell all and join the crusade, could have any certificate that tomorrow his prophet shall not unsay his testimony!" (*CW*, 3:144–5). The self-directed irony that permeates this discussion is clear when we remember that it is Alcott who is selling all and joining the "crusade," and Emerson who has served as his inconstant prophet. Alcott has taken Emerson more sincerely than Emerson has taken himself, a situation that provokes Emerson's ironic dictum: "I am always insincere, as always knowing there are other moods" (*CW*, 3:145).[75]

But the guilt revealed in the passage does not obscure Emerson's genuine exasperation, focused primarily on Lane and Alcott's narrow dogmatism. Emerson noted that "the discourse, as so often, touched character," and by this standard, he found Alcott and Lane wanting. "They were both intellectual," Emerson told them. "They assumed to be substantial & central, to be the thing they said, but were not, but only intellectual, or the scholars, the learned, of the Spirit or Central Life." This elaborate charge of hypocrisy is particularly interesting because under the circumstances we might expect Emerson, aloof from the experiment, to be the most vulnerable to this accusation. But Emerson finds a certain aloofness in Alcott and Lane's very assurance about their course of action: "I felt in them the slight dislocation of these Centres which allowed them to stand aside & speak of these facts knowingly. Therefore I was at liberty to look at them not as commanding fact but as one of the whole circle of facts." They are committed, as he perhaps is not, but they are committed in *theory*, not in experience. Moreover, their theoretical commitment has blinded them to many aspects of experience, a comment that explains his description of them as "divine lotos-eaters." As Emerson explains, "They did not like pictures, marbles, woodlands, & poetry; I liked all these & Lane & Alcott too, as one figure more in the various landscape." It is significant that by the end of this conversation, Emerson has portrayed himself as more attuned to the concrete and particular world, a commitment that prevents his complete immersion in the theories of Lane and Alcott. Emerson notes Alcott's rejoinder about "the injury done to greater qualities in my company, by the tyranny of my taste," an accusation, that is, that Emerson's aesthetic orientation prevents his political commitment. But the conversation has illustrated Emerson's observation, fundamental to "Nominalist and Realist," that "every man believes every other to be a fatal partialist, & himself an universalist" (*JMN*, 8:386–7; see also *CW*, 3:145), and it is with this sense of suspended assent that Emerson, somewhat abruptly, closes the essay. The sense of irresolution with which "Nominalist and Realist" ends is perhaps the appropriate correlative for Emerson's shifting internal dialogue on the nature of the moral life. Certainly the essay suggests how deeply the questions of reform went to the core of his entire philosophy, and how he was struggling to align his more abstract sense of justice and human possibility with the questions of the hour. But there is more here, finally, than suspended assent. Although it does not abandon the universal, the direction of "Nominalist and Realist" is to suggest that theory and generalization, albeit necessary and inevitable, must always be taken with some reserve of skepticism. That skepticism represents the recognition of the inevitable changes of perception that experience will generate, and if we remain open, the essential ability to adapt to experience, an adaptation that is crucial to the transformation of theory into practical power.

FROM SELF-CULTURE TO CHARACTER

"Character is centrality, the impossibility of being displaced or over-set" (*CW*, 3:58).

Emerson's discussion with Alcott and Lane turned on the concept of "character," and from this perspective he pointedly commented that "the centres of their life" were not "coincident with the Centre of Life" (*JMN*, 8:386). This discussion suggests the importance the concept of character had assumed for him in the early 1840s. As he moved toward the view that larger human possibility had to be enacted in the sphere of the particular, his doctrine of self-culture began to evolve into a doctrine of character. The program of self-culture had assumed an available spiritual energy that propelled the soul expansively forward, but by the 1840s Emerson's sense of the need to grow had in part been supplanted by the need for an anchor in a fluctuating and disorienting universe. Character was his term for that moral ballast, a power whose "natural measure ... is the resistance of circumstances" (*CW*, 3:57). This depiction of character as an expression of resistance to outside forces was a reformulated individualism that had its fullest expression in the later essays "Fate" (1860) and "Character" (1866), which rendered human meaning and purpose dependent on the creative transformation of restrictions and limits. *Essays: Second Series* is a crucial volume in the articulation of this doctrine, beginning with the intense epistemological investigation of "Experience" and concluding with the political commentary of "New England Reformers." "Character" was an important bridge in the conceptual territory between knowledge and action, including something of the introspective focus of "Experience" and the moral imperative of the reform movements.

Emerson's conception of character evolved in part from his concept of the "universal man," the idealized figure who served him in the 1830s as a repository of human hope. Inclined toward hero worship, but skeptical about any actual individual's capacity to fulfill all human potential, Emerson had projected instead this abstract embodiment of that potential. It had been his earliest response to the dilemma of the "double consciousness," allowing him to accept the tragic limitations of human history without abandoning an ideal of human nature. The promise of human potential reappears in "Character" as a palpable but nevertheless undefined power of social influence in certain strong individuals. Emerson describes Sidney and Raleigh as "men of great figure, and of few deeds," and he observes that "we cannot find the smallest part of the personal weight of Washington, in the narrative of his exploits. The authority of the name of Schiller is too great for his books." These individuals project a sense of expectation on those who observe them, a perhaps subconscious recognition of their "latent" power. "What others effect by talent or by eloquence, this man accomplishes by some magnetism" (*CW*, 3:53). Mystical as it may at first seem, character as Emerson describes it here is in fact a socially grounded force. The wellsprings of character may rest in the individual's access to the universal soul, but it is brought to life only in social interaction.

This latent power evident in social interactions can be understood as part of the series of polarities in the fabric of nature that were explored in *Essays: Second Series*: "Everything in nature is bi-polar, or has a positive and negative pole. There is a male and a female, a spirit and a fact, a north and a south. Spirit is the positive, the event is the negative. Will is the north, action the south pole. Character may be ranked as having its natural place in the north. It shares the magnetic currents of the system. The feeble souls are drawn to the south or negative pole" (*CW*, 3:57). This list of opposites privileges the abstract over the material, and aligns "character" with "will," "spirit," and "male."[76] But the pairing of these concepts against "fact," "action," and "female" indicates the increasingly intolerable division in Emerson's thinking. "Here or nowhere is the whole fact," he had said to Reed; and his rebuke of Reed's dualism shadows his own attempt here to separate "spirit" from "fact." The accelerating tendency of his work in the early 1840s had been to emphasize the material and the factual. The "double consciousness" that emerged in Emerson's discourse in the early 1840s expressed the concern that the ideal would be starved by its divorce from the material. But Emerson also feared action divorced from principle, a material world divorced from the larger vision available in the spiritual. "Character," an important signpost of Emerson's increasingly pragmatic orientation, attempts to integrate the spiritual into a larger doctrine of informed moral action. Character connotes both the possession of vision and the capacity to bring it to bear in the social world. Its strength originates in disinterestedness, a selflessness that is the touchstone of Emerson's moral valuations.

Character, the "moral order seen through the medium of an individual nature," is a measure of the individual's capacity for acting in a spirit of disinterestedness. "An individual is an encloser. Time and space, liberty and necessity, truth and thought, are left at large no longer" (*CW*, 3:56). Access to such spiritual energy accounts for the magnetic force of character in some individuals: "All things exist in the man tinged with the manners of his soul. With what quality is in him, he infuses all nature that he can reach; nor does he tend to lose himself in vastness, but, at how long a curve soever, all his regards return into his own good at last" (*CW*, 3:56–7). Although character ultimately depends on the individual's access to universal and self-effacing laws, Emerson observed that it manifests itself as "self-sufficingness," a phrase indicating the essay's close relation to "Self-Reliance." The tone of "Character" is less combative, but it returns with new emphasis to the qualities of tenacity and self-possession in moral judgment: "Character is centrality, the impossibility of being displaced or overset. A man should give us a sense of mass" (*CW*, 3:58). This rootedness is not always comforting, and Emerson praises the "uncivil, unavailable man, who is a problem and a threat to society," and whose contribution is to confront society with the hard facts that its expediency has shunted to the side. Such resistance "destroys the skepticism which says, 'man is a doll, let us eat and drink, 'tis the best we can do,' by illuminating the untried and unknown" (*CW*, 3:59). As in "Self-Reliance," eccentricity and stubbornness become modes of virtue in their exposure of the shallowness of social conformity. Character is the rejection of the ease of conformity in the demand for the truth.

Character may also become a source of leadership, as well as determined resistance: "A healthy soul ... stands to all beholders like a transparent object betwixt them and the sun, and whoso journeys towards the sun, journeys towards that person." In the interrelated representations in this passage, the sun is the attractive energy of spiritual law, the ideal that both sustains individuals and remains beyond their reach, an object of pursuit. The person of character is "transparent," a word with a rich history in Emerson's symbolic vocabulary, suggesting both the possession of spiritual energy and a fundamental selflessness that allows it to penetrate the confines of the ego. "Men of character," he concludes, "are the conscience of the society to which they belong" (*CW*, 3:57).

Emerson's praise of character, despite the deep conviction that marks the tone of the essay, does not entirely resolve the fundamental dilemma of his philosophy of self-culture. If the attainment of character represents the highest achievement of self-culture, how shall it be pursued? Is it not, like the ecstatic moment, a kind of gift, the blessing of an inherited temperament or disposition, the calculated pursuit of which might be useless? Emerson makes an important turn away from this dilemma by structuring "Character" as an essay that mediates between the moral emphases of "Self-Reliance" and "Friendship." "Character" begins with images of lonely and resistant eccentricity, but moves toward a celebration of human relatedness in which much of Emerson's later pragmatic project has roots. Friendship, finally, becomes the test of character.

Emerson changes the terms of the discourse, reorienting the reader's sense of the social manifestations of character, when he transforms the bristling individualism that had defined character into a humanly accessible, even congenial, quality: "But if I go to see an ingenious man, I shall think myself poorly entertained if he give me nimble pieces of benevolence and etiquette; rather he shall stand stoutly in his place, and let me apprehend, if it were only his resistance; know that I have encountered a new and positive quality;—great refreshment for both of us" (*CW*, 3:58). Significantly, this hypothetical situation is a social call, a moment whose potential artificiality ("nimble pieces of benevolence and etiquette") is a challenge to the qualities of character that Emerson has been describing. It emphasizes the demand that others place on the individual self. Aware of these dangers, Emerson is able to suggest that such a moment can be positive if a "real" encounter, based in honest and open interchange, rather than an artificial dance of avoidance, can be achieved. Nimble etiquette is contrasted with the prosaic ability to "stand stoutly" in place, and it is the latter that makes it possible for us to encounter "a new and positive quality." Consider how the value of those terms has been augmented by Emerson's foregoing discussions in "Experience," in which he lamented the inability to achieve encounters with other persons or things. "An innavigable sea," he wrote, "washes with silent waves between us and the things we aim at and converse with" (*CW*, 3:29). How bracing, then, to encounter even the resistance, or maybe especially the resistance, of a self-reliant individual. If, as he had also said in "Experience," it is the possibility of surprises that makes life worthwhile, such an encounter is especially valuable in showing us "a new and positive quality." Friendship has become the means by which character is revealed.

In friendship, Emerson found the promise of spontaneous self-forgetfulness, the universal capacity that allowed individuals to transcend their narrowness as they met another person, to be an important counter to skepticism. This is one of the most important indications of the new importance that social life held in his developing philosophy. Such "strict relations of amity" confirmed the spiritual potential of the individual, giving life and solidity to an assumption that might sometimes begin to seem a coldly intellectual axiom in Emerson's thinking: "The sufficient reply to the skeptic, who doubts the power and the furniture of man, is in that possibility of joyful intercourse with persons, which makes the faith and practice of all reasonable men." Emerson's faith had found important confirmation early in his career in the moments of ecstasy that seemed to provide the individual with an access to divinity. But as "Character" suggests, friendship had become a new mode of experiential confirmation of possibility: "I know nothing which life has to offer so satisfying as the profound good understanding, which can subsist, after much exchange of good offices, between two virtuous men, each of whom is sure of himself, and sure of his friend" (*CW*, 3:64). It is important to note that Emerson qualifies this affirmation to prevent its being taken too easily as a promise, rather than regarded as a benefit that has to be earned. The understanding is not an instantaneous product but the result of a history of "exchange of good offices," anchored in the difficult possession of a surety about oneself and one's friend. These are not conditions that can be regarded lightly or achieved casually. But even with its qualifications, it remains a crucial affirmation in what may be Emerson's most tenuously optimistic book.

POLITICS AND ETHICAL JUDGMENT

"We frigidly talk of reform, until the walls mock us with contempt."
(*JMN*, 9:367)

The more fully Emerson was able to articulate the seemingly paralytic fact of the polarities of experience, the better he was able to meet its implied paralysis with the determination to act. Both "Nominalist and Realist" and "Character" advance Emerson's agenda of the pursuit of practical power. Practical power entailed, of course, political power, and although there are important moments of extreme political skepticism in *Essays: Second Series*, it is also important to remember that Emerson made two important public political statements in 1844, his address to the reform society at Amory Hall entitled "New England Reformers" and his address on emancipation in the British West Indies. Needing a ninth essay to round out his book, he considered both, finally deciding to include "New England Reformers." Its inclusion may have been initiated by practical necessity—his publisher wanted a ninth essay—but the piece resonates well with the foregoing volume.[77] The structural movement of *Essays: Second Series* from "The Poet" through the essays on polarity, "Experience," "Character," and "Nominalist and Realist," to the concluding analysis, "New England Reformers," is itself a formal representation of Emerson's emphasis on pragmatic alternatives to perceptual dilemmas.

But the seemingly mystical and aesthetic emphasis of "The Poet" does not take that essay entirely out of the political sphere, broadly defined. In a book of essays in which wrestling with several forms of doubt plays a fundamental role, "The Poet" stands out for its unqualified assurance, grounded in the pragmatic sense of poetry as a form of curative action. This conception of poetry is particularly notable in the light of the threat of paralysis in "Experience." In the work of the poet he found the human intellect capable of exploiting nature's polarity, and his sense of the value of authorship as a form of action deepened as his prominence as an intellectual spokesman grew.[78] The implied politics of "The Poet" further emphasizes that even at his visionary height, Emerson maintained a sensitivity to the social landscape that we may not at first recognize. Although the poet is set apart because of a fuller realization of humanity's capacity for symbolic perception, such a privileging of the poet gives way in the essay to a valuation of the common, and a decidedly democratic emphasis. "The poets are thus liberating gods" (*CW*, 3:18), Emerson concluded, and the liberation was not wholly aesthetic and intellectual: "We do not, with sufficient plainness, or sufficient profoundness, address ourselves to life, nor dare we chaunt our own times and social circumstance" (*CW*, 3:21). The essay memorably calls for the poetic treatment, and thus the broadened moral apprehension, of "our logrolling, our stumps and their politics, our fisheries, our Negroes, and Indians, our boasts, and our repudiations, the wrath of rogues, and the pusillanimity of honest men, the northern trade, the southern planting, the western clearing, Oregon, and Texas" (*CW*, 3:22). Although this passage is usually taken as a celebration of rough-hewn frontier America as contrasted to an effete and overrefined Europe, and thus a blanket endorsement of the American political situation, it is in many respects a carefully constructed list of the politically sensitive issues in the formation of the American nation: electoral politics, slavery and the Southern plantation economy, Northern capitalism, the conquest and removal of the Indians, and the ecological destruction of the West. No wholly apolitical poet could sing these things. The question of America was essentially political, and the democratic poetry that Emerson implied here was in no sense politically naive. The America that was "a poem in our eyes" (*CW*, 3:22) was a nation possessed of political promise and political danger, not political justice.

Whereas "The Poet" implied a politics, "New England Reformers" was the history of the social movement that had begun to ask the necessary questions about the political promise of America. Emerson originally delivered the lecture in a series that included prominent advocates for a wide variety of social and political reforms, and thought of it, as Linck C. Johnson has shown, as a "sermon" to the reformers. Johnson's reconstruction of the context of the address reveals that by comparison with previous lecturers such as William Lloyd Garrison, Charles Lane, and Adin Ballou, Emerson assumed the tone of "a distant observer rather than an active sympathizer" of the reform movement, hoping to "remove that audience to a high ground from which its own activities ... could be viewed with understanding and detachment."[79] Emerson was most attracted to political movements when he saw in them the operation of a religious or spiritual principle, and most inclined to reject them when that principle seemed absent. In "New England Reformers," he described the reform movements as evidence of secularization, the movement of the religious impulse out of the church and into society. Thus, "the Church, or religious party, is falling from the church nominal, and is appearing in temperance and non-resistance societies, in movements of abolitionists and socialists," and in various religious reformers who question the sabbath, priesthood, and the church (*CW*, 3:149). Emerson is thus able to argue that despite the attacks on the church that, as Johnson established, characterized the opening lectures of the series by Garrison (pp. 241–4), the Amory Hall lectures, and the reform movement as a whole, were signs of a new form of the religious sensibility.

The reformers had indeed brought "keener scrutiny of institutions and domestic life than any we had known," but also "plentiful vaporing, and cases of backsliding" (*CW*, 3:150). Emerson found the reformers more capable of identifying social ills than of proposing practical remedies, as typified in their ill-considered enthusiasm for communal "association" as a panacea for human problems: "I have failed, and you have failed, but perhaps together we shall not fail. Our housekeeping is not satisfactory to us, but perhaps a phalanx, a community, might be. Many of us have differed in opinion, and we could find no man who could make the truth plain, but possibly a college, or an ecclesiastical council might" (*CW*, 3:156). The rush to association tended to divert attention from the more basic ethical reform that must be pursued in the individual, the family, and the household.

Political reform obviously was not the complete answer to Emerson's crisis, but insofar as political dissent might sharpen distinctions between the superficial and the real, it had enormous value. Do we want, he asked, "to be pleased and flattered?" No, we rather want "to be shamed out of our nonsense of all kinds, and made men of, instead of ghosts and phantoms" (*CW*, 3:161). Dissent functioned as a means of confronting the hard truth that was usually an object of evasion in modern life: "We are weary of gliding ghostlike through the world, which is itself so slight and unreal. We crave a sense of reality, though it come in strokes of pain" (*CW*, 3:161). This reference to the ghostlike condition echoes the opening paragraph of "Experience," in which the barrage of images of aimlessness and bewilderment results in a haunting insubstantiality: "Ghostlike we glide through nature, and should not know our place again" (*CW*, 3:27). By returning to that image in "New England Reformers," Emerson indicated a closer connection between two apparently unrelated essays. Although "Experience" is intensely introspective, and "New England Reformers" is social commentary, both essays have their roots in the same spiritual struggle. In the failure of vision, can action be made spiritually viable? Does action itself create its own form of vision?

That we would take reality even "in strokes of pain" (*CW*, 3:161), as he said in "New England Reformers," or look to death "with a grim satisfaction, saying, there at last is reality that will not dodge us" (*CW*, 3:29), as he said in "Experience," is evidence of a passion for reality that is a basis for hope. Emerson's plea to the leaders of the reform movement was to recognize the widespread spiritual alienation that might serve as the movement's greatest fuel:

> We desire to be made great, we desire to be touched with that fire which shall command this ice to stream, and make our existence a benefit. If therefore we start objections to your project, O friend of the slave, or friend of the poor, or of the race, understand well, that it is because we wish to drive you to drive us into your measures. We wish to hear ourselves confuted. We are haunted

with a belief that you have a secret, which it would highliest advantage us to learn, and we would force you to impart it to us, though it should bring us to prison, or to worse extremity. (*CW*, 3:163)

The charged passage conveys an aching sense of approaching a precious and long-sought goal, yet being unable to grasp it, a situation that reflects Emerson's sense of political reform as continually renewed, but never wholly realized, promise.

So in the case of politics, as in the case of spiritual fulfillment, Emerson had to learn to read the imperfect as an ironic reflection of the perfect. Even the "secret melancholy" (*CW*, 3:158) to which he referred in "New England Reformers" had its use in proving that humanity could not be satisfied with the superficial or the unjust, and that complacency did not have complete sway in human nature: "Every man has at intervals the grace to scorn his performances, in comparing them with his belief of what he should do" (*CW*, 3:160). He thereby turned his own self-reproach into a principle of hope and made of his political skepticism a mode of dissent.

How did this dissent manifest itself? In 1844, with "some prodding by Henry [Thoreau] and Lidian," as Gay Wilson Allen has noted, Emerson delivered a public address commemorating the tenth anniversary of the British emancipation of slaves in the West-Indies.[80] The issue of slavery had by then become the most pressing political issue of the day, and brought Emerson to his clearest statement of the identity of ethics with politics. His sense of the convergence of those categories strengthened gradually from the 1830s to the 1850s.[81] With "Character" and "New England Reformers," the address constitutes his response to the paralysis and disconnectedness described that same year in "Experience," and is thus an important signpost of Emerson's developing pragmatism.[82] The address offered Emerson an opportunity to take the abstraction of the spiritual into the realm of the social and factual, and it was in this light that he saw the enactment of West Indian emancipation itself: "a day which gave the immense fortification of a fact, of gross history, to ethical abstractions" (*W*, 11:99). Ambivalent as ever about entering ground in which he felt no expertise, he nevertheless put his reticence aside: "The subject is said to have the property of making dull men eloquent" (*W*, 11:100).

Emerson exhibits a surprising tough-mindedness and wisdom of the world in the address. Joseph Slater aptly remarked that the speech makes it "impossible for even the most superficial reader to think of Emerson as a denier of evil," for Emerson cataloged in some detail the savage abuse of slaves. "I am heart-sick," he wrote, "when I read how they came there, and how they are kept there" (*W*, 11:102). His description of their oppression and abuse is moving:

> For the negro, was the slave-ship to begin with, in whose filthy hold he sat in irons, unable to lie down; bad food, and insufficiency of that; disfranchisement; no property in the rags that covered him; no marriage, no right in the poor black woman that cherished him in her bosom, no right to the children of his body; no security from the humors, none from the crimes, none from the appetites of his master: toil, famine, insult and flogging. (*W*, 11:102–3)

Even more appalling are his specifics: "pregnant women set in the treadmill for refusing to work ... a planter throwing his negro into a copper of boiling cane juice" (*W*, 11:104). This is not mincing words, and while Emerson did not dwell on the morbid, he did feel the necessity of making vivid what might have seemed a distant evil to his audience. "The blood is moral," he declared. "The blood is anti-slavery: it runs cold in the veins: the stomach rises with disgust, and curses slavery" (*W*, 11:104).

As Joseph Slater and Len Gougeon have established, Emerson was deeply affected by the sources he had used to prepare his speech—Thomas Clarkson's *History of the ... Abolition of the African Slave Trade* and James A. Thome and J. Horace Kimball's *Emancipation in the West Indies*.[83] He had, moreover, another source close to his heart, William Ellery Channing's last public address in 1842, which had celebrated the same anniversary of emancipation in the West Indies. All of these sources were partisan histories, which used their chronicles of the evil of slavery, and the British success in outlawing it, as evidence for the abolitionist cause.[84] As Emerson dwelt on the facts of slavery, his realization of its incalcitrant evil grew. He had approached the question with the same assumptions as his mentor Channing, who had seen the emancipation of the West Indies slaves as "the fruit of Christian principle acting on the mind and heart of a great people."[85] Emerson adopted the same millennial tone when he saw the emancipation of the slaves as a "moral revolution": "Other revolutions have been the insurrection of the oppressed; this was the repentance of the tyrant. It was masters revolting from their mastery. The slaveholder said, 'I will not hold slaves.' The end was noble and the means were pure. Hence the elevation and pathos of this chapter of history" (*W*, 11:135). But part of Channing's hope had been based on an assumption that the slaveholders, if not ripe for a "moral revolution," were at least susceptible to economic persuasion. Rebutting the theory that Southerners clung to slavery out of a fear that the freed slaves would massacre their former owners, Channing insisted that economic motives were essential: "The master holds fast his slave, because he sees in him, not a wild beast, but a profitable chattel" (p. 295). Channing then referred to an estimate by Henry Clay that the slaves are worth "twelve hundred millions of dollars," and found himself in curious agreement with Clay on one issue: "It is not because they are so fierce, but so profitable, that they are kept in chains" (pp. 295–6).[86]

In an 1844 journal entry, Emerson had echoed much the same idea:

> The planter does not want slaves: give him money: give him a machine that will provide him with as much money as the slaves yield, & he will thankfully let them go: he does not love whips, or usurping overseers, or sulky swarthy giants creeping round his house & barns by night with lucifer matches in their hands & knives in their pockets. No; only he wants his luxury, & he will pay even this price for it. (*JMN*, 9:127–8)

Emerson's hope in the reasonable greed of the slave owners seemed to have helped him to justify his own aloofness from the abolitionist movement. This same journal entry includes an indictment of the abolitionist who would reform the South, but who continues to use sugar, cotton, and tobacco, and to maintain servants in his own home. The slave owner and the abolitionist manifest versions of the same form of greed, for neither is sufficiently free from material aspirations and the social system that supplies them. Thus he argued that a consistent self-reliance was in fact the best way to promote the antislavery cause: "He who does his own work frees a slave. He who does not his own work, is a slave-holder" (*JMN*, 9:127). Emerson hoped that enough of such self-reliant moral action, coupled with compensation to slave owners, might loosen their grip on the slaves and lay the groundwork for a legislative solution in America similar to the one in the West Indies.

But as he continued to think about the issue that summer, he also realized that there was an element of wishful thinking in that formula, and he said so to his Concord audience. He repeated in the address almost word for word the idea that the planter "has no love of slavery, he wants luxury, and he will even pay this price of crime and danger for it," but he headed that opinion with the qualifying "We sometimes say ..." He then made his change of mind explicit: "But I think experience does not warrant this favorable distinction, but shows the existence, beside the covetousness, of a bitterer element, the love of power, the voluptuousness of holding a human being in his absolute control" (*W*, 11:118). Here was the heart of darkness. Emerson's immersion in his sources had not been wasted effort, for he came to the address with a graver sense of the hardened evil of slavery.[87]

Emerson's determination to give the desire for power its full measure was also evident in his brilliantly caustic depiction of the evasions of the Northern middle class: "The sugar [the slaves] raised was excellent: nobody tasted blood in it. The coffee was fragrant; the tobacco was incense; the brandy made nations happy; the cotton clothed the world. What! All raised by these men, and no wages? Excellent! What a convenience!" Moreover, any reminder that economic relations with the South carried moral responsibilities was not welcomed: "If any mention was made of homicide, madness, adultery, and intolerable tortures, we would let the church-bells ring louder, the church-organ swell its peal and drown the hideous sound" (*W*, 11:124). Significantly, Emerson and his audience had been denied access to any of the churches in Concord for the address.[88]

Emerson had not abandoned his old faith in the maturing progress of the spirit, but he did seem to be recognizing new modes in which the spirit worked. Although he saw "other energies than force, other than political" (*W*, 11:139) at work in the modern world—moral energies—he finally seemed to imply that even those energies might manifest themselves as a will to power. Thus he returned to his favorite organic metaphor of unfolding life, but couched it in new terms, which have a surprisingly post-Darwinian ring: "the germ forever protected, unfolding gigantic leaf after leaf, a newer flower, a richer fruit, in every period, yet its next product is never to be guessed. It will only save what is worth saving; and it saves not by compassion, but by power" (*W*, 11:143). The political implications of this metaphor are clear enough: That which is worth saving is sometimes saved by force. An evil that is invulnerable to compassion or moral appeal, even to economic calculation, must of necessity be confronted with power. This outcropping of a rugged pragmatism in Emerson's thinking is made clearer in his struggle to come to terms with slavery.

Power is, of course, slippery ground, for it could certainly be argued that abuse of power had resulted in slavery. Emerson is not entirely free of racial bias, and he assumes that the Negro is in part a victim of racial weakness, one that is, however, gradually being overcome. "When at last in a race a new principle appears, an idea,—*that* conserves it," he writes. "Ideas only save races. If the black man is feeble and not the best race, the black man must serve, and be exterminated" (*W*, 11:44). The operation of power that Emerson depicts here serves in some senses to justify the wrongs of the past, and can be taken to mean, in the worst sense, that those who are oppressed have deserved their oppression.

But he is determined to draw a different conclusion from it, by arguing that the Negro is crucial to the future of human civilization: "But if the black man carries in his bosom an indispensable element of a new and coming civilization; for the sake of that element, no wrong nor strength nor circumstance can hurt him: he will survive and play his part." He cites the examples of "Toussaint, and the Haytian heroes, or ... the leaders of their own race in Barbadoes & Jamaica" (*W*, 11:144), as evidence of the presence of such a principle, thereby making the international movement for abolition a vanguard of the human future.

The underlying faith of his argument is that in the long view, force and moral sense are not in essential opposition—an increasingly difficult assumption in the building slavery crisis. Nevertheless, he takes the example of the West Indian emancipation, and the growing awareness in America of the evils of slavery, as signs that can augment his faith. His concluding argument is that "the sentiment of Right" is "the voice of the universe," moving inevitably to the destruction of slavery and the affirmation of freedom. "The Power that built this fabric of things affirms it in the heart; and in the history of the First of August, has made a sign to the ages, of his will" (*W*, 11:147).

NOTES

70. Stephen E. Whicher, *Freedom and Fate*, pp. 123–40. Whicher's influence on Emerson studies was extended through his *Selections from Ralph Waldo Emerson: An Organic Anthology*.

71. The essay has been given significant consideration recently in David Van Leer's *Emerson's Epistemology*, pp. 189–93.

72. See Merton M. Sealts, Jr., *Emerson on the Scholar*, pp. 159–60, for a discussion of the connections between "Nominalist and Realist" and the later *Representative Men*. Sealts points out that "Representative" was a working title for "Nominalist and Realist."

73. See David Van Leer, *Emerson's Epistemology*, pp. 191–2. He finds irony in Emerson's opening discussion of the concept of universals and notes that Emerson's emphasis "although not antiessentialist, tends to direct attention away from absolute questions" (p. 192).

74. Emerson's distrust of the experiment is revealed in an interesting journal entry of 1846: "When Alcott wrote from England that he was bringing home Wright & Lane I wrote him a letter, which I required him to show them, saying, that they might safely trust his theories, but that they should put no trust whatever in his statement of facts. When they all arrived here, he & his victims,—I asked them if he showed them that letter; they answered that he did: So I was clear" (*JMN*, 9:397).

75. Ralph L. Rusk explains how Emerson solicited money for Alcott's trip to England in 1842 and supplied most of it from his own pocket: "The thankful Alcott wanted to include a miniature of Emerson in his baggage and had loyally read his copy of the *Essays*, conjuring up memories of home, while approaching the English shore in the last days of May, 1842" (*The Life of Ralph Waldo Emerson*, p. 297). Alcott had returned from this trip with Lane, and their plans to launch Fruitlands had met with Emerson's skepticism.

76. The male bias here is confirmed in Emerson's further characterization of the

differing valuation of these opposite poles: "The feeble souls are drawn to the south or negative pole. They look at the profit or hurt of the action. They never behold a principle until it is lodged in a person. They do not wish to be lovely, but to be loved" (*CW*, 3:57). It is also notable that the list runs counter to the usual forms of sexual stereotyping. The world of fact and action was, by most nineteenth-century standards, a male world, whereas that of the spiritual was largely female. One might instructively compare the associations of "masculine" and "feminine" in Margaret Fuller's contemporary *Woman in the Nineteenth Century* (1845), based on an article written for the Dial in 1844. Both Fuller's and Emerson's discussions suggest the difficulties of extended symbolic uses of the terms "male" and "female." For an informative discussion of the concept of the feminine in romantic discourse, with particular reference to Fuller, see Julie Ellison, *Delicate Subjects*, pp. 5–14, 217–25.

77. See Joseph Slater's discussion of Emerson's decision to include "New England Reformers" (*CW*, 3:29–31).

78. In speaking of authorship as a form of action, one must consider Emerson's conceptual and vocational term for this role, the "scholar," as Merton M. Sealts, Jr., has noted. He has traced the genesis and implications of the term, demonstrating that it became the synthetic formulation through which Emerson could continue to balance the competing demands of intellectual work and social engagement. See *Emerson on the Scholar*, passim.

79. Linck C. Johnson, "Reforming the Reformers," pp. 258 and 255. Maurice Gonnaud has noted that the lecture "was delivered less than two months after the disbanding of Fruitlands, and in the circumstances became something of an assessment of it." He also notes that one important context of the lecture was the conflict Emerson felt between the call of political reform and the necessity of living an inner life. See Maurice Gonnaud, *An Uneasy Solitude*, pp. 318–23, quotation from p. 318.

80. Gay Wilson Allen, *Waldo Emerson*, p. 427. See Allen's discussion of the background of the address.

81. Len Gougeon's *Virtue's Hero* is the definitive study of Emerson's involvement in the antislavery movement, and will do much to increase our awareness of the centrality of this issue to Emerson's career after the middle 1840s.

82. Sealts has commented perceptively on what must have been an underlying psychological dynamic arising from Emerson's grief over Waldo: "Emerson's grasping for some tangible objective 'reality' after the death of Waldo may account to some degree for his increasing preoccupation with outward affairs during ensuing years" (*Emerson on the Scholar*, p. 143).

83. Joseph Slater, "Two Sources for Emerson's First Address on West Indian Emancipation"; and Len Gougeon, *Virtue's Hero*, pp. 75–8.

84. For information on the development of Channing's antislavery views, see Douglas Stange, *Patterns of Antislavery Among American Unitarians, 1831–1860*; and Andrew Delbanco, *William Ellery Channing: An Essay on the Liberal Spirit in America*. For the influence of Channing's antislavery stance on Emerson, see Len Gougeon, *Virtue's Hero*, pp. 42–51.

85. *William Ellery Channing: Selected Writings*, p. 287. Further quotations will be cited parenthetically.

86. For Clay's speech see *The Works of Henry Clay*, 6:139–59.

87. Len Gougeon comments on this passage: "Despite several scholarly assertions to the contrary, Emerson understood quite well man's inherent capacity for evil" (*Virtue's Hero*, p. 362 n. 73).

88. Gay Wilson Allen, *Waldo Emerson*, p. 427.

GEORGE KATEB

Friendship and Love

If we say that self-reliance is the true principle of Emerson, we then ask, Does the self-reliant individual need others? Obviously no one, no matter how self-reliant, can live without others. Emersonian self-reliance is not perpetual solitariness. When we ask whether the self-reliant individuals need others, we mean to see what human relationships Emerson posits as ideally suited to self-reliant individuals. Our distinction between mental and active self-reliance is relevant here. Of greatest concern to Emerson is the prosperity of mental self-reliance. Our purpose now is to show that the relationships Emerson praises most are those that improve the work of mental self-reliance, the attempt to think one's own receptive thoughts and think them through. It is a weighty fact that human relations most conducive to mental self-reliance are simultaneously valuable as expressions of active self-reliance (in the sense of trying to be or show oneself more adequately, more fully). But the contribution that a relationship makes to mental self-reliance matters most. In the next two chapters, I will discuss human relations that display active self-reliance but do not simultaneously improve the work of mental self-reliance.

The furtherance of mental self-reliance provides a perspective on the whole range of relationships that comprise society. In more than one lecture or essay Emerson actually does survey many relationships from that

From *Emerson and Self-Reliance*. © 2000 by Alta Mira Press.

perspective. The first thing we notice is that Emerson takes no sort of relation for granted; none, no matter how long established or revered, can go unexamined. Each must somehow earn the acceptance of the self-reliant individual, and some relationships are especially resistant to acceptance. Rather than advancing one's mental self-reliance they may retard it. Before turning to what Emerson has to suggest about particular relationships, it would be well to pause and simply say that in Emerson's theorization of self-reliance, no sort of relationship should come easily, even if the self-reliant individual accepts it as valuable. But there must and will be relationships. The ideal is that they be truthful and that they also promote a greater receptivity to truth about what is external to them—truth about the world.

I have already taken up Emerson's idea (in "Experience") of the "innavigable sea" that cuts us off from one another, and hence of the near impossibility of honestly experiencing and being experienced. The honesty increases with self-reliance and hence the difficulty of connection may also increase. Allowing for Emerson's pedagogic extremism, we can still find nourishment in his despair. We can be left with a sobering reminder of the gaps between persons and try to discover whether and how Emerson, in the name of mental self-reliance, tries to narrow them, even if he is unable to close them. When I mentioned Emerson's report on the grief he felt or failed to feel over his son's death, I discussed his view of the difficulties of relation in the most general, existential way. However, he has more to say. We should not take as final Emerson's exasperated (or is it exultant?) remark that "All men, all things, the state, the church, yea the friends of the heart are phantasms and unreal beside the sanctuary of the heart" ("Introductory Lecture," *Lectures on the Times*, p. 163). He may posit a "metaphysical isolation" of each person, but he enters a sizable qualification:

> This solitude of essence is not be mistaken for a view of our position in nature. Our position in nature, nature will severely avenge. We are tenderly alive to love and hatred. ("The Heart," *Early Lectures*, 2, p. 280)

The enterprise is, precisely, to discover that others are real, as real as oneself, and that what is outside oneself consists not of phantasms, but of reality. But, for Emerson, with his strenuous concern for truth, it is an arduous enterprise. One's best relations must be both an instrument of truth and an instance of it. One must not have drowned in the innavigable sea while thinking that one is safely ashore. But can the sea be somewhat navigable?

As we take up Emerson's thought on how one may break out of isolation, we should keep to mind that when he was young, and hence more able to adhere to others, he found in intimacy only the confirmation of feelings of isolation. His early words, from 1835, express a recurrent and important mood:

> 'Tis very strange how much we owe the perception of the absolute solitude of the spirit to the affections. I sit alone, and cannot arouse myself to thoughts. I go and sit with, my friend and in the endeavor to explain my thought to him or her, I lay bare the awful mystery to myself as never before, and start at the total loneliness and infinity of one man. (Notes in *Society and Solitude*, p. 347)

*   *   *

The very title of Emerson's book, *Society and Solitude*, announces both an antagonism and a complementary connection. As we have seen, the Emersonian sense is that any human phenomenon, even though indispensable, is inevitably incomplete and must be completed and balanced by what is antithetical or at least contrasting. Emerson's title implies that society is better off if people have a taste for solitude, but also that proper solitude looks to the perpetual interruption of itself by relationships, by social involvement. But we must never make Emerson evenhanded, certainly not with respect to the contending and cooperative claims and benefits of society and solitude. The core of Emersonian individualism, the mental self-reliance that he theorizes, demands a larger place for solitude than many other conceptualizations of how to live, what to do, more than many other conceptualizations of individualism. He does not finally say that solitude is the most natural and favorable condition of any self-reliant individual. But its advantages serve as a standard by which to judge many relationships: not all of them—not, for example, being a parent (about which Emerson speaks rapturously); but self-reliance certainly allows one to judge some of the most important ones. Indeed, solitude provides an initial measure for the evaluation of intimacy.

In his Dartmouth college lecture of 1838, "Literary Ethics," Emerson gives his most succinct expression of the high worth of solitude. He is addressing students and advising them, but his words, as always, have a general application. The self-reliant individual, no matter what his walk in life, is, after all, a lifelong student. Emerson asks why the student must often be solitary and silent, embracing solitude as a bride and having his "glees and glooms" alone (p. 104). Why must one often be one's own bride? In periods of marriage to oneself, he says, one "may become acquainted with his thoughts" (104). One lies passive to one's thoughts and thus becomes self-reliant, because self-reliant thinking is built on self-acquaintance. This is not exactly Socratic self-knowledge, which seems tied to the attempt to find out what one really wants and what is really satisfying. Such self-knowledge is not as close to Emerson's heart as it is to, say, Thoreau's. Rather, Emersonian self-acquaintance is the effort to fix one's attention on the steady but confused and elusive stream or sea or ocean of consciousness or semiconsciousness as well as on one's dreamlife. What is happening inside oneself? What is one really thinking? Emerson's premise is that it is too easy to forget to listen to oneself, and to settle, instead, for the thoughts of others, whether others are close to hand or part of some large, anonymous network. Somehow, anyone's own thoughts, often secret or at least unexpressed, are better—more real, more just, more truthful—than thoughts that are held in common and that circulate, whether in a large group or a small one. And this is the case even though, and especially because, many thoughts come unbidden just as dreams do, and despite the fact, which Emerson gives many indications he knows, that one is frequently helpless in relation to the contents of one's inner life, and not only when dreaming. One must try to become self-acquainted. One must try to retrieve what is valuable from the flow of evanescence. The first paragraph of "Self-Reliance" concentrates this advice. In solitude, we grow self-acquainted. In turn, self-acquaintance prepares us for a self-reliant reception of the world.

On numerous occasions, Emerson says that if an individual pays attention to his or her inner life, one gains access to the mind of the universe. In becoming self-acquainted one discards the untruth, the imperception, the slothful sensuality that invariably characterize the thoughts that are socially held in common and that circulate. One makes room for the universe's intelligence to register itself on one's attention. Every person's intuition—that is, untaught perception—derives from participation in the universal mind. This view is part of the core of Emerson's religiousness. We must not allow his religiousness, however, to spoil our reception of him. I want to separate Emerson from his religiousness for the sake of his truth. Therefore, if I am told that, for Emerson, the only point of self-acquaintance is to put oneself in touch with the universal mind, then I would have to say, I hope not. As I have tried to suggest, Emerson himself is much more cagey. He endows his words with the capacity to be detached from his transcendental ambitions, lending themselves to uses more secular. "Literary Ethics" climaxes in the religious insistence that the student "is great only by being passive to the superincumbent spirit" (p. 109). But counsel to the unreligious also works its way throughout the essay. Quite simply, it is good to grow self-acquainted because it is good to know what is one's own—to know oneself in distinction from others. Literal solitude is indispensable to self-collection and self-recollection.

Though solitude is necessary for self-acquaintance, which, in turn, matters most as the indispensable preparation for self-reliant thinking about the world, the reality that encloses one's solitude. As I have already tried to indicate, Emerson thinks that the most immediate knowledge of experienced reality often comes not during immersion in it but afterwards. The closest encounter is retrospective. There is a radical split in Emerson between doing (or being) and knowing (or seeing). Emerson regularly maintains that we most truly know, we get nearest to reality—whether our own experiences or the life around us—after the fact, and, for the most part, in solitary contemplation. That is the great work of solitude: to know oneself, of course, but also (and perhaps this thought seems ironical) to know everything but oneself. Emerson shows little of the hesitation about solitude that Montaigne expresses in his essay, "Of Solitude": "There are ways to fail in solitude as well as in company" (*The Complete Essays* [D. Frame, Trans.], pp. 182–183).

But solitude is not sufficient for the purposes of solitude. There is society. Emerson says:

> Of course, I would not have any superstition about solitude. Let the youth study the uses of solitude and of society. Let him use both, not serve either. The reason why an ingenious soul shuns society, is to the end of finding society. ("Literary Ethics," p. 105)

Although a person must depend for various reasons on various sorts of relationships in society, only one sort turns out to be from its very nature intrinsic to both self-acquaintance and self-reliance; only one sort of relationship helps solitude accomplish its major work of receiving the world in truth. That is friendship. Finding society means finding the right company; it does not mean looking for the good society. Emerson explains himself:

> You say, I go too much alone. Yes, but Heaven knows it is from no disrelish for love and fellow working. I shun society to the end of finding society. I quit a society which is no longer one. I repudiate the false out of love of the true. I go alone that I meet my brother as I ought. ("The Protest," *Early Lectures, 3*, p. 96)

In the central essay, "Friendship," from *Essays: First Series*, Emerson says:

> The soul environs itself with friends that it may enter into a grander self-acquaintance or solitude; and it goes alone for a season that it may exalt its conversation or society. (p. 344)

Only friendship establishes the true reciprocity between society and solitude—a reciprocity that cancels the question as to which of them is a means and which is the end. Society and solitude exist for each other, as friends do. And they both serve the highest purpose, which is truth, as friends do.

The demands made of friendship, then, are tremendous. Though the following words from *Nature* are about the difference between all human beings and the rest of nature, the subsequent paragraph makes clear that the favor shown human beings over nature actually derives from Emerson's high estimation of the possibilities of friendship. He says:

> Words and actions are not the attributes of brute nature. They introduce us to the human form, of which all other organizations appear to be degradations. When this appears among so many that surround it, the spirit prefers it to all others. It says, "From such as this, have I drawn joy and knowledge; in such as this, have I found and beheld myself; I will speak to it; it can speak again; it can yield one thought already formed and alive." … far different from the deaf and dumb nature around them, these all rest like fountain-pipes on the unfathomed sea of thought and virtue whereto they alone, of all organizations, are the entrance. (pp. 30–31)

Even if Emerson claims a year later (1837) that "every being in nature addresses me," I think he believes that the address of one speaking creature to another is what makes all other reception possible, and that the speaking of friends intensifies both the need and the power of reception ("Introductory," *Human Culture, Early Lectures*, 2, p. 226).

Emerson sees two elements, as he calls them, that compose a friendship. He claims that the elements are of equal worth and that there is "no reason why either should be first named" ("Friendship," p. 347). But he does name truth first, and tenderness a bit later. I think that Emerson's tendency is to give the element of truth the larger place. Perhaps it is better to say that the mysteries of tenderness make possible the search for truth, even if tenderness is not itself a vehicle of truth. A friend is, then, an accomplice in truth. What truth? I read Emerson as suggesting, first, that friends help each other approach the truth about all the reality that is external to them, the truth about the world. As I have said, the point of self-reliance is to see or perceive the world honestly and accurately, free of the depression and falsehood of church religions. Friends encourage mental self-reliance in each other. Second, a friend is the most real being outside oneself, and in getting to know that person, I can think that I have at last truthfully experienced a reality as genuine as myself (when I attend to myself in a fully awakened and withdrawn state). What is more, Emerson suggests, in an Aristotelian vein, that a friend can help me feel my own being as more real. My friend is myself externalized. "Other men are lenses through which we read our own minds" ("Uses of Great Men," *Representative Men*, p. 616). (Emerson thus reworks Plato's analogy of the letters.) I can watch him or her as I cannot watch myself and learn otherwise unknowable truths about myself by watching this other, provided the two of us are—to borrow Mill's phrase about both friends and lovers in *The Subjection of Women*—"not too much unlike" (*Collected Works of John Stuart Mill*, 21, p. 334). Emerson would have found the phrase congenial. Yet Emerson can also praise the bond of substantial difference, as when he says:

> Each man seeks those of different quality from his own, and such as are good of their kind; that is, he seeks other men, and the *otherest*. ("Uses of Great Men," p. 616)

Quite programmatically Emerson states:

> Some perceptions—I think the best—are granted to the single soul; they come from the depth, and are the permanent and controlling ones. ("Inspiration," *Letters*, p. 292)

But then he allows that it takes two to find other perceptions. He goes so far as to say:

> In excited conversation, we have glimpses of the universe, hints of power native to the soul, far-darting lights and shadows of an Andes landscape, such as we can hardly attain in lone meditation. Here are oracles sometimes profusely given, to which the memory goes back in barren hours. ("Considerations by the Way," *The Conduct of Life*, p. 1093)

These possibilities lead Emerson to say that "the best of life is conversation" ("Behavior," *The Conduct of Life*, p. 1049). The role of friendship is, however, not usually exaggerated. An almost grudging quality is present when Emerson says:

> If men are less when together than they are alone, they are also
> in some respects enlarged. ("Clubs," *Society and Solitude*, p. 228)

The qualifications and hesitations reflect Emerson's constant sense that it is
only with difficulty that either a truthful or a truth-serving sort of human
relationship can be had. Friendship is not a conquest, but it is an
achievement.

Perhaps all of Emerson's qualifications and hesitations come close to
being canceled, however, when he comes out and says:

> Our affection towards others creates a sort of vantage or purchase
> which nothing will supply. I can do that by another which I
> cannot do alone. I can say to you what I cannot first say to myself.
> ("Uses of Great Men," p. 616)

The one to whom we can say what we cannot say to ourselves is
"inestimable." Being known by another whom one trusts is indispensable to
self-acquaintance:

> What else seeks he in the deep instinct of society, from his first
> fellowship—a child with children at play, up to the heroic
> cravings of friendship and love—but to find himself in another
> mind, to confess himself, to make a clean breast, to be searched
> and known, because such is the law of his being that only can he
> find out his own secret through the instrumentality of another
> mind? ("Address on Education," *Early Lectures*, 2, p. 200)

An acknowledgment of the capacity to hide from oneself, from one's own
most thorough introspection, is rare in Emerson. It goes well with the magic
he attributes to the eloquent public speaker: namely, the ability to state a
truth that the listener is "most unwilling to receive," that the listener "did
not wish to see." Indeed, the statement of truth which one is unwilling to
receive may be "so broad and so pungent that he cannot get away from it, but
must either bend to it or die of it" ("Eloquence," *Society and Solitude*, pp.
91–92). I doubt that Emerson wants friendship to be as risky as this, but these
formulations about public eloquence also fit, up to a point, the office of
private friendship as Emerson pictures it. Friendship can also be a rescue
from imperviousness: "I cannot tell what I would know; but I have observed
there are persons who, in their character and actions, answer questions which
I have not skill to put" ("Uses of Great Men," p. 617).

Let us also be aware that before "Self-Reliance" was published,

Emerson appears to value what he regrets in "Self-Reliance." In "Society" (1837), he writes:

> What constitutes the charm of society, of conversation, of friendship, of love? This delight of receiving again from another our own thoughts and feelings, of thus seeing them out of us, and judging of them as of something foreign to us. The very sentiment you uttered yesterday without heed shall sound memorable to you tomorrow if you hear it from another. Your own thought and act you shall behold with new eyes, when a stranger commends it. (*Early Lectures*, *2*, p. 100)

In the first paragraph of "Self-Reliance," Emerson memorably rebukes us for dismissing our thought without notice just because it is ours. He says:

> In every work of genius we recognize our own rejected thoughts; they come back to us with a certain alienated majesty. (p. 259)

Yet the earlier words are more suitable to the best meanings of self-reliance than the later ones.

The way to approach truth is to practice what Emerson calls sincerity. One can be sincere only with a friend. Emerson says in "Friendship" that ordinarily:

> Every man alone is sincere. At the entrance of a second person, hypocrisy begins. (p. 347)

But, against the odds:

> A friend is a person with whom I may be sincere. Before him I may think aloud. I am arrived at last in the presence of a man so real and equal that I may drop even those undermost garments of dissimulation, courtesy, and second thought, which men never put off, and may deal with him with the simplicity and wholeness with which one chemical atom meets another. (p. 347)

Friendship is mutual intellectual nakedness. Between friends there are "no terrors, no vulgarities" because "everything can be safely said" ("Social Aims," *Letters*, p. 90). Sincerity is thus one of the main solvents of conformist perception and utterance. It helps me to understand what the world means and to mean what I say. Therefore a self-reliant person relies on a friend as he relies on himself ("Behavior," p. 1049).

The medium of friendship is conversation, and the best company is made up of just one other person: one friend at a time. Sincerity permits the proper influence of one on another, which is a kind of contagion that is utterly dissimilar from the unconscious contagion of conformity to convention or public opinion or episodic public moods. Emerson says:

> We are emulous. If the tone of the companion is higher than ours, we delight in rising to it ... it is because one thought well that the other thinks better: and two men of good mind will excite each other's activity, each attempting still to cap the other's thought. ("Inspiration," *Letters*, p. 293)

As I have said, these formulations on friendship concern the need a self-reliant individual has for others, when they are friends, to the end that he or she can improve a truthful understanding of the world and gather the courage to express it. In this way, friendship enhances one of the principal aims of solitude. In addition, friends assist the self-reliant individual to progress toward a particular and especially personal acquisition of truth: the sense that some other being in the world is as real as oneself. Of course every being is as real to itself as I am to myself. That should go without saying, but it cannot. Rather, a friend is as real to me, perhaps, as I am to myself. Sincerity is once again the key. When two persons are mutually sincere, each can also hope to know the other's reality. Pretense, play-acting, and conformity are gone. The most real is the least social, the most personal. Yet the most personal is also the most universal. We touch human nature by getting near to a true friend. In "Friendship," Emerson says:

> There can never be deep peace between two spirits, never mutual respect, until in their dialogue each stands for the whole world. (p. 352)

Then, in one of the climaxes of the essay, Emerson writes:

> A friend therefore is a sort of paradox in nature. I who alone am, I who see nothing in nature whose existence I can affirm with equal evidence to my own, behold now the semblance of my being, in all its height, variety and curiosity, reiterated in a foreign form; so that a friend may well be reckoned the masterpiece of nature. (p. 348)

A semblance is a likeness. My friend is like me and is, as it were, me. In being with a friend, I am with myself yet outside myself. In seeing my friend, I can see myself in a way that is not otherwise possible. I can therefore add to my self-acquaintance. I add to my knowledge of the truth about myself.

Emerson here approaches agreement with the Aristotelian dictum that a friend is another self—that is, another who is myself, another who is also myself. When in an earlier lecture, "Society," Emerson explicitly likens a friend to "another self," he interprets the phrase in an un-Aristotelian spirit to mean that the friend "occupies another point of view, and sees the same object on another side" (*Early Lectures*, 2, p. 102). In the essay "Friendship," Emerson again departs from Aristotle. He does not base the feeling of having another self on a kind of selfless self-love, as Aristotle does, but on some affinity that does not seem to have anything to do with self-love. He writes:

> The only joy I have in his being mine, is that the *not mine* is mine.
> (p. 350)

The *not mine* must not become merely mine if it is to be mine in a worthwhile way. It must remain its own simultaneously. I, too, must not be merely mine, and I must also remain my own. (Recall how in *Nature* he tries to show that the "NOT ME" is, with great struggle, me.) We are admonished that "We must be our own before we can be another's" (p. 351), and that "There must be very two, before there can be very one" (p. 350). Genuine separation alone can constitute a genuine union. It is a union of wholes, not parts.

Emerson makes a little effort to theorize the affinity, the initial attraction between friends:

> We are associated in adolescent and adult life with some friends, who, like skies and waters, are co-extensive with our idea; who, answering each to a certain affection of the soul, satisfy our desire on that side; whom we lack power to put at such focal distance from us, that we can mend or even analyze them. We cannot choose but love them. (*Nature*, p. 31)

He also says, "We talk of choosing our friends, but friends are self-elected," and adds:

> Friendship requires that rare mean betwixt likeness and unlikeness that piques each with presence of power and of consent in the other party. (p. 350)

These last are rather strange words—opaque, maybe evasive. Or perhaps they are Emerson's tribute to the arbitrariness or contingency that determines attraction. Emersonian friendship does not calculate advantages; it only derives them. Elsewhere he explains the consent of friendship as "consent of will and temperament" ("Considerations by the Way," *The Conduct of Life*, p. 1093). It may be that what Emerson says about falling in love also applies to coming to have a friend:

> There is the illusion of love, which attributes to the beloved person all which that person shares with his or her family, sex, age, or condition, nay, with the human mind itself. 'Tis these which the lover loves, and Anna Matilda gets the credit of them. As if one shut up always in a tower, with one window, through which the face of heaven and earth could be seen, should fancy that all the marvels he beheld belonged to that window. ("Illusions," *The Conduct of Life*, p. 1120)

Nevertheless, friendship appears as the one sort of human relationship that manages to take us out of what Emerson calls our "eggshell existence" ("Considerations by the Way," p. 1093) and allows us to find and give reality in the realm of human relationships. And perhaps it also deepens the sense of one's own reality beyond what a practiced introversion gives.

Let me observe in passing that Emerson does not make friendship monogamous, as he says other philosophers may. One friend at a time is best for company, not a gathering, if friendship is to yield its greatness. But the self-reliant individual will have a number of friends:

> I please my imagination more with a circle of godlike men and women variously related to each other and between whom subsists a lofty intelligence. ("Friendship," p. 349)

What of tenderness, the second element of friendship? It seems obvious that the emphasis on a friend as an accomplice in truth and in the search for ever more reality need not put much value on warmth—if warmth is what tenderness means. In discussing friendship the word "love" is sparingly or only lightly and teasingly used. I think that Emerson really believes that the transactions of friendship involve feelings that are more important than comradeship and infatuation. To be sure, tenderness is not merely a means to the end of finding truth and reality, or merely a residual form of gratitude for success in attaining that end. Still, it is acceptable in Emerson's theorization of friendship only when it is compatible with that end. The self-reliant individual wants light more than intimacy, which may obscure the light.

Emerson speaks of distance between friends. Let me make some distinctions. He sometimes advocates distance, knowing that the passion of friendship is to overcome distance; he sometimes seems troubled that since the growth of individualism in the 1820s, all sentiments have weakened and an extreme distance or detachment, not intrinsic to the human condition, has developed; and he sometimes resigns himself sadly to the inevitable existence of distance, to the "infinite remoteness" in even the closest sorts of relationships, including friendship ("The Heart," *Early Lectures*, 2, p. 279). Passages in his work sustain all three positions. But his most radical passages, I think, are those in which he speaks as the advocate of more distance—that is, of distance recognized as such, accepted as inevitable, and deliberately turned into a source of benefit. Distance always exists, whether we care to acknowledge the fact or not. People, even friends, are separate beings, in life, in consciousness, in death. The point is; to face the fact and make good come out of it. And the good is not the mere advantage of abating one's annoyance at constant proximity, although a journal entry does in fact speak of this practical advantage to distance:

> Our virtues need perspective. All persons do. I chide and rate my wife or my brother on small provocation if they come too near me. If I see the same persons presently after in the road, in the meeting-house, nay, about the house on their own affairs, heedless of me, I feel reverence and tenderness for them. (*Journals*, 7, p. 419)

Tenderness between friends, therefore, must respect distance; it will resemble kindness more than a loss of self in the other. Emerson says that between friends:

> The joy of kindness is here made known, the joy of love which admitteth of no excess. ("Society," *Early Lectures*, 2, p. 104)

And he advises that friends should "Leave this touching and clawing" ("Friendship," p. 351). With friends, "We will meet as though we met not, and part as though we parted not" (p. 354). Friends live in thoughts about each other.

Emerson complains at moments about distance, but the reason for the complaint is that the friend (or at least, the regular companion) unwittingly blocks Emerson's access to the knowledge the friend has but cannot impart.

The friend becomes an imperfectly useful resource. Emerson's spoken but unpublished words are not tender at all; they are an impersonation of the institution of social clubs, and they are also a little frightening:

> Barriers of society, barriers of language, inadequacy of the channels of communication, all choked up and disused ... Each man has facts I am looking for, and, though I talk with him, I cannot get at them, for want of the clew ... I cannot have society on my own terms (Quoted in Notes to "Clubs," *Society and Solitude*, p. 419).

Emerson knows men of many different kinds of learning:

> I would fain see their picture-books, as they see them.—This was the very promise which mesmerism made to the imagination of mankind. Now, said the adept, if I could cast a spell on this man, and see his pictures, by myself, without his intervention,—I see them, and not he report them ... lift the cover of another hive, see the cells, and suck the honey ... draw the most unwilling mass of experience from every extraordinary individual at pleasure ... Here was diving bell, but it dived into men. (He was the thought vampire.) He became at once ten, twenty, a hundred men, as he stood gorged with knowledge ... hesitating on which mass of action and adventure to turn his all-commanding introspection. (Quoted in Notes to "Clubs," *Society and Solitude*, pp. 419–421. See also Notes to "History," *Works*, 2, pp. 386–387)

If Emerson had the ring of Gyges, he would steal knowledge somehow, not power and sex.

The most radical passage in the essay, "Friendship," is a plea for a certain kind of distance:

> Worship his superiorities; wish him not less by a thought, but hoard and tell them all. Guard him as thy counterpart. Let him be to thee forever a sort of beautiful enemy, untamable, devoutly revered, and not a trivial conveniency to be soon outgrown and cast aside. (p. 351)

It is hard for me to know what to make of the idea that a friend is a "beautiful enemy." The thought seems to exceed even Nietzsche in its daring, in its espousal of "the pathos of distance," although the passage on "star friendship" in *The Gay Science* (sect. 279, pp. 225–226) has a likeness to Emerson's concept. Is Emerson just playing? Aristotle, Montaigne, and Bacon all influence Emerson's reflections on friendship, but I find this thought in none of them. Emerson is certainly not taking any idea he has found elsewhere and impersonating it, trying to say for it words that are more adequate than those of its committed partisans. The idea had no partisans.

Certainly the idea is not adequately explained in Emerson's early remark (1832) that "every man must learn in a different way. How much is lost by imitation. Our best friends may be our worst enemies" (Quoted in Notes to "Self-Reliance," *Works*, 2, pp. 388–389). The point here is that we may imitate those we love best and thus lose our originality, forfeit "the significance of self-education." But that point is meanly self-regarding. Nor is the grand suggestiveness of the idea of a friend as an enemy suitably framed when Emerson says in "Friendship":

> I hate, where I looked for a manly furtherance or at least a manly resistance, to find a mush of concession. Better be a nettle in the side of your friend than his echo. (p. 350)

In a lecture given before "Friendship" was published, Emerson refers interestingly to enemies in the context of describing friends (and lovers). He says:

> ... sitting with a friend in the stimulated activity of the faculties, we lay bare to ourselves our own mystery, and start at the total loneliness and infinity of one man. We see that man serves man only to acquaint him with himself, but into that sanctuary, no person can enter. Lover and friend are as remote from it as enemies. ("Society," *Early Lectures*, 2, p. 105)

Here, enemies are only enemies: friends are not enemies, although, to be sure, enemies are no further away from one's center than friends are. This passage is not conventional, but it is much less radical than the words in "Friendship," and is not a preparation for them. Furthermore, Emerson is not saying that friendship is a process by which those who are initially hostile are eventually reconciled, as opposites are united. This latter sentiment, the reverse of Emerson's, Nietzsche idealizes as the only genuine love of enemies: "How much reverence has a noble man for his enemies!—and such reverence is a bridge to love.—For he desires his enemy for himself...." (*On the Genealogy of Morals* [W. Kaufmann, Trans.], first essay, sect. 10, p. 475).

But Emerson tries not to have enemies in the usual sense; he fights personal enmity, but he will not exclude tension from affection.

Often when Emerson is being radical, he takes a thought from the Gospels or from Plato's *Republic* or *Symposium* and reworks it, making it more fit for the uses of self-reliance. But he does not take the idea of a friend as a beautiful enemy from these sources; it seems to lack precedents. It is not really the privatization of the agonistic ideal of citizenship. Nor is it Homeric. William Blake's line, "Opposition is true Friendship" means that your enemy is, unknown to you, your friend, your benefactor (*The Marriage of Heaven and Hell*, p. 262). (This sentiment, by the way, is certainly present in Emerson.) It does not mean that your friend is, ideally or really, your enemy, but that person is your special enemy because he or she has a beautiful form to which you cannot help being attracted. Let us content ourselves by saying that for Emerson, friends have to remain somewhat strange to each other; actually, the more they know each other, and the more sincere they are, the more strange to each other they should, in certain respects, grow. Friends, like lovers, "should guard their strangeness" ("Manners," p. 522). In this way, tenderness does not interfere with truth. Friends should continue to surprise one another, catching each other off guard, refusing to become familiar and hence wrongly reassuring. Familiarity should dissolve itself by permitting an opening out into strangeness. What makes friends enemies is not that they are, in the usual sense, competitive. They are not competitive in Aristotle's sense, either: they do not try to see which of them can do more good to the other, and thus turn perhaps into mutually overbearing rivals. They are *beautiful* enemies; they retain an aura for each other. Perhaps when in the first Duino Elegy Rilke says (in Leishman-Spender's English) that "Each single angel is terrible" (p. 21), we have some approximation to Emerson's meaning. (Rilke's German word *schrecklich* is, however, too strong.)

At the same time I do not wish to deny that even in regard to friendship Emerson may very well engage in the kind of excess of statement he thinks that accuracy requires. But his work seems not to offer a contrasting excess. He seems to be of one mind on the subject of friendship.

A reasonable question, I suppose, is whether he was or tried to be a friend in the way his theory prescribes. It may be worth mentioning that Thoreau thought that Emerson spoke the needed truth to him only after their friendship waned: "When he became my enemy he shot it to me on a poisoned arrow." If Thoreau is accurate, Emerson did not practice his precepts—at least with Thoreau in this period. Yet Thoreau could also complain of candor: "I am more grieved that my friend can so easily give utterance to his wounded feelings—than by what he says." (See Robert

Sattelmeyer, "'When He Became My Enemy': Emerson and Thoreau, 1848–49," pp. 190, 201.) A more general characterization of Emerson's friendship is made by Henry James, Sr., in his remarkably vivid and violently ambivalent memoir of Emerson:

> In his books or public capacity he was constantly electrifying you by sayings full of divine inspiration. In his talk or private capacity he was one of the least remunerative men I ever encountered.... He had apparently no private personality.... I could find in him no trivial sign of the selfhood which I found in other men ... he only connected with the race at second-hand ... he recognized no God outside of himself and his interlocutor, and recognized him there only as the *liaison* between the two. (*The Literary Remains*, pp. 299–302)

But a more measured critique is made by Henry James, the son, who, in his first essay on Emerson, a review of the Carlyle–Emerson correspondence in 1883, said:

> Emerson speaks of his friends too much as if they were disembodied spirits. One doesn't see the color in the cheeks of them and the coats on their back. (Henry James, *Literary Criticism*, p. 247)

James wants to see novelistically; Emerson does not. James knows as much, and in a later essay, which may have no peers in the writing about Emerson, he complains that Emerson kept away from novels. Let us say that Emerson's radicalism includes an anti-novelistic sense of beauty and of truth. He does not want us to be especially interested in his or our friends' cheeks or coats. He defines heaven as the place without melodrama. It is nevertheless good to hear James's reproach.

In the second essay, the 1887 review of James Elliot Cabot's *A Memoir of Ralph Waldo Emerson*, James intensifies the reproach. He says:

> Courteous and humane to the furthest possible point, to the point of an almost profligate surrender of his attention, there was no familiarity in him, no personal avidity. Even his letters to his wife are courtesies, they are not familiarities. He had only one style, one manner, and he had it for everything—even for himself, in his notes, in his journals. (Henry James, *Literary Criticism*, p. 260)

So be it. Emerson tries to be what James does not want him to be. But is James consistent? Emerson, in life and thought, revises human relationships individualistically—a great theme in James himself. He is more equivocal than Emerson, but closer in spirit than he allows.

I cannot help thinking, all in all, that friendship is the only sort of human relationship that Emerson believes is intrinsic to mental self-reliance. It alone helps to do the work of solitude, and that, because friendship alone assists both self-acquaintance and (without paradox, without compromise) self-reliance. Only friendship's tie to the search for truth and for reality is unaccidental. Its tenderness does not directly advance the work of solitude. But there is no friendship without tenderness, which is a need and a passion relieving us of an otherwise unendurable solitude. Clearly, Emerson reconceptualizes friendship, not merely adapting an old practice.

But what of love—sexual and passionate love? What does Emerson say about it? What does he suggest about the connection between love and mental self-reliance? The brief answer is that to the extent that love includes or turns into friendship, all that can be said in behalf of friendship can be said for love. But that brief answer is not quite adequate, especially when we notice how easily Emerson applies his formulations about friendship to love and how quietly he drifts into discussion of unsexual friendship when his ostensible subject is sexual love.

In two essays on love and in other pieces on domestic life, Emerson tries to look at love—even at personal love—from the perspective of mental self-reliance. It is not always easy to say whether he is being unsettlingly radical or just prudish or cold. Maybe the line between the two is indistinct: radical individualism of Emerson's sort is in principled opposition to possessiveness and exclusiveness in human relations because these qualities are interwoven with the vices of envy, jealousy, and spite. What binds too tightly also blinds: exclusive love presumptuously defines the lover and the loved. None of this suits the effort to know oneself or the world. If exclusive love must be allowed, it cannot be celebrated.

In any case, Emerson as a theorist of self-reliance is not an enthusiast of the sexual passion. He is temperamentally ascetic: "Appetite shows to the finer souls as a disease, and they find beauty in rites and bounds that resist it" ("Prudence," p. 362). That these words of distaste appear when Emerson impersonates the quality of prudence does little to diminish the force of their sincerity. In a rare off-color metaphor he says that "We may all shoot a wild bull that would toss the good and beautiful, by fighting down the unjust and sensual" ("History," p. 253). The sensual male is unjust, if not mean: too vigorous and hence unmindful. He also says:

> The preservation of the species was a point of such necessity, that
> Nature has secured it at all hazards by immensely overloading the
> passion, at the risk of perpetual crime and disorder. ("Culture,"
> *The Conduct of Life*, p. 1016)

These words occur when Emerson speaks on behalf of culture, understood
as the restraint on the "goitre of egotism" and hence on all assertive passions.
In the strongest voice, he makes the case of culture, a case which he will
elsewhere correct. But Emerson repeats the sentiment when later, in *Society
and Solitude*, he speaks on behalf of old age. Perhaps we are in the presence
of his true or nearly true feelings when he says the same thing from two
different perspectives.

Emerson would prefer a less sexed world; perhaps that is what self-
reliant individuals may prefer. Then again, maybe not, for he can also say:
"When we speak truly—is not he only unhappy who is not in love? his
fancied freedom and self-rule—is it not so much death?" ("The Method of
Nature," p. 128). Furthermore, he regularly pays tribute to human physical
beauty, male and female. In the section, "Beauty," in *The Conduct of Life*, he
says:

> The felicities of design in art, or in works of nature, are shadows
> or forerunners of that beauty which reaches its perfection in the
> human form. All men are its lovers.... It reaches its height in
> woman. (p. 1107)

To be sure, in one of Emerson's reworkings of Plato's doctrine of love's
ascent in the *Symposium*, the lowest rung is not sexual desire but a sensation
more merely physical, but solely human. In the same section, "Beauty," from
which I have just quoted, he says:

> Thus there is a climbing scale of culture, from the first agreeable
> sensation which a sparkling gem or a scarlet stain affords the eye,
> up through fair outlines and details of the landscape, features of
> the human face and form, signs and tokens of thought and
> character in manners, up to the ineffable mysteries of the
> intellect. (p. 1112)

The love of beauty, although it guides the soul from one thing to something
else better, is not at root sexual. It seems to have no root, but is born in a
child's eye. The romance of love itself is partly rooted in such splendid
superficiality. In this passage, therefore, Emerson departs from Plato: he does

not think that sexual arousal and its imaginative sublimations provide the basic adhesive to reality. Thus, in the space of a few pages, Emerson speaks a bit dissonantly. The idea of beauty makes him say that all earthly beauty aspires to the beauty of the human body and is perfected in it; but the idea of culture makes him say that sexual love is love of beauty, but love of beauty is not originally sexual. As we shall see, when he speaks directly on behalf of love, he is less ambiguous. But his reputation for being unsexual or antisexual is partly deserved, I suppose.

Early in the essay, "Love," which was published in *Essays: First Series*, and was a revised version of a lecture given a few years before, Emerson writes:

> I have been told that in some public discourses of mine my reverence for the intellect has made me unjustly cold to the personal relations. (p. 329)

The lecture of 1838, also called "Love," already finds Emerson worried that his views on education disparage love of persons (*Early Lectures, 3*, p. 56). I assume that Emerson is haunted by the way in which Socrates, in the *Phaedrus*, turns from impeaching love as hopelessly irrational and begins to defend it so as not to give offense to Eros, who is, after all, a god. To love is to worship and hence to be pious. Emerson, too, will try to compensate for any coldness. The essay "Love" praises human love. "Persons are love's world" (p. 329); love is the "deification" of persons (p. 335). And Emerson will try to defend, at least up to a point, the inclination to single out just one person for the bestowal of a love that excludes everyone and everything else. Friendship too is exclusive, but is so for the sake of opening one's perception of the world. Love seems to have no such purpose and shrinks the world to one person.

Yet Emerson's praise of love reaches its highest point when he describes the effect of love on the ability of the lover to perceive the world with fresh eyes. In a couple of pages he describes this effect in such a way as to bring it close to his constant and overriding ambition, which is to open one's perception of the world. He writes:

> The passion rebuilds the world for the youth. It makes all things alive and significant. (p. 331)

These words seem to catch the essence of self-reliant thinking and to indicate that personal love, quite without trying, causes an epistemological miracle. The passage culminates, furthermore, in a formulation that gives to love a power equal to friendship in calling forth knowledge of one's powers and hence increasing self-acquaintance:

> In giving him to another it still more gives him to himself. He is a new man, with new perceptions, new and keener purposes, and a religious solemnity of character and aims. He does not longer appertain to his family and society; *he* is somewhat; *he* is a person; *he* is a soul. ("Love," p. 331)

The trouble is that much of this passage does not seem sincere. Some sentences are willed or fanciful, and one may finish thinking that whatever else sexual love may mean to Emerson, and howsoever grand a place he establishes for it in the structure of life and its necessities, it does not have a lot to do with mental self-reliance understood as the desire to think one's thoughts and think them through. Love seems off to the side. Most people may not care that love appears unconnected to a poetical or philosophical reception of the world. But Emerson does, and so must anyone who takes the aspirations of democratic individuality seriously.

Here are a few of the sentences that illustrate the effect of love:

> The clouds have faces as he looks on them ... Behold there in the wood the fine madman! He is a palace of sweet sounds and sights; he dilates; he is twice a man; he walks with arms akimbo; he soliloquizes; he accosts the grass and the trees; he feels the blood of the violet, the clover and the lily in his veins; and he talks with the brook that wets his foot. ("Love," p. 331)

I grant that the last phrases have a fine poetic diction and come from Emerson's best skills. Still, if looked at sternly, these words become a parody of self-reliant thinking, which tries to stare the world into beauty and find the world worthy of affirmation. It is as if in such words Emerson illustrates the truth of his remark that the relation of unsexual friendship "is a kind of absolute," and that it is so "select and sacred that it "even leaves the language of love suspicious and common, so much is this (sc. friendship) purer, and nothing is so much divine" ("Friendship," p. 346). Emerson's case for love is not helped when he avers that overwhelming and world-opening love is not a passion that anyone over the age of 30 can feel, even though he hastens to add:

> The remembrance of these visions outlasts all other remembrances, and is a wreath of flowers on the oldest brows. ("Love," p. 329)

These remembrances do not strike me as being those in which the meanings of one's experiences and encounters in the world, or of one's observations of the larger world, are distilled and turned into truthfully poetic perception, either in solitude or with the help of a friend. (I do not deny that other writers may have more successfully portrayed the alliance of sexual passion, self-acquaintance, and mental self-reliance. Who, if not Proust?)

Emerson condescends to love. This becomes clearer when we see how he conceptualizes the relation between the sexes, especially married love. In the lecture, "Society," he says:

> The first Society of Nature is that of marriage, not only prepared in the distinction of Sex, but in the different tastes and genius of Man and Woman. This society has its own end which is an integrity of human nature by the union of its two great parts, Intellect and Affection. For, of Man the predominant power is Intellect; of Woman, the predominant power is Affection. One mainly seeks Truth, whose effect is Power. The other delights in Goodness, whose effect is Love. (*Early Lectures*, 2, p. 102)

The writing is straight; every noun, almost, is capitalized; the abstractions are simple and dualistic. In the preliminary lecture on love, he extends his point by noticing the respective vices of men and women and says that men and women "must balance and redress each other" (*Early Lectures*, 3, p. 63). He also attributes will, daring, and experimentation only to men, while confining women to sympathy, and sympathy to women. I would say that Emerson's commitment to seeing the world as comprised of salutary antagonisms and contrasts and of competing and divergent claims is reduced in these thoughts to a crude dichotomy and hence to a too easy aestheticism, to bad poetry—the kind of all-too-human response to life that Emerson usually deplores and tries to cure so that a superior, democratized aestheticism can take its place. Even at its most conventional, however, Emerson's thought does not exhibit the crassness that denies women any share in the life of the mind. He readily associates the advance of civilization with their ever greater involvement in public and social life. But he makes men or masculinity *represent* the life of the mind.

If we were to leave Emerson's treatment at this point, we would have to conclude that self-reliance neither gains anything from sexual love nor gives anything to it. The relationship of personal love, though fully compatible with democratic individuality, seems immune to its most significant aspect: self-reliance understood as mental self-possession for the sake of affirming the world. Of course, we could say that the sexual love that

Emerson theorizes is more than merely compatible with another and lesser aspect of self-reliance—namely, self-expressive activity. Sexual love, when so intensely personalized and made romantic, is, after all, usually thought as the *result* of individualizing tendencies in society that existed well before the establishment of modern democracy. Thus Emerson could be seen as working out in his own way the meaning of those tendencies. I grant validity to this point. But if I am right in holding that the main Emersonian form of self-reliance is shown and must be shown in thinking and perceiving rather than in expressive activity, then this valid point does not reach to the most fundamental issue.

To gain relevance to mental self-reliance, sexual love must surpass itself and become friendship. Emerson further suggests that friendship growing out of sexual love may be even more valuable for perception of truth and the experience of reality than a friendship that does not. This thought is the culmination of the essay, "Love." But the friendship of lovers or former lovers cannot be based on the continuous dualism of masculine and feminine, which is conventionally a dualism of unequals. Friends are equal. A truthful and truth-seeking relationship must be a relationship of equals. This sentiment accounts for a passage in the essay "Character" (*Essays: Second Series*) in which unsexual friendship is definitively elevated above sexual love:

> I know nothing which life has to offer so satisfying as the profound good understanding which can subsist, after much exchange of good offices, between two virtuous men, each of whom is sure of himself and sure of his friend ... Of such friendship, love in the sexes is the first symbol. Those relations to the best men, which, at one time, we reckoned the romances of youth, become, in the progress of the character, the most solid enjoyment. (p. 506)

In his time, Emerson is reckless in explicitly locating the source of male friendship in romance. But he remains bound by convention to the extent he finds that the love between men and women must be a relationship of unequals and hence philosophically inferior to the friendship of equal men. Sexual love at its best is reduced to a symbol, an imperfect copy of something better, the higher relation of unsexual (or sexually unconsummated) friendship.

If Emerson is to escape convention, he must see through the dualism of masculine and feminine. The dualism must give way, or at least allow its rigidity to be loosened. The most desirable traits of intellect and character must be seen, to a decisive degree, as floating free of biological identity.

One must be disposed to regard men and women as equally available for the kind of friendship that is centered in a companionable quest for more truth, more reality. The self-reliant eye, unimprisoned by gendered thinking, will see equal potentiality in men and women to become self-reliant individuals. The project would be to promote the equal education of women so that there may be a marriage of equals. We must go to other writings, some of which are roughly contemporary to "Love," to see evidence that Emerson tries to break free of the conventional dualism that gives men not so much a monopoly of intellect as a monopoly of the highest traits of intellect.

For the most part, Emerson loosens but does not abandon the dualism of masculine and feminine. He follows two loosening strategies. Common to them both is the decision to describe mental activity solely by reference to the categories of masculine and feminine. One strategy is to value masculine mental traits above feminine ones for the purposes of intellectual self-reliance, but also to say that some women show masculinity. (This is not to say that most men are relevantly masculine.) The other strategy is to claim that the most self-reliant person manages to combine in himself or herself both masculine and feminine intellectual traits and that both sets of traits are equally indispensable. What pervades Emerson's views is a readiness to detach intellectual gender from biological sex and point the way to an ideal hermaphroditism. Let me add that even when Emerson's emphasis is on mental life, his words on masculinity and femininity expand to cover the whole character.

I grant that to use the concepts of "masculine" and "feminine," even though distributed apart from the sex of persons, is to fix the possibilities of identity in a manner not consistent with the theory of democratic individuality. The founder of the theory does not think it through to its end. What cannot be denied, I believe, is that much of the time Emerson seems to regard the masculine traits, whether mental or more broadly characterological, as superior to their necessary feminine complement. Still, in loosening the dualism Emerson does unconventional work, the kind of work needed by the theory of democratic individuality, the heart of which is self-reliant perceiving and knowing, but which must also, of course, encompass being and acting.

The first strategy, then, is to suggest that just as many men lack intellectual masculinity, so some women may have it. In *The Conduct of Life*, Emerson says:

> In every company, there is not only the active and passive sex, but in both men and women, a deeper and more important *sex of*

mind, namely, the inventive or creative class of both men and women, and the uninventive or accepting class. (p. 973)

It is well to notice that this sentence comes from the chapter titled "Power." As Emerson says at the start of the book, he will speak as favorably for each phenomenon as possible. This sentence thus expresses a sentiment of those who are especially given to the pursuit or admiration of power—namely, all of us much of the time. To repeat: Emerson is impersonating a sensibility. As it stands, his thought at least breaks with the custom of unalterably dividing the world into masculine men and feminine women, even if it reserves for masculinity the better role in mental life. Bad hermaphroditism is common because many men combine a male body with a feminine mind (uncreative, passive); good hermaphroditism means that some women, despite having women's bodies, have masculine minds (creative, active). The natural ideal remains the mentally masculine man.

But this line of thought is not the only one, and I think it is further away from Emerson's true beliefs than other passages where he praises femininity and places it equal to or better than masculinity in mental life, and admires any man or woman who is mentally both masculine and feminine. (This is the second strategy.) After all, it would not be consistent—that is, it would not be honest—for Emerson to celebrate perceptual reception and hospitality and then depreciate passivity when it is as mentally alert and vigorous, indeed as rapacious, as he preaches and practices it. If one is willing to receive, to be impinged upon, to be invaded, to be open to the world, one is not conventionally deemed masculine. For Emerson to call such traits feminine is not ideal, but he nevertheless engages in a radical undertaking. He is dignifying the feminine in a way very few others then did. With a radical simplicity he says, "The stronger the nature, the more it is reactive" ("Uses of Great Men," p. 616).

In a journal entry (1843) he expresses an almost pained tribute to femininity:

> Poets ... do not appear to advantage abroad, for ... sympathetic persons, in their instinctive effort to possess themselves of the nature of others, lose their own, and exhibit suppliant manners, whilst men of less susceptibility stand erect around him ... like castles.
>
> It is true that when a man writes poetry, he appears to assume the high feminine part of his nature.... The muse is feminine. But action is male. (*Journals, 8*, p. 356)

At one point he goes the length of citing with approval the words of Henry James, Sr.:

> To give the feminine element in life its hard-earned but eternal supremacy over the masculine has been the secret inspiration of all past history. ("Character," *Lectures and Sketches*, p. 121)

Emerson gives a political slant to this thought in his lecture, "Literature" (1837), where he says that "from their sympathy with the populace arises that humanity even feminine and maternal, which always characterizes the highest class of geniuses" (*Early Lectures*, 2, p. 62).

In a journal entry from 1839, Emerson writes:

> Women see better than men. Men see lazily if they do not expect to act. Women see quite without any wish to act. Men of genius are said to partake of the masculine and feminine traits. They have this feminine eye, a function so rich that it contents itself without asking any aid of the hand. (*Journals*, 7, p. 310)

Emerson's escape from categorical rigidity is effected by praise of the exceptional individual, the genius, although the class of genius seems exclusively made up of men. Yet women as a class are praised for having better perception, the thing that is central to Emerson's depiction of intellectual activity and is a possession Emerson covets for himself.

In a later journal entry (1843), Emerson says:

> Much poor talk concerning woman, which at least had the effect of revealing the true sex of several of the party who usually go disguised in the form of the other sex. Thus Mrs. B is a man. The finest people marry the two sexes in their own person. Hermaphrodite is then the symbol of the finished soul. It was agreed that in every act should appear the married pair: the two elements should mix in every act. (*Journals*, 8, p. 380)

To call Hermaphrodite the symbol of the finished soul is surely noteworthy. Emerson thus extends the idea of hermaphroditic perception to take in the person as such, and now the finest people, not just men, can be ideally hermaphroditic.

Afterward, in *English Traits* (1856), Emerson calls the English national character hermaphroditic for combining kindness and military prowess:

> The two sexes are co-present in the English mind ... The English delight in the antagonism which combines in one person the extremes of courage and tenderness. ("Race," *English Traits*, p. 802)

These words seem, once again, to confine to men the ability to be hermaphroditic: men alone fight in wars. (The English are "rather manly than warlike.") The feeling is irrepressible that whenever Emerson publishes his work, he reserves the highest privileges of hermaphroditism to men, but grants women the same privileges only in the privacy of his journal. But, as we shall see, he does publish thoughts more radical than any that appear only in his journal. We should also remark that Emerson indicates that only when we *delight* in hermaphroditic antagonism can we achieve the heights. The antagonism is not between ideas or between phenomena, or between us and others, but between one element in ourselves and another element at a distant extreme. The best character and the best mind feel this delight. To feel it to the extent of welcoming or cultivating one's hermaphroditism is the most authentic sign of self-reliance.

Emerson complicates his sense of the hermaphroditic by further loosening the dualism of masculine and feminine. He suggests that as people improve, as they grow more self-reliant, they grow more fluid in character and mind. In his lecture, "Swedenborg; or the Mystic," which was published in *Representative Men* (1850), he entertains the thought that gender, divided between "virility" and "the feminine" (p. 679), is a universal quality that pervades every human phenomenon and stamps the whole human world with its dualism. But he turns on the thought and says:

> God is the bride or bridegroom of the soul.... In fact, in the spiritual world we change sexes every moment. You love the worth in me; then I am your husband: but it is not me, but the worth, that fixes the love; and that worth is a drop of the ocean of worth that is beyond me. Meantime, I adore the greater worth in another, and so become his wife. He aspires to a higher worth in another spirit, and is wife or receiver of that influence. (p. 680)

The progress of mental life becomes perpetual worship that is always instigated and accompanied by perpetual self-dissatisfaction. Someone, in some way or on some matter, is wiser than oneself. One opens oneself to him or her. The categories of gender are drastically renovated by being destabilized and made to serve unconformist purposes. This passage may be Emerson's most advanced statement on love.

A related point is made in ungendered language in the essay "Compensation":

> The radical tragedy of nature seems to be the distinction of More and Less. How can Less not feel the pain; how not feel indignation or malevolence towards More? ... It seems a great injustice. But see the facts nearly and these mountainous inequalities vanish. Love reduces them as the sun melts the iceberg in the sea ... If I feel over-shadowed and outdone by great neighbors, I can yet love; I can still receive; and he that loveth maketh his own the grandeur he loves.... It is the nature of the soul to appropriate all things. (p. 301)

Identification with the superior proceeds from incorporation; the receiver's active love converts the receiver, otherwise passive, into the equal of the superior and thereby abolishes envy. This is not identifying with the aggressor. Rather it is pleasure in thinking that although one does not share privileges, they exist in the world and enhance it. In abandoning resentment, one loses sight of one's lack. To use gendered language, the feminine thus becomes masculine, or overcomes it.

A journal entry (1842) that is a little later than the meditations that found their way into the eventual lecture on Swedenborg fills out the thought in that lecture:

> A highly endowed man with good intellect and good conscience is a Man-woman and does not so much need the complement of woman to his being as another. Hence his relations to the sex are somewhat dislocated and unsatisfactory. He asks in woman, sometimes the Woman, sometimes the Man. (*Journals*, *8*, p. 175)

Unfortunately, these words, like the passage from the lecture on Swedenborg, still seem to place the masculine above the feminine and still seem to assume that the good hermaphroditic opportunity is for men, not women. But the appearance is partly deceptive: a true man expects a woman to be able to be a man episodically, just as he becomes a woman. What is more, that as a man in the middle of the 19th century, Emerson can say before a popular audience, as he does in the lecture on Swedenborg, that a developed man becomes the wife of the man from whom he learns is remarkable. Virility is potency to instruct. We may, of course, wish that Emerson could have found an unsexed or ungendered language to express the desirability of being inwardly full of contrasts and antagonisms that are acknowledged, then mastered and made mobile. But I think that Emerson carries self-reliance into new territory. Later radicals can perfect his intuitions. His language conveys in an especially forceful way the idea that the independent mind has no categorial fixity, that receptivity is absent of such fixity. And as the mind is, so should the character endeavor to become. Emerson's reflections suggest that because a true individual is hermaphroditic, a pair of friends, whether or not they are or have been lovers, must each strive to be hermaphroditic so as to grant full play to each other's nature and full scope to each other's thought.

The fact is Emerson believes everyone is hermaphroditic. He says:

> The spiritual power of man is twofold, mind and heart, Intellect and morals; one respecting truth, the other the will. One is the man, the other the woman in spiritual nature. One is power, the other is love. These elements always coexist in every normal individual, but one predominates. ("Natural History of Intellect," *Natural History*, p. 60)

If one element must predominate, the individual will not allow it to injure the claims of the other element. "Each has its vices, its proper dangers, obvious enough when the opposite element is deficient" (p. 61). One must therefore tend both the masculine and the feminine in oneself.

To some appreciable extent, then, Emerson tries to efface the stark distinction between men and women and hence between conventional masculinity and conventional femininity. The point—Emerson's point, not just our own—is to see whether sexual love can, like unsexual friendship, help the intellectual work of self-reliance and not merely be a relationship that is compatible with it or that may have some of the coloration of expressive individuality in a democracy. Lovers must become friends. In "Of Friendship," Montaigne quotes Cicero's *Tusculan Disputations*, 4: "Love is the attempt to form a friendship inspired by beauty" (*The Complete Essays* [D. Frame, Trans.], p. 39). The idea of hermaphroditism is a large step towards theorizing love as friendship, yet a kind of friendship that grows out of sexual love and very nearly replaces it—a kind of friendship that treasures the memory of sexual passion but transmutes the decay of passion into the perfection of friendship. The question in Emerson reduces to whether a husband and a wife can befriend each other.

I believe that a key formulation is found in the lines I quoted from his journal. Let me repeat them:

> A highly endowed man with good intellect and good
> conscience is a Man-woman and does not so much need the
> complement of woman to his being as another. Hence his
> relations to the sex are somewhat dislocated and unsatisfactory.
> (*Journals*, *8*, p. 380)

I read that passage as saying that, contrary to the myth on love that
Aristophanes offers in the *Symposium*, a true individual has progressed to the
point where one has engendered in oneself the half that most people, still
imperfectly individualized, miss in themselves and seek in others. True
individuals self-reliantly complete themselves from within. They grow to
resemble the original, undivided double self; they have tried to become self-
healed. Emerson produces a ferocious statement of the individual's self-
sufficiency in "Perpetual Forces," a lecture from 1862, in the time of the
Civil War:

> The last revelation of intellect and of sentiment is that in a
> manner it severs the man from all other men; makes known to
> him that the spiritual powers are sufficient to him if no other
> being existed; that he is to deal absolutely in the world, as if he
> alone were a system and a state, and though all should perish
> could make all anew. (*Lectures and Sketches*, p. 83)

Emerson's more moderate view is that what the true individual lacks is
nothing that another person can steadily supply. Rather, what is required is a
company of friends, perhaps one's spouse included, who take turns in
supplying what is lacking. The very need to be supplied is diminished: One
tends to supply oneself. What is most urgently wanted is not sexual embrace
but help toward intellectual fulfillment: the ecstasy of reception of the world.
"Hence his relations to the sex are somewhat dislocated and unsatisfactory."
The reason is that women, in Emerson's time and place, were not expected
to be intellectual.

In a journal entry, Emerson tries to suggest that love is not desire, and
that desire diminishes as love increases:

> Remember the great sentiment, "What we love that we have, but
> by Desire we bereave ourselves of the love," which Schiller said,
> or said the like.

Schiller's lines, as quoted by Emerson's editors, are:

One *loves* what he has; one *desires* what he has not; Only the rich soul loves; only the poor one desires. (*Journals*, 7, p. 214)

Emerson finds his thought captured perfectly by another.

Of course, no one is literally self-sufficient. The point is that what one needs from lovers and friends is nothing so tremendous as half a self, as in Aristophanes's story. In relations with the loved one, the source of dislocation is the difficulty in converting love into friendship. Luck is necessary; the project can never be easy. Yet each partner in love, like each unsexual friend, has (or can cultivate) a mixture of masculine and feminine traits, even though they are in different emphases and proportions. In this way they become equals, while remaining diverse. Despite having the same capacities as the other, each necessarily has a different temperament, different experiences, and different tastes, and hence will have a different perspective on life. The couple will never run out of things to say. All this is possible when two persons are "not too much unlike." The mutually attractive unlikenesses, which must also exist between two individuals, can be assured without the cultural system of gender once inner hermaphroditism is encouraged.

To repeat, Emerson does not actually say that lovers or unsexual friends should be or become a pair of hermaphroditic individuals. His thought is hinted, not worked out. But I believe I am taking it in a direction he suggests.

Do I need to add that Emerson's ideal of hermaphroditism is not a doctrine of bisexual activity? The only time Emerson writes about homosexual love is in an undergraduate essay, composed when he was 17, called "The Character of Socrates." He does not speak the name of such love, but seeks to clear Socrates of a want of "temperance" and does so indignantly (*Two Unpublished Essays*, ed. by Edward Everett Hale, 1896, pp. 21–23). Emerson's explicit sexual world is comprised of straight sex, aiming for marriage, and then, despite aversions, maintaining it. Nevertheless, implicit in his view is the thought that if sexual desire is dependent on the mutual need of contrasting selves (or half-selves) for each other, then the hermaphroditic soul, being more complete, will be less psychologically needy, not more sexually adventurous. In Walt Whitman, however, a link between the hermaphroditic and the bisexual is intimated.

*   *   *

I have already said that Emerson varies his sentiment on the distance between people who are close. He advocates more distance than is customary; he also regrets the increased distance that democratic individuality has created, and he considers distance a permanent fact that must be honestly acknowledged. This variation appears in his discussion of married love as it does in his discussion of friendship that was never sexual. As with friendship, so with married love, it is possible to see Emerson above all as an advocate of distance.

In the case of married love, the advocacy of distance has mixed sources. On the one hand, he says that after the early days of sexual infatuation, things change: insecurity, displeasure, pain enter the relationship. What, after all, could be expected when "two persons, a man and a woman, so variously and correlatively gifted, are shut up in one house to spend in the nuptial society forty or fifty years?" ("Love," p. 337). Surely, a new relationship must grow out of the old one if some relationship is to be preserved. Emerson never mentions divorce; so, permanent marriage frames his discussion of sexual love. If society were starting from scratch, perhaps the institution of marriage would be replaced ("Religion," *English Traits*, p. 883). But it is here: make the best of it; make something really fine out of it—finer even than the early days of infatuation. Let it grow into the worthiest friendship, which is partly defined by distance. On the other hand, Emerson is committed to the belief that the highest relationship cannot be to persons, but to the world. Yet he allows that the best preparation for becoming attached to the world, for praising and affirming it, for beholding it as beautiful, is to be attached first in a relationship of sexual love. With Emerson, then, the much greater reason for advocating distance is philosophical yearning, not the "incongruities, defects and disproportion" he says that one will find in the spouse ("Love," p. 336). Even if infatuation could last, it exists to be superseded. Let distance come, and with effort it will not be the distance of dissatisfaction, but the proper distance, the distance of sympathetic detachment.

Emerson's famous poem "Give All to Love" actually suggests the thought that though love, a god, deserves the lover's complete self-giving, the lover should not give all to love. The lover acts properly when he honors the emotional freedom of the beloved:

> Cling with life to the maid;
> But when the surprise,
> First vague shadow of surmise
> Flits across her bosom young,
> Of a joy apart from thee,
> Free be she, fancy free

What is good for one is good for the other:

Though thou loved her as thyself,
As a self of purer clay,
Though her parting dims the day,
Stealing grace from all alive;
Heartily know,
When half-gods go,
The gods arrive. (*Works, 9*, p. 92)

Persons are only half-gods; they are partly material. Love is only one of the gods. The greatest gods are truths. The gods arrive when the truth about the imperfections of sexual love are faced. The distance that lovers should need is not literal separation; rather it comes from an unpossessive attitude that only time may grant and with it, the gift of philosophical freedom.

In the lecture, "Home" (1838), Emerson speaks his most fervid words on the excellence of distance between people who are closest:

> I have said that a true Culture goes to make man a citizen of the world ... at home in nature. It is the effect of this domestication in the All to estrange the man in the particular. Having learned to know the depth of peace which belongs to a home in the Soul, he becomes impatient and a stranger in whatsoever relation or place is not like it eternal. He who has learned by happy inspiration that his home and country are so wide that not possibly can he go forth out of it, immediately comes back to view his old private haunts, once so familiar as to seem part and parcel of himself, under an altered aspect. They look strange and foreign. Now that he has learned to range and associate himself by affinities and not by custom he finds himself a stranger under his own roof. (*Early Lectures, 3*, p. 31)

The aim of glad estrangement is to come to know that not only are those whom one loves infinitely beautiful, but all persons are such to those who love them. Everyone loves arbitrarily, but because everyone does, there is no injustice. But the limits intrinsic to personal love must be overcome. Love can aspire to impartiality. We cannot love the world as we love what we know close to hand and is ours, but we can develop the imagination of love and take to heart the fact that anyone known well can be loved well. Everyone deserves to know and to be known well. "Love," he says, "shows me the opulence of nature, by disclosing to me in my friend a hidden wealth, and I infer an equal depth of good in every other direction" ("Nominalist and Realist," p. 585). Distance between persons whose relationship began in sexual infatuation can enable the best perception of the lovely world, the love-worthy world that houses infinitely more, infinitely more love, than their special love. If, then, Emerson is cold about sex, he has a passionate reason. His entire conception of personal love is determined by his wish to see it serve the end for which mental self-reliance exists: reception of the world, especially other human beings. He gives exclusive love a telos beyond itself, rather than making it the highest condition of life.

In the essay "Love" Emerson says that "even love, which is the deification of persons, must become more impersonal every day" (p. 335). Married love puts the couple "in training for a love which knows not sex, nor person, nor partiality" (p. 337). In one paragraph he reworks the idea of love's ascent in the *Symposium*, but gives less to beautiful bodies than Plato does. (Another version of love's ascent is found in his poem "Initial, Daemonic and Celestial Love.") He thinks that the body is "unable to fulfill the promise which beauty holds out," and continues to say:

> if, accepting the hint of these visions and suggestions which beauty makes to his mind, the soul passes through the body and falls to admire strokes of character, and the lovers contemplate one another in their discourses and their actions, then they pass to the true palace of beauty, more and more inflame their love of it, and by this love extinguishing the base affection, as the sun puts out fire by shining on the hearth, they become pure and hallowed. (pp. 333–334)

We notice that Emerson ingeniously inserts a trope from Plato's parable of the cave in the *Republic* into his super-Platonized picture of the metamorphoses of sexual love. Then he suggests that the lover ideally passes from the beauty of the good character of the beloved to an appreciation of the good character of all persons:

> so is the one beautiful soul only the door through which he enters to the society of all true and pure souls ... And in beholding in many souls the traits of the divine beauty, and separating in each soul that which is divine from the taint which it has contracted in the world, the lover ascends to the highest beauty, to love and knowledge of Divinity, by steps on this ladder of created souls. (p. 334)

Emerson is carried away; rather he is impersonating the lover and thus magnifies the phenomenon of love. Though his ladder of love reaches beyond persons to "Divinity," Emerson is intensely concerned to show the continuity between love of one person and love of all persons—not love between one person and love of what is other than or more than persons. Of course, even the continuity between love of one and love of all must seem implausible or unwanted to anyone who thinks that being in love with a person is thoroughly discontinuous with any other kind of love, because no one or nothing exists like the beloved or is as good. Emerson is radical in affirming the continuity; he means it, but not quite as Socrates's Diotima urges it when she insists that sexual love of one person should lead to sexual desire toward all. For Emerson, it is only the illusion of love that blinds lovers to the fact that love of any one person is a love of qualities or attributes shared with other persons. One unknowingly loves the type through a single person, the essence through an accident. The beloved is actually an imperfect realization of a complex ideal, whether imagined or vaguely remembered, that can never in truth be perfectly realized. The lover should try to climb to a love of the ideal itself and descend again to a particular love, but now enlightened by an understanding of the nature of love.

Emerson may doubt he will ever be believed. He may have his own doubts. For that reason, the praise of unsexual friendship may be more sincerely congenial to him than praise of love. But he must praise personal love, and what induces the strain of ecstasy in his voice is the possibility that such love can provide the surest access to knowledge of reality, to truth about the world. I think when Emerson says that "Divinity" is the ultimate reality, the place where the ladder of love ends, his best sense is that this place is not love of a theist substitution for Plato's metaphysical absolute beauty, but love of the world. Love of the world, however, is not continuous with or like sexual (or unsexual) love of persons. The beauty of the human and nonhuman world is not like the beauty of persons. The world is not in the image of a person. Friendship, is a relation which, thanks to love, whether sexual or not, brings to birth and nurtures impressions of truth about the world and its beauty. If Emerson, on one occasion, can locate the root of the desire for beauty in a child's bewitchment by a scarlet stain, the love of persons is obviously not a mere bewitchment by surface. Correspondingly, the passage of love leading persons to love of the world is not direct. Emerson's Platonism is revisionary and incomplete. He says:

> whilst every thing is permitted to love, whilst man cannot serve man too far, whilst he may well and nobly die for his friend, yet are there higher experiences in his soul than any of friendship or love,—the revelations of impersonal love, the broodings of the spirit, there is nothing at last but God only. ("Prospects," 1842, *Early Lectures*, 3, p. 381)

Mental self-reliance begins and may very well end in solitude, but its point, which is love of the world, gathers indispensable help from the friendship in sexual love as well as the love in unsexual friendship.

PAMELA SCHIRMEISTER

From Philosophy to Rhetoric

I cast away in this new moment all my once hoarded knowledge, as
vacant and vain. Now, for the first time, seem I to know any thing rightly.
The simplest words,—we do not know what they mean, except when we
love....   —Emerson, "Circles"

LETTING GO

Despite Emerson's eloquent call for a new mode of letters that will
replace philosophy as such, its representative—the American scholar—no
more exists at the end of the essay than he did at the beginning. Emerson has
been quite clear about what American letters are not, but he fails to delineate
what they shall be. It would be typically Emersonian if the American scholar
and letters themselves were by definition prospective, but at this point, all
that one can really say about Man Thinking is that he is not to bear the image
of the traditional philosopher. As "The American Scholar" suggests, by this
Emerson means that his thinking is to participate neither in what he
elsewhere calls "a paltry empiricism," nor in the forms of conceptualization
and system building associated particularly with Kant and his ancestors. We
are, in some sense not entirely clear, to let go of philosophy. Such an idea of
course returns us to the image of the hand with which Emerson opens his
address to the scholar and that, in turn, structures his argument throughout

From *Less Legible Meanings: Between Poetry and Philosophy in the Work of Emerson*. © 1999 by the
Board of Trustees of the Leland Stanford Jr. University.

the essay. If taking from letters is associated with the hand divided into fingers in order to close round something, to grasp or comprehend it in a teleological fashion, giving to letters might well be represented by an opposite image, that of an open hand. Such an image does not appear in Emerson's text, any more so than any image of what American letters might be. But is it likely that Emerson, well read in the pre-Socratics, could fail to have known that with a closed hand Zeno represented dialectics or philosophical argument? With an open hand, he represented eloquence.[1]

The subject of this chapter is precisely Emersonian eloquence or rhetoric as performance and persuasion, but before attempting to understand what that might mean and how it might replace a more traditional philosophical project, recall that an open hand can invite or repel. It may be as much a shield as a greeting, a warning as a welcome. I say this at the outset because if thinking as the potential receptivity embodied by the open hand is to replace the activity of conceptualization, it does so in complex ways that imply more than a sequential transition from one discourse to another. Transition is one of Emerson's central tropes, and it is never simple. Perhaps the most trenchant instance occurs in "Self-Reliance": "Life only avails, not the having lived. Power ceases in the instant of repose; it resides in the moment of transition from a past to a new state, in the shooting of the gulf, in the darting to an aim."[2] This passage will become emblematic of the process that Emersonian rhetoric attempts to engender in the reader, but in the meanwhile, it serves as a reminder that Emerson's interest lies neither here nor there, in neither past nor future, but rather somewhere in between, in the interstitial process of moving from one point to another. His project for American letters takes shape as just such a process or trajectory between what are on their own ground reified disciplines or conceptual fields. The difficulty is that the opposition between those disciplines, between philosophy and rhetoric, is not itself definitive for Emerson but merely encloses the transitional process between them.

Emerson himself provides a paradigmatic example of the problems attendant to the transition from philosophy to letters, fittingly, at the close of the essay entitled "Intellect," the penultimate piece in *Essays: First Series*. At the beginning of this essay, Emerson announces, "Intellect and intellection signify to the common ear consideration of the abstract truth."[3] The point of the essay will be to subtilize the common, to revise our notions of what is called thinking so that we no longer see thought as bound up solely with abstract truth. The essay concludes, as might be expected, with a brief meditation on different types of knowing. Speaking of the man who would know "truth," Emerson begins:

> The circle of the green earth he must measure with his shoes, to find the man who can yield him truth. He shall then know that there is somewhat more blessed and great in hearing than in speaking. Happy is the hearing man; unhappy the speaking man. As long as I hear truth, I am bathed by a beautiful element and am not conscious of any limits to my nature ... but if I speak, I define, I confine, and am less.[4]

In an immediate sense, the passage echoes a number of Emerson's concerns in "The American Scholar." If we must measure the earth with our shoes, then it is because knowledge is to be experiential or nothing; as Emerson insists earlier in the essay, "I would put myself in the attitude to look in the eye an abstract truth, and I cannot" (420).

The turn away from such truth is a turn toward mediation, toward the Other who can yield truth, and indeed, throughout the essay, the emphasis falls on just such mediation. The implication of the first two sentences in the above passage is that once we recognize that knowledge is mediated, something reflected back to us through the circuit of the Other, then we must understand thinking as reception rather than as reaching after, a difference further underscored by the passivity of hearing itself. As Emerson notes several pages earlier, "Our thinking is to be a pious reception. Our truth of thought is therefore vitiated as much by too violent direction given by our will" (418–19). Receptivity implies affectability—that is, the susceptibility to being affected by the Other, and it is for this reason that the later part of the passage shifts the opposition between receptivity and activity into a different register. In the interplay with the Other, we learn that hearing is more "blessed" than speaking, and the three terms—"hearing," "blessing," and "speaking"—continue to figure centrally as the essay comes to its conclusion. If the opposition between receptivity and activity is relocated specifically in terms of speech, then it is because knowing is in the process of becoming the province of rhetoric and persuasion, of the ways in which language affects us, make us receptive to it. This dynamic is, in turn, conceived as making us more, just as the kind of conceptualization that defines and confines makes us less.

Emerson will address this transition more specifically at the close of the essay, but in the meantime, it is worth noting that the connotations of the word "blessing," particularly as it appears in the Hebrew Bible (*berakha*), have always had to do with more-ness and increase, particularly in the sense of "more life." To be blessed, by giving ourselves up to hearing, then, would mean in some sense to be more of who we are. What might otherwise seem like no more than the replacement of one discourse with another is thus complicated by the fact that, as in "The American Scholar," the passage from philosophy to rhetoric subtends the larger trajectory of self-creation, or *Bildung*. The beginning of the paragraph quoted above indicates Emerson understood the connotation of blessing as more life; it is a connotation he then makes explicit at the close of the paragraph and with which he reveals the stakes of the confrontation with traditional philosophy. Echoing the preceding essay in the series, "Circles," he continues in "Intellect":

> Every man's progress is through a succession of teachers, each of whom seems at the time to have a superlative influence, but it at last gives place to a new. Frankly let him accept it. Jesus says, Leave father, mother, house and lands, and follow me.... Each new mind we approach seems to require an abdication of all our past and present possessions. A new doctrine seems, at first, a subversion of all our opinions, tastes, and manner of living. Such has Swedenborg, such has Kant, such has Coleridge, such has Hegel or his interpreter Cousin, seemed to many young men in this country. Take thankfully and heartily all they can give. Exhaust them, wrestle with them, let them not go until their blessing be won. (426–27)

I quote this passage at length because it encapsulates the nature of the Emersonian way of both inheriting and disowning traditional philosophy. At the beginning of the paragraph, the emphasis is on learning and knowledge as occurring by overwhelming influence or reception, both of which proceed by abandonment of current investments. Yet these influences will themselves one day give way to abandonment. In between these two moments, Emerson inserts the striking idea of one's encounter with philosophy as that of Jacob wrestling with the angel for the blessing. Coupled with the mention of Jesus, it is in part as if Emerson is simply suggesting that knowledge, and philosophy in particular, are spiritual pursuits, or rather the nineteenth-century way of inheriting religion. The passage, however, goes further than that.

In the Biblical account, Jacob's encounter with the angel itself occurs as a transitional moment.[5] Having fled the house of Laban, Jacob returns to the Holy Land after twenty years. His first move is to send gifts ahead to his brother Esau, asking for reconciliation and peace. As Avivah Zornberg puts it, "The central image that expresses Jacob's dilemma at this period of his life ... is of Jacob behind."[6] By "Jacob behind," Zornberg intends something like his temporal lastness and lateness. The last of the patriarchs and second-born, he nonetheless steals the birthright and the blessing from Esau, and now he sends his propitiatory gifts of livestock ahead, along with his servants and his camp, remaining behind on the far side of the Jabbok. Indeed, the classic reading of his position of birth is that of a man whose destiny is deferred. That destiny, however, will accomplish itself as he wrestles with a nameless one until daybreak, finally wresting the blessing from him. Who is this nameless one? Midrashic tradition holds that it is Esau's guardian angel, but also it surely must be an image of Jacob himself, who is in any case Esau's twin.[7] Angels are named for their mission, and this one's mission is to give Jacob a new name, to show him in a face-to-face confrontation how to become Israel. It is perhaps for this reason that in response to Jacob's question, ("Tell me, I pray thee, thy name"), the angel responds, "Wherefore is it that thou dost ask after my name?" Jacob already knows the answer, for he is facing himself in the moment at which he is leaving one identity behind to take on a new one. Evidently, such leave-taking is not possible on one's own. Jacob somehow needs this angel, and even then, the blessing comes hard. The angel only blesses Jacob in order to escape, as if facing ourselves literally means letting go of ourselves. The wrestling match thus becomes an opportunity for self-understanding and -discovery won at the cost of a battle. Not least significantly, this is a battle unfolding on the threshold between private and public identities. After asking Jacob his name, the angel says, "Thy name shall be called no more Jacob, but Israel: for as a prince hast thou power with God and with men, and hast prevailed."[8] Jacob will become a new nation.

So, lateness or behindness, and winning the blessing, means the possibility of being more than one has been by achieving a new and larger identity.[9] I emphasize these two aspects of the Jacob story because I think they bear on Emerson's use of the trope to describe the American confrontation with European philosophy. Like Jacob, Americans, too, as individual readers, always come after when it comes to European philosophy, not just because they are Americans but also because the philosophic conception of truth is something always already there, immutable and universal. In our confrontation with European philosophy, what we stand to gain is precisely the possibility of our own identity as makers, rather than onlookers. This holds both at the personal and cultural levels. Jacob's story represents this moment as the passage from private to public identity, suggesting that for Emerson, an American's individual grappling with European philosophy will lead to an American way of inheriting or disowning that tradition, although at this point, the nature of the passage from private to public remains uncertain.

The central idea is still that philosophy represents the decisive battleground on which the war for identity is to be won or lost. Thus

Emerson insists at the opening of the passage that one must abdicate all past and present possessions, including oneself, if one is to make any progress. To win a new name, one must give up the old. And, to make such progress, to win the blessing from philosophy, means to overcome it on its own ground. It is not a matter, as de Tocqueville had insisted, of being ignorant of all of the schools of European philosophy.[10] We must wrestle with it, hand to hand, grasp it, see ourselves face to face in it, to see how we find or fail to find ourselves there. Only then can we let go, just as Jacob lets go of the angel once its blessing is won. It is as if, in this decisive confrontation, one grasps conceptualization itself, thereby overcoming it and replacing it with the receptivity of the open hand.

Nonetheless, Emerson here worries about losing, and indeed, in Jacob's story itself, the outcome is equivocal. Jacob wins a new name, but he is crippled. One might construe this to mean that neither Jacob nor the angel exactly triumphs, but rather that both prevail. For Emerson, the anxiety generated by the conflict with European philosophy manifests itself as a fear of overinfluence. But as he writes immediately following the passage on winning the blessing, "After a short season, the dismay will be overpast, the excess of influence withdrawn, and they [the philosophers] will be no longer an alarming meteor, but one more bright star shining serenely in your heaven, and blending its light with all your day."[11] There is something in our confrontation that unmakes us, but I take this passage to say as well that European philosophy will no longer be a call to arms, a reason to do battle. Having wrestled with it and won its blessing, we will be remade, but we will also have changed it, domesticated it into the common light of our day. To make philosophy part of the everyday would surely mean to make it experiential, to transform conceptualization into living, into something in which we recognize ourselves, see ourselves face to face. The possibility of such a confrontation provides at least one of the reasons that Emerson alludes to Jacob in the first place. Wrestling involves bodily contact, direct experience, as well as an etymological root that includes the idea of twisting or turning. The way in which Emerson figures our encounter with European philosophy involves both.

In the first place, we are not simply to take what the other gives, but rather to experience it, to make contact with it in a direct way—to live it. It is just this dimension of the encounter that makes possible the transition from private to public. If we are not looking an abstract truth in the eye, but taking on the teachings of philosophy experientially, seeing ourselves face to face, then we must each do it individually. As we upbuild ourselves, so we inherit philosophy as part of a collective day. This type of contact implies a subversion, or a twisting of the usual relation between the subject seeking to grasp the object of truth, into a more dynamic process of receptivity in which the subject and its truth might no longer be distinguishable. Wrestling requires two participants who, in their confrontation, are far less separable than opposing sides in a battle would be. Such perhaps would be the American way both of letting go of a European philosophical inheritance and, at the same time, of taking something of it afterward.

The closing paragraphs of "Intellect" make clear that thinking as experience, and particularly the experience of self-understanding, has been Emerson's tangent all along. Speaking of the difficulty of European philosophy, Emerson is simply dismissive: "The Bacon, the Spinoza, the Hume, Schelling, Kant, or whosoever propounds to you a philosophy of the mind, is only a more or less awkward translator of the things in your consciousness.... Say, then, instead of too timidly poring into his obscure sense, that he has not succeeded in rendering back to you your consciousness" (427). According to this logic, the reading of philosophy becomes, far from a search for abstract truth, an exercise in self-recognition, just as Jacob's confrontation with the angel leads to self-understanding. But the drift here is negative, for in the remaining paragraph of the essay, Emerson worries over whether or not the type of philosophy with which he has been grappling has anything to do with the laws of intellect at all. He announces his reservation with the statement, "I will not, though the subject might provoke it, speak to the open question between Truth and Love" (427). For Emerson, who has little or nothing to say about love, what could such a question mean? If, however, the subject of intellect provokes this question, it is because philosophy may be the way of Truth, but if truth cannot speak to us, and if we cannot hear it, engage with it, then it means nothing.

To understand what is at stake in the open question between truth and love, we perhaps need to move to the closing sentence of the essay: "The angels are so enamoured of the language that is spoken in heaven, that they will not distort their lips with the hissing and unmusical dialects of men, but speak their own, whether there be any who understand it or not" (428). Aside from an echo of Emerson's earlier dissatisfaction with the ministry, there is also an echo here of the well-known passage from Chapter 13 of Paul's first letter to the Corinthians: "Though I speak with the tongues of men and angels, and have not love, I am become as sounding brass, or a tinkling cymbal."[12] What is missing, of course, in this musical language of truth as spoken by men or angels is precisely love. In the context of the earlier distinction between speaking and hearing, with the latter as the more blessed, Emerson here ironically wrests the blessing from the angels who speak but are not heard and transfers it to those who deal in the hissing and unmusical dialects of men. If this dialect is hissing, then it is perhaps because the language of men, like that of the serpent, entails speaking with a double tongue, that is, in the language of metaphor, of figure, of self-conscious rhetoricity, rather than transparency. Similarly, to speak the language of men must also mean to be heard, and being heard implies persuasion. This leaves us with love. In "Friendship," Emerson had suggested that "our intellectual and active powers increase with our affections,"[13] which is perhaps another way of stating that all of our intellectual progress is through a series of teachers. Truth on its own, say the kind of truth that Emerson presupposes by European philosophy, never persuades us. It is always the Other who does so, always our affections for the Other that lead. And how does the Other do this? It would seem, given Emerson's emphasis on the involuntary nature of hearing itself, through our own passivity, or call it receptivity. But receptivity to what? The answer at this point can only be "rhetoric."

Put another way, if the purpose of letters is a form of self-creation, itself not yet clear, then there is no point in Emerson or anyone else reporting that this is so. To do so would be similar to Descartes having formulated the cogito in the second person. As with the cogito, the project of American letters is one which each reader, each potential scholar, must take up for him- or herself. Indeed, the project consists precisely in the taking up of it, which can only be done by being drawn to it through its rhetorical pull. If the Other speaks to us and we hear it, then the connection is everything, and the connection is established through the way in which the Other speaks and in which we hear. Insofar as this connection must be experiential rather than a statement of what is to be, "The American Scholar" cannot properly be said to constitute part of the project of American letters. It is no more than an announcement of what is to come, a sketch or a blueprint. The actual transition from philosophy to letters occurs later, in *Essays: First Series*, as I have been trying to demonstrate by way of examining the close of "Intellect." But as I have also just suggested, the transition itself eludes discursive statement or else loses itself in such statement. The real work of transition will have to be performed rhetorically, in such a way that the reader can be receptive to it, persuaded by it. Only then will we have let go.

READING

Transitions necessarily occur briefly, quickly, say, for example, through an allusive moment within a text, or in the turning of a single word. But lest it seem I have placed too much weight on the single reference to Jacob in what is in any case an obscure essay in Emerson's canon, let us return to the beginning of *Essays: First Series*, to the essay entitled "History." The assumption in doing so is that we take the book's title itself seriously, for the *First Series* is just that, a continuous meditation on the nature of letters in all of their senses. It is an explanatory meditation at times, but primarily a serial exemplification of the type of thinking with which we are to replace philosophy, as well as an act of performative rhetoric designed to put the reader on the path of that thinking. Emerson implies as much midway through "History" when he writes in a paragraph comprised of a single sentence, "His onward thinking leads him into the truth to which that fact or series belongs."[14] In short, each of the parts of a series represents a single idea, but the purpose of serial presentation is to foster onward thinking, to give us up, as Emerson has it in "Intellect," "unreservedly to that which draws [us]."[15] This is not to say that a series always proceeds continuously; as "Experience" demonstrates, a series may equally imply discontinuity. In either respect, whether as continuity or discontinuity, *Essays: First Series* is aimed just at onward thinking itself, and particularly onward thinking construed as the activity of self-creation through letters.

To say that *Essays: First Series* proceeds serially in an attempt to draw the reader into onward thinking raises the question of why Emerson begins with an essay entitled "History." The answer must surely be that the topic is somehow necessary for the understanding of the purpose of the series as a whole and, more specifically, preparatory for the lessons of the essay immediately following, "Self-Reliance." There is, of course, in a general sense nothing in the least unusual about Emerson writing an essay on history. He would simply be sharing in the nineteenth-century preoccupation with the use of historical method and, particularly, genealogy, as tools of self-understanding. Whether they be tales of our biological origins, of our economic system, of Western morality, or of individual human development, the historical fictions of the nineteenth century all make the assertion that identity cannot be understood outside of the historical matrix. Indeed, as Emerson puts it in the second paragraph of the essay, "Man is explicable by nothing less than his whole history."[16] In the most general sense, it is from this perspective of history as constitutive of self-understanding that the essay's inaugural position in the series makes sense. Emerson, however, differs from Darwin, Marx, Nietzsche, and Freud not simply by virtue of preceding them, but quite specifically in his use of the genealogical method. One assumption usually underlying this method is that the past informs the present: tell me who you were, and I'll tell you who you are. It is clear that Emerson found this kind of determinism distasteful, and yet, the genealogical method remains important for him for reasons tangential to determinism. From Marx through Freud, genealogies may expose the lineaments of the past in the face of the present, but they also show just how tenuous the links are between origins and ends. Paradoxically, the very connection between past and present that implies determinism also reminds us again and again of the contingencies by which the present became what it is. Rather than a record of natural fact, history thus becomes the medium in which we have constructed ourselves and can do so again and again.

I take this belief in the constructedness of history to underlie the architectural tropes pervading Emerson's "History." It is not simply that architecture belongs to the material record of culture but also that architecture serves as a reminder of the purpose of reading or writing history as constructed, and therefore as perpetually educative or upbuilding. For the same reason, it should not surprise us in the least that the essay on history has little to do with history as material record and everything to do with the reading and writing of history. In order to understand the nature of Emerson's emphasis on reading and writing, it is important to specify that by history, Emerson intends more than the mere record of events: "There is one mind common to all individual men.... Of the works of this mind history is the record" (237). These apparently simple sentences, both of which express well-known Emersonian truisms, lay the groundwork for the theory of self-creation that takes shape throughout the *First Series*.[17] It is precisely because there is one mind that we can begin to read the record of history at all. Reading, then, becomes an identificatory process, a kind of identification of ourselves with the one mind, or, say, a recognition of ourselves through and as that one mind. As the record of the one mind, the writing of history then is not simply the cataloguing of events or facts, any more than the reading of history would be the grasping or comprehending of such a catalogue. Instead, history becomes a medium in which we find ourselves through the processes of reading and writing, or, as Emerson puts it, "The advancing man discovers how deep a property he has in literature,—in all fable as well as in all history."[18] The fact that Emerson refuses to distinguish between fable and history is simply one more indication that the essay is less about history per se than about reading and writing. If as we advance we learn that we have a deep property in such activities, then it is precisely because they are proper to us, the means through which we define ourselves.

If, however, Emerson does not more straightforwardly entitle the essay "Reading," then it is perhaps because the reading process itself marks our advent in history. To say we find ourselves in history is not precisely accurate insofar as finding implies that a self already exists, perhaps in the same way that history implies a past that exists. If everything already has sense in it, if we already exist as particulars identical with the one mind, then history in a sense is a meaningless term. But just as Emerson insists, in an uncanny anticipation of Nietzsche, that "all inquiry into antiquity... is the desire to do away this wild savage and preposterous There or Then, and introduce in its place the Here and Now" (241), so, too, as the essay continues, it elaborates a theory of reading in which the self, far from already existing, comes into being as it reads. This idea is made explicit early in the essay: "So all that is said of the wise man by Stoic, or oriental or modern essayist, describes to each reader his own idea, describes his unattained but attainable self. All literature writes the character of the wise man. Books, monuments, picture, conversation, are portraits in which he finds the lineaments he is forming" (239). Perhaps the most notable feature of this passage is the ambiguity of the pronouns. In the simplest sense, the passage would seem to be saying that the essayist merely describes himself in his representation of the wise man, but this construction contradicts Emerson's entire drift in "History." We are to esteem ourselves the text, and books the commentary. In fact, the grammar of the sentence allows that in the representation of the wise man, the idea to which Emerson refers may belong both to the essayist and to the reader, so that in either case the identificatory nature of reading alluded to in the opening paragraph of the essay is here confirmed. The shifting pronouns that govern the double sense of this passage thus indicate a kind of process or interaction in which it is impossible to tell whose ideas are whose. Far from being the passive absorption of "material," reading becomes an active experiential encounter defined precisely by the slippages between text and reader. It is in our reading of the other's text that we form an idea—literally, an image—not of what we are, if we are indeed anything, but of what we might become. Yet it is impossible to say where that image originates.

Let me take this a little further. When Emerson says that all literature writes the character of the wise man, he may simply be suggesting that the task of literature is to depict wisdom. But surely he is working as well with a kind of pun on the etymological meaning of "character" as a written thing. Originally in the Greek, "character" designated a stylus, and by extension from the active to passive voice, the marks it makes, as for example in the contemporary sense of the "characters" of the alphabet. But the word was also extended to mean distinguishing characteristic, as that which marks one. It is only later, perhaps with Aristotle's *Rhetoric*, that the meaning of "character" extends itself still further, coming to mean not only that which typifies but also that unique interior state or quality that makes one who one is and no other. It is an etymological history that implicitly defines one's characteristic—or, in Emersonian terms, "representative"—self as a written, constructed thing. The written nature of the self is furthered with the final sentence of the paragraph in which reading provides "a portrait in which he [the reader] finds the lineaments he is forming" (239). In this sense,

Emerson's insistence that literature writes the character of the wise man is equivalent to the statement that the reading of literature creates or gives birth to character. More specifically, we might say that in our acts of reading, we author or script the lines of the text of our future selves.

The corollary, of course, is that until we learn how to read history properly, we do not properly exist as characters. As Emerson writes in the opening paragraph, "Who hath access to this universal mind is a party to all that is or can be done" (237). Prior to the reading that gives access to this mind, we are evidently limited. We cannot do what can be done. And what can be done, in the terms of the essay, is always something constructed, be it the building of architectural monuments, the writing of literary texts, the making of sculptures, or the making of men. We are to identify ourselves precisely with such activities, not necessarily in the specific sense but more generally as activities involving the construction of things. As we do so, as we learn to read history aright, we identify with those figures who occupy the historical record, not with their creations per se but with their creative activity, just as in "The American Scholar." The implication is that once we begin reading, we pass from some natural chronology—say, history conceived as a mere transcription or record of what we already are, as mere repetition of the one mind—into a perpetual self-construction, the writing of our own characters. This form of self-creation differs from brute chronology or repetition precisely in its reference to that nonhistorical point, the one mind. It duplicates the one mind, but with a difference, the difference being just that consciousness of itself as a form of the one mind. If we manage this passage, then our "annals" would be "broader and deeper," as the end of the essay has it, and "we would trulier express our central and wide-related nature, instead of this old chronology of selfishness and pride" (256). The shift from the attained to the attainable self as it occurs in the reading and writing of history, which is nothing other than the reading and writing of ourselves, thus marks the difference between prehistorical and historical being.

It is here that the connection between self-creation and reading becomes explicit for the first time, and in essence, it is rhetoric that forms the nexus. This is the nexus that will become so crucial for the later pragmatism of William James, Charles Peirce, and Richard Rorty.[19] The self is not something there and given, but rather something arrived at interpretively, or, more precisely, a text that is always giving birth to itself through its interpretive acts. Our concerns for the moment, however, are more immediate, especially in the way that "History" lays out the central principles that will inform "Self-Reliance." In the first place, it suggests that the activity of self-creation is to be understood and undertaken as a form of reading, that is, under the guise of letters. To say so, of course, brings us close to Cavell's understanding of what he calls "Emersonian perfectionism." Cavell in fact deploys the above passage about our unattained but attainable selves as the centerpiece of his very persuasive argument about what constitutes that perfectionism. His agenda entails assimilating Emerson to a philosophical tradition of moral perfectionism that extends from Plato to Wittgenstein, with particular attention to Kant. Cavell lists no less than twenty-eight characteristic features of philosophical texts that participate in such a tradition. Essentially, however, moral perfectionism involves a process in which the self transforms itself for the better with the help of an Other, a transformation, which, in turn, prepares for larger social change as well. According to Cavell's reading, Emerson's work falls into this category not simply because of the emphasis on transformation and upbuilding but also because Emerson's text presents itself as that Other making such transformations possible. Thus the modern essayist in the passage quoted above is Emerson himself. In this respect, Emerson is presenting his own text as the path by which we each, in our reading, begin to move toward our future or unattained selves. Were it possible to quote Cavell's entire commentary on Emerson I would do so, since it informs at every step what I wish to do here. But here is a representative passage:

> Emerson's turn is to make my partiality itself the sign and incentive of my siding with the next or further self, which means siding against my attained perfection (or conformity), sidings which require the recognition of an other—the acknowledgement of a relationship—in which the sign is manifest. Emerson does not much attempt to depict such a relationship (film may call it marriage, philosophers have usually called it friendship), but the sense I seek to clarify is that Emerson offers his writing as representing this other for his reader.[20]

For Cavell, Emersonian perfectionism is that movement whereby one achieves a new identity—for within any perfectionism, identity is not something one has, but something to be attained—by rejecting one's former self. One does so by reading a sign of one's future self in the text of the Other.

Cavell's interpretation differs from most kinds of reader-response theories in that his interest lies neither in determining the universal operations of the text that enlist the participation of some generic reader nor even in the more psychologized version of American reader-response theory. Instead he focuses more pointedly on what might be Emerson's hopes for both the individual words of his text and each reader. The idea that the text requires the reader's completion and at the same time completes the reader is by no means new. One might think of Roland Barthes's *S/Z* as a primary example, but one need not take any Gallic detours to arrive at similar constructions of the relation between reader and text. Arthur Danto, for example, in an article fittingly entitled "Philosophy As/And/Of Literature," suggests thinking of the literary text in general as a kind of mirror:

> Each work of literature shows in this sense an aspect we would not know were ours without benefit of that mirror: each discovers, in the eighteenth-century meaning of the term, an unguessed dimension of the self. It is a mirror less in passively returning an image than in transforming the self-consciousness of the reader who in virtue of identifying with the image recognizes what he is. Literature is in this sense transfigurative.[21]

What interests me about both Cavell and Danto is that even as they open up the possibility that reading might become constitutive of the self, they tend to ignore precisely how the relation between reader and text works. In a later section, I will suggest that one of the reasons for this evasion has to do with the fact that the relation between reader and text in Emerson itself lies beyond representability, such that one can speak neither of a reader nor a text, but only of relation. That this undoing of the subject and the text is also the foreclosure of the tradition of moral perfectionism about which Cavell speaks must wait for later consideration.[22]

Indeed, as Cavell says, Emerson himself does not much represent that relationship, except to designate it as a form of reading, and one must wonder about the vagueness of the word. What precisely does it mean to say that the self authors itself by way of an encounter with the text of the Other? It is surely appropriate that Emerson calls such an encounter "letters," but as we move from conceptualization to rhetoric, we are also moving from the simple opposition between reader and text, subject and object, to a more complex kind of relation. This is implicit in Cavell's argument, although he never states it as such, an absence revealed in his diffidence about how Emerson's text attracts us to itself in the first place and how we actually then go about moving from our attained to unattainable self. Nonetheless, Cavell provides an important starting point, for if the Emersonian text is to perform the work that he attributes to it, it begins to function more like another subject in its own right—Lacan would say as a subject of desire—than like a static entity waiting to be grasped. Moreover, the fact that the self comes to itself only through the detour of the Other implies a self always other than itself, or at least elsewhere from itself. Indeed, if the Emersonian text were no more than a mirror reflecting a given and fixed subject, then one would be wholly on the ground of early speculative idealism. Although at times Emerson does seem to remain on this ground, the transformative work he posits for his text situates him neither as a philosopher nor purely as a rhetorician. His work does not seek to posit our preconditions, nor, properly speaking, to persuade us of anything. Persuasion, however, will remain at the forefront; Emerson then is a rhetorician with a difference. In other words, the Emersonian project of letters can no longer be formulated simply as the opposition between philosophy and rhetoric. A third term is necessary, and once we are talking about persuasion, about intersubjective relations, or about the absence of subjectivity perhaps implied by desire itself, that term must be psychology.

ALIENATED MAJESTIES: BEYOND REPRESENTATION

"Self-Reliance" indeed begins by positing a psychological self, but also and first with what we already know in at least several senses. Not only is it Emerson's most widely read essay, the centerpiece of his work (and, therefore, in a sense, the least readable of his works), but also it returns us as well to the problem of the subject present to itself. It does so by reminding us of what we already are. Here is the inescapable beginning:

> I read the other day some verses written by an eminent painter which were original and not conventional. The soul always hears an admonition in such lines, let the subject be what it may. The sentiment they instil is of more value than any thought they may contain. To believe your own thought, to believe what is true for you in your private heart is true for all men,—that is genius. Speak your latent conviction, and it shall be the universal sense; for the inmost in due time becomes the outmost,—and our first thought is rendered back to us by the trumpets of the Last Judgment.... A man should learn to detect and watch that gleam of light which flashes across his mind from within, more than the lustre of the firmament of bards and sages. Yet he dismisses without notice his thought, because it is his.[23]

Note first the prevalent images informing this paragraph. Emphasis falls overwhelmingly on vision and speech. Emerson begins by reading verses written by a painter, with words created by a maker of images. The very opening of the essay deals with the visual as it coincides with language. This pattern repeats itself when Emerson concludes with the idea of learning to detect, that is, to see as if from the outside, the gleam of light that flashes from within. A flash is something that we might simply see or fail to see, but once we have detected it, it is recognized thought, something we might formulate in language. Both of these statements, in turn, approximate the idea that the inmost should become the outmost when we speak. What is inmost is precisely what is not spoken, and therefore perhaps no more than an image, if that. By wording or speaking the image, inmost becomes outmost. Language is thus linked with representation in a way that the merely visible is not. Vision and speech here are united in the sense that speech posits or represents that which is as yet merely latent or invisible from the outside, a point that bears also on Emerson's repeated injunctions throughout the essay that we do our work. Emerson's other favorite word for work is vocation—the acts through which we make manifest what otherwise was undone or unspoken.[24]

The passage from latent to manifest is also the passage from private to public, but before one can understand how that passage occurs, it is important to note just how Emerson positions himself in order to get underway. In one sense he would seem to be announcing, here at the beginning of an essay that Nietzsche might have titled "How One Becomes What One Is," that he is working well within the Cartesian tradition of subjectivity. For surely that gleam of light flashing across from within is akin to Descartes's natural light, and if Emerson chooses to represent this as a gleam or flash, then it is perhaps simply to underscore the instantaneous nature of the cogito.[25] Emerson thus opens the essay with the inaugural moment of the subject itself, with the whole question of how the self gets started, and he does so at least in part on the Cartesian model, of the auto-foundation or auto-positioning of a subject presenting itself to itself as consciousness. We should remember that the Cartesian subject only knows that he exists, only confirms the cogito, when he pronounces it to himself, and this is very much part of the pattern of Emerson's essay.[26] The visual is exactly that which, paradoxically, is not represented except as spoken. Thought and speech alone constitute the means by which we present ourselves to ourselves, both in the opening paragraph and throughout the essay. In a central passage Emerson tells us that when his genius calls, he "would write on the lintels of the door-post, *Whim*," a word already inscribed with an etymological history that goes back to "wandering with one's eyes." But "whim" is not simply that internal state allowing one to do as one pleases. It is also a word marking that state. Similarly, when Emerson gets around to asking on what precisely are we to ground our reliance, his well-known answer is a "primary wisdom" called "Intuition." Intuition of course means "to look upon," and were that insufficient, it is nothing other than intuition that furnishes Descartes with the originary act of auto-foundation, wherein he formulates his doubt and thereby knows himself to exist.[27] Like the Cartesian subject who poses before himself by speaking himself, the Emersonian subject begins by trying or wanting to be the subject of representation. What is at issue, or seems to be, is why we let others steal from us that unseen gleam or flash with which we might have illuminated ourselves to ourselves in the first place.

Perhaps, however, the question is less how we have lost something than the possibility of obscurity present in the language of flashes and gleams from the beginning. If the visual here marks precisely what remains unrepresented, then it is because the flash from within can illuminate. But it can also eclipse sight; hence the mystical idea of the "black sun." The light by which the invisible becomes visible is itself invisible in this paragraph. This structure also underlies Emerson's emphasis on speaking one's latent thoughts. In both instances the idea is that there is something we are doing all the time—say, thinking—that nonetheless escapes us. We evidently have latent thoughts and regularly send gleams of light abroad from within, but we do not know it; that is, we do not represent it to ourselves, mediate it in graspable form. In this respect, "Self-Reliance" is less an essay about what we do not have than a description of what we do or are all the time without being aware of it. For just this reason, as David Van Leer has persuasively suggested, the obstacles to self-reliance are merely impossibilities. Consistency may be the hobgoblin of little minds, but properly speaking, a self that is a self at all cannot "consist." Consistency simply implies nonbeing.[28] The idea that self-reliance is a version of the self-existence of the self also helps to explain the shift that occurs about midway through the essay, where Emerson moves from his admonitions about why we fail ourselves to more fatalistic statements about what we are. He writes, "I suppose no man can violate his own nature"; or "A character is like an acrostic or Alexandrian stanza; read it forward, backward, or across, it still spells the same thing."[29]

Let us not forget, however, that we remain acrostics, puzzles to ourselves. The weight of the opening paragraph remains on the latent and the invisible. It could not be otherwise, for as soon as the self is understood as representational consciousness, as the image wherein we appear to and speak ourselves, the largest portion of our activity will become, as Nietzsche concluded again and again, invisible, or unconscious. It is on this basis that Lacan, for example, can insist upon the thread that connects the Cartesian and the Freudian subjects.[30] In any case, the opening paragraph begins in paradox. On the one hand, as long as the subject remains the subject of representation, it is bound to seek after an image of itself. On the other hand, every such desire, be it for the clear and distinct, or for the inmost to become the outmost, proves only the existence of another place where we are not, that is, the place where things are latent, unrepresented, and, it may be in some sense, unrepresentable.

What Emerson sets up, then, in the first paragraph of the essay is, properly speaking, not simply a philosophical self, not simply the centered, transcendental, absolute "I think" of the cogito, but rather a cogito that thinks me—a psychological self divided into the light of representational consciousness and the other of the unconscious.[31] The central interpretive problem of the essay hinges on how one construes Emerson's stance toward this subject that is split between the known and the unknown, the seen and the unseen, the represented and the unrepresentable, which in turn, bears on the matter of self-reliance as the self-evidence of the self. This ambiguity reaches its most intense pitch in the famous sentences following the passage quoted above: "A man should learn to detect and watch that gleam of light which flashes across his mind from within, more than the lustre of the firmament of bards and sages. Yet he dismisses without notice his thought, because it is his. In every work of genius we recognize our own rejected thoughts: they come back to us with a certain alienated majesty."[32] Typically, these lines are read as stating the central problem the essay seeks to solve, and therefore, as an admonition to reappropriate one's rejected thoughts, retrieving them from their alienation in the Other. To do so would be to reclaim all that is latent, unconscious, and invisible into the light of representational consciousness: "Wo Es war, soll Ich werden."

As such, the idea of alienated majesty underpins nearly all readings of the essay as a whole, that is, all of the readings in which the soul of Emersonian individualism takes shape. Do not reject your own thoughts, rely on yourself, on no other, or, as the epigraph has it, "Ne te quaesiveris extra." One might object that when Emerson later complains, "Man is timid and apologetic; he is no longer upright; he dares not say 'I think,' 'I am,'" (270), he would seem to be equating achieved self-reliance with the transcendental auto-foundation of a Cartesian cogito. We may think, and exist, but we dare not say it. I want to return to these lines later, but for the moment, it is sufficient to say that read in the light of representational consciousness, the essay has one task: its goal would seem to be to teach us how to become conscious of our latent thoughts by representing them to ourselves, by consciously making them our own and voicing them rather than waiting for them to return through the Other.

Perhaps, then, Emerson is being careless when he gets started in this same paragraph with the words, "I read." And one must wonder why, when Emerson has been so careful from "The American Scholar" onward to distinguish his idea of thinking from the representational conceptualization of modern philosophy, he would now, in his central essay, attempt to rescue a divided subject precisely as the unified subject presenting itself to itself. The very lines, however, that seem to enjoin us to reappropriate our rejected thoughts point in a different direction when we remember that if the only way in which we know ourselves is through a representation of ourselves, that is, by a kind of posing ourselves before ourselves, then alienated majesty comes to define not the problem but the necessary state of affairs from the start. In this respect, alienated majesty marks the primary instance of the self-existence of the self, a description of what we are doing all the time without being conscious of it. There is, however, one key distinction here: in the instance of alienated majesty, one finds the additional suggestion that without the Other, one cannot get started at all. If I did not first read my thoughts in the text of the Other, I would simply have no thoughts of which to be aware. I could hardly be said to exist.

Properly speaking, then, my relation to the Other becomes the inaugural moment of subjectivity, for what Emerson is suggesting in this opening paragraph is that the imperative of self-consciousness, the auto-foundation of the self, always and only occurs in the act of reading the text of the Other. There is no question of short-circuiting alienation, for without exteriorizing itself first, thought necessarily remains latent and invisible. Why, after all, according to Emerson, do we reject our own thoughts in the first place? Simply, "because they are ours," as if one's own thought is, by definition, always rejected, always elsewhere.[33] That is why those thoughts, whether dismissed or repressed, reappear as the thought of or in the work of genius, the work of the Other. If this were all, we would say that alienated majesty is at once the problem and the solution—a problem so long as it remains an unconscious identification with the text of the Other, and a solution insofar as we recognize that Other as ourselves, even if we first need that Other as a medium in which to collect ourselves. Read, however, against "History," Emerson's apparent chagrin in "Self-Reliance" becomes puzzling. Like "History," "Self-Reliance" is very much an essay about becoming ourselves, but the reading process that oriented that project in "History" seems here to have gone awry. In the earlier essay, the emphasis falls on precisely this apparently dialectical process of reading the text of ourselves through the commentary of others, and there is no anxiety on Emerson's part about the question of to whom the thoughts belong. The example is the gothic cathedral which "affirms that it was done by us, and not done by us. Surely it was by man, but we find it not in our man but ... we put ourselves into the place and state of the builder."[34] Once we have done so, once we have identified ourselves in it, we, too, are builders, both of the cathedral and of ourselves. This is simply to say that it would be impossible to read any work of genius if the thoughts were not ours to begin with, and we discover it experientially. This is why Emerson insists in "History" that "every mind must know the whole lesson for itself,—must go over the whole ground. What it does not see, what it does not live, it will not know" (240). If the lesson were not we ourselves to begin with, then we could not see or live it at all. History would be no more than "a dull book." If it is otherwise, then it is because the text we read is both ours and not ours, just as the thoughts that return to us in alienated majesty belong to us and do not belong to us.[35] In "History," however, the mediations of reading simply "remed[y] the defect of our too great nearness to ourselves." In "Self-Reliance," this remedy would seem to become the illness. We are not too close, but rather too far from ourselves.

Why the reader in "History" should be any less alienated than the one in "Self-Reliance" is not at all clear, and yet, the tone of "Self Reliance" is unmistakably admonitory, even as its opening paragraph rehearses all that "History" so calmly asserted. In order to understand this difference we need to understand more precisely what Emerson means by reading, and what he means changes somewhat in the space between the two essays. As Emerson remarks toward the close of "History," "I will not now go behind the general statement to explore the reason of this correspondency [between ourselves and what we read]. Let it suffice, that in the light of these two facts, namely, that the mind is One, and that nature is its correlative, history is to be read and written."[36] In short, Emerson has done no more than to state the mimetic nature of the relation between reader and text, without explaining why that relation occurs as it does. Moreover, it can hardly matter to whom the thoughts belong if they all proceed anyway from the One Mind. The first essay would seem to deal with reading that is a kind of reflective mimesis that works on a specular model. History is simply a mirror for us—one we must recognize as such. Such a construction assumes that the task of Emersonian reading remains always to return us to ourselves as a kind of representation, which is, in turn, a representation of the One Mind. Despite the emphasis on an attainable or future self, reading as presented in "History" implies a preexistent self that must simply be brought back to itself, in which case, one would have to ask if Emerson himself were not siding with all of the philosophers from whom elsewhere he wishes to distance himself. Moreover, it is hard to understand why a self that already exists would need the text of the Other in the first place, why such a subject would subject itself in this way.

I think Emerson himself raises precisely these questions at the close of "History." Having steadily asserted that history is nothing but a mirror, he abruptly asks, "Is there somewhat overweening in this claim? Then I reject all I have written, for what is the use of pretending to know what we know not? But it is the fault of our rhetoric that we cannot strongly state one fact without seeming to belie some other. I hold our actual knowledge very cheap" (256). Emerson's strategy here is to shift the frame of reference, to remind us that even as we read history, we read his essay, and that as such, we have been engaged in an active interpretive and self-creative encounter with his text. That encounter may be mimetic insofar as we find ourselves in that text, but it is before all of that, rhetorical: if we have found ourselves in the mirror of Emerson's text, then it is because his rhetoric has persuaded us to do so, not because we have "understood" the essay and, thereby, ourselves. In this sense, we do not appear before we read, any more than the meaning of the text appears after we read; we are constituted in our relation to it. As the passage jolts the reader back to the realization that he or she does not finally know what the text means, the register of meaning is itself made problematic, and doubly so, because Emerson himself claims not to know what he means. Whose thoughts would here be emerging? Mine? The text's? These questions cannot be answered, because in point of fact, no thoughts are emerging at all, thus suspending the priority of both text and reader. Emerson's rhetorical punctuation of what he calls "fact," which is nothing other than what we conceive our own interpretation to be, cancels any kind of representational or mimetic logic, or at least calls it into question, for as the last sentence of the passage indicates, rhetoric exceeds and betrays representation. The moment that it states a fact, represents something, it is wrong. Its strength is its very slipperiness and changeability. Not only, however, is it changeable but also it operates independently of any "message" it may convey, even when that message seems to mime the reader. In a sense, rhetoric as here conceived does no more than to operate a passage, one without origin or destination. This suggests that Emersonian reading consists less in the stability of a specular mimetic relation and more in the uncertain and almost unspecifiable draw of rhetoric itself, a draw in which it is no longer quite clear whether meaning resides in the text, in the reader, or in both and neither.

Such issues reorient Emerson in "Self-Reliance." When our thoughts come back to us with alienated majesty, when "we are forced to take with shame our own opinion from another,"[37] we do not speak our latent conviction, another speaks it for us, speaks us. And why is this the case? Oddly enough, because the Other always seems to mean more than we do. No sooner does Emerson report that our thoughts return with alienated majesty than he adds, "Great works of art have no more affecting lesson for us than this. They teach us to abide by our spontaneous impression with good-humored inflexibility then most when the whole cry of voices is on the other side. Else, tomorrow a stranger will say with masterly good sense precisely what we have thought and felt all the time" (259). Given the position of the first sentence, the most affecting lesson may be that of alienated majesty, or it may be the apparent lesson of self-reliance: abide by your spontaneous impression. In fact, there is no difference between the two. We are to abide specifically by our impression, that is, by what impresses us, what comes back or on to us from the outside, and yet, as the passage continues, that "outside" escapes thematization and so cannot strictly speaking be named. If that impression differs from all of the voices "on the other side," then it is perhaps because those voices, unlike the "rhetoric" at the close of "History," can be located somewhere and convey a thought. But we have already been told that the sentiment that a text instills is more important than any thought it might contain, which is perhaps just another way of saying that our spontaneous impression is precisely a matter of feeling, of affect. For this reason the lesson of which Emerson speaks is "affecting." It is what draws us to it, influences us, disposes us in a certain way, and attaches us to it, without, in the least voicing itself as a particular thought, as a representation. In one sense, this passage anticipates the open question between truth and love that Emerson raises at the close of "Intellect." Reading is no longer a specular or mimetic circuit wherein we encounter the truth, but rather it is a matter of being affected by an Other. Here that affect is no longer grounded by the mythical authority of the One Mind. If we are attracted to the work of art, then it is not because that work presents us with a truth, or represents the One Mind, but rather because the work seems to exert a kind of power over us, to affect us in this way. It draws us into a process that can no longer be assimilated to a specular or mimetic model, unless of course we wish to call reading affective mimesis. In what does such a process consist? Nothing other than identification. What we think and feel all along, the Other thinks and feels all along, and it is no accident that this identification proceeds through how the Other "speaks." The implication is that the rhetorical effects of the text, of its speaking, are precisely affective. Conversely, it implicates affect itself as rhetorical effect. We are bound to the text, identified by and in it, because we desire it, and we desire it because of its rhetorical power over us. It is just this strange power that fuels Emerson's admonitory tone at the opening of "Self-Reliance."

But why does this Other affect me? What makes me desire it, or, to use Emerson's word, receptive to it in the first place? How does it achieve rhetorical power over me? I am not sure these questions can be answered at this point. Indeed, we are left in the opening paragraph of "Self-Reliance" with anything but the certainty of clear and distinct ideas. On the one hand,

Emerson would seem to want us to learn to make the latent manifest, the invisible visible, but on the other hand, the whole notion of affectivity, which is the very suggestibility or receptivity that Emerson everywhere emphasizes, resists the sort of reappropriation implied in the passage from invisible to visible or spoken. Rhetoric and affectivity consistently cancel representational meaning in Emerson. I think that this is a genuine impasse in much of his work, first because a purely rhetorical reading, independent of any thematic "content" would be impossible, but also because Emerson himself seems to want his readers to do a great many things at once, specifically in the sense of the transitional activities I mentioned earlier. The actual workings of an Emersonian essay consistently, if one can say so, evade the straightforward exposition of discursive thought. That evasion is, as I have been suggesting, their central dynamic. Yet if there is nothing but such a dynamic, then the essays become unreadable. To understand the rhetorical maneuvers within any given essay more fully, then, would itself involve a kind of detour through an Other, that is, a reflection through a discourse that lies outside of the Emersonian essay itself. Without this detour, we would have nothing but the oscillations of our own encounter with the text in a close reading that would remain in constant and, therefore, incomprehensible transition.

NOTES

1. Brewer, 524.

2. Emerson, "Self-Reliance," *EEL*, 271.

3. Emerson, "Intellect," *EEL*, 417.

4. Ibid., 426. Already here we can see that the effects of eloquence, literally our hearing, and therefore passive reception, of the Other's words, removes limits of the self. Once this is the case, the listener would, of course, neither be able to represent himself to himself nor to thematize the source of his reception.

5. *Genesis*, 32:17–30.

6. Zornberg, 230.

7. Ibid., 234–35.

8. *Genesis* 32:28–29.

9. Given the passivity that emerges as central to Emersonian receptivity, it is interesting that Zornberg accentuates both Jacob's concern with control over his experience and the way in which he must eventually learn to relinquish such control (217–30).

10. De Tocqueville, II:3.

11. Emerson, "Intellect," *EEL*, 427.

12. *Corinthians I* 13:1–2.

13. Emerson, "Friendship," *EEL*, 341.

14. Emerson, "History," *EEL*, 247.

15. Emerson, "Intellect," *EEL*, 427.

16. Emerson, "History," *EEL*, 237.

17. In "History," the One Mind still appears to have the mythical status of an origin that the One Man has in "The American Scholar." As I suggest later, however, the theory of reading sketched in "Self-Reliance" demythologizes the One Mind by doing away with origins altogether. If there is One Mind, then it would only be in the sense that we can no longer tell where our ideas, and, indeed, our very subjectivity, originate at all.

18. Emerson, "History," *EEL*, 250.

19. In James's and in Rorty's works, the importance of rhetoric and belief carry the weight of what Emerson calls reading; in both cases, they are the means through which we create and recreate ourselves. In Peirce, this connection is perhaps less clear, but as Walter Benn Michaels has shown, Peirce, too, declares the subject/object problem false and replaces it with the idea that the self is an interpretation and performs interpretations; put otherwise, reading is constitutive of the self, and readers are therefore constituted (Michaels, 185–200).

20. Cavell, *Conditions*, 31–32. In terms of the passage from "History" on which Cavell's interpretation depends, moral perfectionism does seem to ground Emerson's project. The concept of receptivity, however, as developed in "Self-Reliance" is the very undoing of moral perfectionism if such perfectionism is seen to require a particular Other as a guide. The whole point of receptivity, as I suggest in the next sections, is to undo any thematizable source of reception.

21. Danto, 79.

22. In "The Politics of Interpretation," an essay that predates the Emerson material in *Conditions*, Cavell intriguingly suggests in passing that reading in general is nothing other than our transference to the text (52–54). Provocative as this idea is, Cavell never specifies what he means by transference, although overall, he seems to assimilate it to an idea of seduction as instruction. In *Conditions*, the idea of transference to the text is implicit throughout, a link that underscores the instructional nature of the transference as Cavell formulates it earlier. I would say, however, that seduction is probably the more important dimension in Emerson, and since we are dealing with texts, its seductions can only occur rhetorically, an idea that Cavell does not develop. In the following sections, I take up this question of how the text might seduce us, and why it does so by formulating transference in a quite specific way, a way that precludes instruction in any straightforward sense. This is perhaps only to suggest that therapy need not be instructive in the usual sense of the word.

23. Emerson, "Self-Reliance," *EEL*, 259.

24. "Vocation" is, of course, literally, a calling, that which singles me out as most precisely myself. This sense of vocation as calling will become particularly important in "Experience" as that which institutes my responsibility. But it is equally the case in "Self-Reliance" that "vocation," a call of which neither the origin nor the destination can be specified, remains a highly charged word.

25. So far we would be well within the classical phenomenological reduction for which the cogito provides the initial model. If this provides the starting point, however, then Emerson will diverge wholly from this model as rhetoric comes to replace any possibility of representation.

26. Here is Descartes in the second Meditation: "I am, I exist, is necessarily true every time that I pronounce it or conceive it in my mind" (24). This makes quite clear the link between thought and representation.

27. "I would not doubt in any way what the light of nature made me see to be true, just as it made me see, a little while ago, that from the fact that I doubted I could conclude that I existed" (Descartes, 37).

28. Van Leer, 128–31.

29. Emerson, "Self-Reliance," *EEL*, 265–66.

30. "Freud's method is Cartesian—in the sense that he sets out from the basis of the subject of certainty" (Lacan, *Four Fundamental Concepts*, 35).

31. For Freud, this opposition is really nonoppositional, since everything finally must be reduced to the light of representational consciousness or consigned to oblivion. Take, for example, the relation between the drives and their representatives: "Even in the unconscious, moreover, an instinct cannot be represented otherwise than by an idea. If the instinct did not attach itself to an idea or manifest itself as an affective state, we could know nothing about it" ("The Unconscious," *Standard Edition*, 14:122). (Hereafter the *Standard Edition* is referred to as *SE*.)

32. Emerson, "Self-Reliance," *EEL*, 259.

33. In a curious way, Emerson anticipates the Freudian notion of primary repression, an act that technically occurs before there is anything to be repressed.

34. Emerson, "Self-Reliance," *EEL*, 241.

35. Cavell notes this feature of Emersonian reading as well and adds, "to think otherwise, to attribute the origin of my thoughts simply to the other, thoughts which are then, as it were, implanted in me—some would say caused—by let us say some Emerson, is idolatry" (*Conditions*, 57). This may be the case, but at the same time, as I suggest in the next chapter, because the source of the thoughts cannot be thematized, there is a necessary moment in the reading process in which thoughts do indeed seem to be implanted in us.

36. Emerson, "History," *EEL*, 255.

37. Emerson, "Self-Reliance," *EEL*, 259.

KERRY LARSON

Justice to Emerson

> Justice is not postponed. A perfect equity adjusts its balance in all parts
> of life. The dice of God are always loaded. The world looks like a
> multiplication table, or a mathematical equation, which, turn it how you
> will, balances itself. Take what figure you will, its exact value, nor more
> nor less, still returns to you. Every secret is told, every crime is punished,
> every virtue rewarded, every wrong redressed, in silence and certainty.
>
> —Emerson,"Compensation"

W hen, over the course of his lifetime, Emerson singled out certain
institutions or practices and called them unjust, we do not find his action
strange or unexpected. We do not think it odd for him to welcome the
abolition of slavery in the West Indies and to speak out for its elimination
elsewhere; we do not think him foolish or self-deceived when protesting the
forcible removal of the Cherokee people from their land by the U.S.
government. It is not hard to understand why he should be alarmed at the
unchecked growth of the division of labor in modern society nor is it difficult
to explain his position against the war in Mexico. Some have questioned
Emerson's depth of commitment in taking up these and other causes, while
others have wondered why, in speaking against certain forms of oppression,
he remained silent on others. Still, without turning the man into a saint, it

From *Raritan* 21, no. 3 (Winter 2002). © 2002 by *Raritan: A Quarterly Review*.

seems reasonable to infer from even this quick list of examples that Emerson retained a conception of justice more or less comparable to that of many other citizens of his time—or to that of our own, for that matter.

On the other hand, when Emerson talks about justice in more abstract terms, one's reaction is likely to be bafflement, suspicion, or even disgust. The topic seems to bring out the worst in him. His serene assurance that "every calamity will be dissolved in the universal sunshine" has long been a source of inspiration for satirists. Melville, one of the first, goaded by this seemingly mindless optimism, got it right when he hit upon the name of Mark Winsome for the transcendental hustler lampooned in *The Confidence-Man*. For all his emphasis on the need to provoke, to unsettle, and to transgress, a certain cosmic complacency insinuates itself into much of Emerson's writing. Pronouncements to the effect that "in the soul of man there is a justice whose retributions are instant and entire," that in fact there is "a rapid intrinsic energy work[ing] everywhere, righting wrongs [and] correcting appearances," surpass, in their glibness, even the most pious platitudes of some of Emerson's fellow Victorians. Justice to Emerson is evidently something given rather than sought after, a necessary and ongoing feature of the world rather than a goal to achieve. Not surprisingly, many have wondered whether this faith in the inevitable presence of justice does not mask an indifference to justice altogether. That is certainly the point behind Melville's sketch of Mark Winsome, whose inane remarks on "the latent benignity of that beautiful creature, the rattlesnake" soon evolve into chilling fantasies over "the joyous life of a perfectly instinctive, unscrupulous, and irresponsible creature," its "whole beautiful body one iridescent scabbard of death." If, in the history of negative opinion on Emerson, the charge of social irresponsibility has been predominant, the primary reason has been what many take to be Emerson's cavalier and unpardonably smug ideas about justice.

The apparent disconnection between Emerson's protests on behalf of social justice in real life and his more unreal notions about justice on the page does suggest one line of response. Perhaps these notions, when situated within the full range of topics and concerns engaged by Emerson's writings, are not all that significant or influential. Perhaps his religiosity and all the baggage that comes with it can be safely set aside so that we may go on to pursue other, more timely themes his work does address. Among Emerson's admirers, George Kateb has been the most explicit about pressing this view, arguing that the more transcendental Emerson can be "severed" from the secular prophet of democratic individualism that modern commentators are more likely to value. The glib theodicy that stands behind his ideas about justice, as well as an assortment of related metaphysical enthusiasms, "may not pose an insuperable obstacle," writes Kateb. "I would like to think," he adds, "that we can judge the problem of his religiousness as minor." And yet as Kateb's phrasing suggests, and as he would be the first to acknowledge, his account gives rise to as many questions as it lays to rest. And even if it didn't, his position does not challenge skepticism over Emerson's religiosity so much as it seeks to contain it. In the meantime, variations on the theme of Emerson's social irresponsibility show no sign of diminishing. In the past five years alone, a century and a half after Melville's novel, reports continue of his "barbarous idealism" (Sharon Cameron), his "rampant sentimentality" (Judith Shklar), and his "cruelty, eccentricity, and insularity" (Cornel West).

In what follows, I try to make sense of Emerson's apparent refusal to take justice seriously. I begin by showing that this refusal is more than just apparent, that in fact it derives from a deliberate rejection of standard preconceptions about what morality is or should be. Critics are right to suspect that Emerson cares little about the obligations of social justice. What they have been slow to see is that it is *their* justice he doesn't care for. Thus in essays like "Compensation" and "Spiritual Laws" he attacks conventional understandings of justice in the name of what he takes to be a more enlightened view, one drawn from the laws of compensation. And while it may seem as though these laws underwrite a justice that is in truth no justice at all, a closer reading of both essays shows that Emerson's motives for equating justice and compensation are neither perverse nor irresponsible. Far from evading social reality, Emerson's concept of morality, in all its otherworldliness, is nothing if not an attempt to cast off the mystifications of a conventional moralism that is itself judged to be hopelessly evasive. Far from betraying his interest in a self-reliant, democratic individualism, Emerson's appeals to a universal, unconditional justice are best understood as an effort to engage the needs and forestall the seductions of that individualism. This takes us in particular to his ideas about envy and its complicated relation to justice in democratic culture.

*   *   *

"Compensation" asks us to imagine the world and all that it contains as governed by a perpetual oscillation of antagonistic extremes. It starts with the assumption that "every thing in nature is made of one hidden stuff" and that it is an essential feature of this "stuff" to be constituted by division. "An inevitable dualism bisects nature," we are told at the outset, "so that each thing is a half, and suggests another thing to make it whole." The examples listed directly after this statement are not particularly helpful ("in, out; upper, under; motion, rest; yea, nay"), but the general idea that everything contains its opposite is clear enough. The further proposition is that because these opposites are in some sense symmetrical they offset each other. So, for example, "every excess causes a defect; every defect, an excess ... for every thing you have missed, you have gained something else; and for every thing you gain, you lose something." Where every action generates its equal and opposite reaction, "the varieties of conditions tend to equalize themselves." By compensation, then, Emerson has in mind a self-regulating system of offsetting polarities that "balances every gift and every defect."

Characteristically, Emerson's discussion freely runs together the natural and the human realms, refusing to draw a firm line between the two. He claims to see signs of compensation everywhere: from the laws of gravity to the evolution of plants and animals, from theories of mechanic forces to the precepts of human morality. Importantly, this "law of laws" is no more susceptible to human manipulation than it is owing to providential design. Compensation is written into the nature of things, a universal condition that can be neither accepted nor rejected. Since Emerson thinks that this compensatory pattern informs human nature as much as it does the laws of nature, the distinction between facts and values does not trouble his discussion (however much it may trouble some of his commentators). How things are and how we ought to behave are not, in his view, conflicting considerations; what lurks within the soul as a "sentiment," he tells us at one point, we recognize "outside us [as] a law." It is on this basis that Emerson declares "all things are moral."

But Emerson's interest in the moral significance of compensation does have a more specific application. By foregrounding features such as commensurability, proportion, balance, and, above all, a supreme disinterestedness, the essay reveals its true focus in the subject of justice. This is anticipated in the title, which calls to mind the plaintiff seeking compensation for damages, the worker just compensation for his labor, or the virtuous compensation for a lifetime of earnest sacrifice. Sorting out the world in terms of weighable equivalences ("Tit for tat; an eye for an eye; a tooth for a tooth; blood for blood; measure for measure; love for love"), Emerson's compensation indeed seems to approach something like the very quintessence of justice: universal, self-executing, and always secured. Scottish Common Sense philosophy, the dominant source of ethical reflection for Harvard Unitarians at the time, held that the capacity to discern right from wrong was an ingrained trait of human nature. Ethical knowledge or a "moral sense" was, in other words, innate. Emerson would seem to go this tradition one better, seeing justice as a natural and innate property not of minds but of the world at large. For him, the adage that "all things are moral" takes as its corollary the insistence that "justice is not postponed."

Emerson is so enamored of this theme that at the outset of the essay he reproaches a minister who preaches, unremarkably enough, that the virtuous shall find their reward in heaven while the wicked shall be punished. The minister's mistake, Emerson thinks, is to believe that "the bad are successful and that justice is not done now." Those who grasp the true import of compensation know, on the other hand, that "the world must be just."

To say that justice is somehow fated to occur here and now obviously flies in the face of standard conceptions of what justice is all about. Presumably, any system of ethics recognizes the centrality of an *evaluative* dimension; we use the terms "good" and "bad" to appraise possible states of affairs in the course of deciding which we ought or ought not to bring about. But Emerson's logic divorces judgment from justice by refusing to treat justice as the outcome of practical deliberation. Indeed, this logic does not simply make judgment irrelevant by making justice inevitable; it also makes a mockery of the very need to establish separate categories marking off the "good" from the "bad." In a world where every extreme attracts its opposite, such a project is doomed from the outset: "if the good is there, so is the evil; if the affinity, so the repulsion; if the force, so the limitation." The idea that unqualified good or unqualified evil attaches itself to human action becomes nonsensical. The sheer duality of things, coupled with "the universal necessity by which the whole appears wherever a part appears," is too ubiquitous and too intransigent for anyone to shave off one side of experience and retain the other. Those who seek to detach pain from pleasure or to divide the bad from the good are wasting their time, for "nature hates monopolies and exceptions." Another way of coming at the same point is to say that if we cannot grasp the whole neither can we escape it: "the parted water reunites behind our hand ... we can no more halve things and get the sensual good, by itself, than we can get an inside that shall have no outside, or a light without a shadow."

Anticipating the connection Nietzsche draws between the rise of modern morality and an exaggerated attachment to free will, Emerson's attack on moral evaluation is at bottom an attack on the notion that fairness falls within our power to control. Basing ethics on freedom of action shows a confusion of priorities, for "our moral nature is vitiated by any interference of our will." Emerson wants us to see that virtuous conduct follows from human flourishing and not the other way around: thus virtue for him is synonymous with "easy, simple, spontaneous action." No doubt the temptation to contrive moral outcomes to our liking—"to act partially, to sunder, to appropriate ... to get a *one end* without an *other end*"—is natural enough, but when this (futile) selectivity gets codified in the laws of church and state, the consequence is a vision of justice "chained to appearances."

Like the minister who promises eternal rewards in return for a lifetime of privation, worldly justice rests upon what amounts to a vulgar theory of compensation, a wishful misreading that tries to rig the system in order to eke out a net gain. And yet "there is always [some] vindictive circumstance stealing in at unawares"—always "this backstroke, this kick of the gun"—that renders such endeavors pointless and that makes conventional morality an encumbrance. In a reversal Emerson never wearied of performing throughout his writing career, it is the mundane, the everyday, the preeminently "practical" rhetoric of social justice that here gets exposed as facile, evasive, and convoluted, while it is the transcendental conception of nature's "stern Ethics" to which we must turn if we wish to derive a truly demystified understanding of what justice means.

Moreover, according to Emerson, this is an understanding that most people accept, albeit in a dim, semiconscious way. Cling as they will to the "superstitions" of "popular theology," people are "wiser than they know" and what they know are the laws of compensation. Pieties heard from the pulpit and greeted by automatic, unthinking acceptance are, when repeated on the street, met with silent disbelief. The point is not that good Christian folk are morally confused or hypocritical. It is, rather, that deeper than sanctioned morality runs a more enduring ethics, what the essay on "Circles" calls "the transcendentalism of common life" and what "Compensation" finds underlying the folk wisdom and folkways of that life. The "documents" from which this "doctrine" is drawn are "the tools in our hands, the bread in our basket, [and] the transactions in the street." Indeed, that "which the pulpit, the senate, and the college deny, is hourly preached in all markets and workshops by flights of proverbs, whose teaching is as true and as omnipresent as that of birds and flies." Although there are a number of source studies of the essay's main idea—Xenophon, Anaximander, Lucretius, and Montaigne are regularly cited—it is nevertheless worth noting that virtually all of the sources cited within the essay are nonphilosophical—proverbs, myths, literary fables, and observed behavior. Emerson takes himself to be elaborating less a philosophical treatise than something more akin to an ethnographic report, one responsive to the beliefs and desires of his readership.

As the reference to "the pulpit, the senate, and the college" suggests, Emerson's disenchantment with religious morality extends to other moralities in the public sphere. Liberalism, as a political philosophy, found its true voice in the seventeenth century when it started to speak a language of natural or subjective rights. Emerson, though considered by many to be, for better or for worse, America's premier exponent of liberal individualism, does not speak this language. He shuns talk of entitlement or obligation; he is not interested in telling people what's owed them or what they owe each other. Parting company from Lockean tradition, "Compensation" views labor as "one immense illustration" of the "absolute balance of Give and Take," not as the source for claims to ownership and to the battery of rights surrounding them. Indeed, the "knowledge and virtue" we derive from labor "cannot be counterfeited or stolen," for "the law of nature is, Do the thing, and you shall have the power [while] they who do not the thing have not the power." The drift of the discussion is to moot questions of security, the point being not to establish a right to something but to set such concerns aside as if they were of secondary importance. His enthusiasm for the rhetoric of natural rights is nicely summed up in a later essay when he deadpans: "we have as good a right, and the same sort of right to be here, as Cape Cod or Sandy Hook have to be there."

Emerson is of course notorious for his zeal in *abandoning* himself to a topic, of giving himself over to one side of a theme or issue and pushing it to extremes, only then to relinquish that emphasis and pursue a different or opposing perspective with equal exuberance. This tacking back and forth of statement and counterstatement, the stylistic enactment of compensation made vivid on the page, not only makes his prose seem engaged in a perpetual process of self-revision, but can also make it difficult to determine when Emerson is asserting a belief and when he is, so to speak, entertaining one. And his equally notorious distaste for logic and systematic thinking only underscores this difficulty. In "Compensation," as elsewhere, Emerson's declarations, in their headlong momentum and stark certainty, can at times take on the appearance of taunts (e.g., "you cannot wrong do without suffering wrong") as if daring us to confute them. How much should his reflections on a cosmic justice independent of human judgment be taken as a series of willful exaggerations—as an occasion for provocation rather than instruction, to recall one of his aphorisms? No one can doubt that he meant for us to take the idea of compensation seriously—it is too persistent and too entrenched throughout his writings, dominating other major essays such as "Circles" and "Fate," for us to think otherwise. But seriousness may assume different guises, the playful and the parodic included. In an essay whose opinions are at once so categorical and perverse, it's worth inquiring further into the nature and extent of the author's commitment to what he calls "the doctrine of compensation."

One way to get at this question is to turn to the second half of the essay, where Emerson pauses to consider one obvious objection to the theory he has been developing. Rehearsing the essay's main idea ("Every thing has two sides, a good and an evil. Every advantage has its tax"), he imagines some listeners recoiling at the moral nihilism of such a position. "The thoughtless say, on hearing these representations,—what boots it to do well?" In the zero-sum world of compensation, "if I gain any good, I must pay for it; if I lose any good, I gain some other." The conclusion is irresistible: "all actions are indifferent." When Emerson takes up a version of the same objection in "Circles," his attempted self-defense is brief and purposefully superficial ("I am only an experimenter. Do not set the least value on what I do"). In "Compensation," however, he is intent on developing a more extended response. Because some readers have suspected that Emerson backs away from the more radical implications of his "doctrine" at this point, this response is worth reviewing in further detail.

Emerson essentially has three things to say to "the thoughtless." First, insisting that "the doctrine of compensation is not the doctrine of indifferency," he notes that "the soul is not a compensation, but a life. The soul is." Because sheer existence or "the aboriginal abyss of real Being" is "not a relation or a part, but the whole," it is immune to the workings of compensation. In good Platonic fashion, "Nature, truth, virtue" are understood to descend from this wholeness, just as "Vice" is said to be "the absence or departure of the same." And to the degree that virtue derives from a transcendent wholeness beyond our power of comprehension, it moves toward us and not the other way around. In short, we should cultivate indifference not to virtue but to the pursuit of it. No doubt Emerson's grand talk about "the soul" is meant to sound heartening, but the basic point here clearly builds upon his polemic against moral evaluation evident earlier in the essay.

Second, Emerson acknowledges that while wrongdoers often *seem* to go unpunished, "in some manner" retribution will occur. Here, too, he seems to put the best possible face on things: if we can't get the good without the bad, at least we should recall that the reverse holds true, that evil is invariably accompanied by its opposite. Needless to say, this does nothing to alter our understanding of compensation and its fundamental laws. Lastly, Emerson assures the thoughtless that "there is no penalty to virtue, no penalty to wisdom"; a "virtuous act" constitutes a clean gain. Unlike the first two replies, this one does seem a substantial departure from the preceding discussion, for if the onset of love, virtue, or wisdom constitutes a pure gain, exempt from "the doctrine of Give and Take," then surely this provides an incentive for striving for such things. But this is another concession that concedes nothing. Virtuous action, Emerson hastens to add, is not properly an action at all but "the incoming of God himself, or absolute existence, without comparative." Virtue is always possible, but on the understanding that the virtuous are vehicles of a higher power and not themselves agents in any legitimate sense. Here, as in the other two cases, Emerson does not so much engage the original concern—"what boots it to do well?"—as talk around it.

The truth is that Emerson has no satisfactory answer to offer the thoughtless; to have one would mean playing by the rules of a game he wants to overturn. In the question we might pose as "why bother to be good" we find another illustration of how moral concerns succumb to a vulgar theory of compensation, with its unspoken expectation of rewards in return for sacrifices. In a certain sense, then, Emerson's reply to the thoughtless is less significant than what prompts the need for a reply in the first place. For Emerson has in effect imagined a group of skeptical listeners who, upon hearing an argument asking them to reconsider some basic assumptions about their moral framework, promptly revert to that framework in balking at Emerson's argument. (Something of the same procedure can be seen in latter-day skeptics who, baffled by Emerson's strange opinions about justice, seek to explain the strangeness by speculating on various causes, ranging from the personal [a psychological incapacity to admit the reality of pain both in himself and in others], to the social [a complacency about the suffering of the less fortunate born of class bias], to the national [the construction of an ideological subject founded on the suppression of racial difference]. In the suggestion that ideas make up for defects felt elsewhere in experience or that they advance hidden agendas for particular gains, such assessments likewise fall back on a mode of evaluation that Emerson is asking us to reconsider.) As if in anticipation of such question-begging treatment, Emerson concludes his reply to the thoughtless by recapitulating, in plain language, the essay's basic proposition ("The gain is apparent; the tax is certain") and by suggesting that, in the end, there is nothing our reason can do with regard to compensation's laws beyond recognizing their intransigence. By using our reason to recognize the limits of our reason, we can at least "contract the boundaries of possible mischief"; by cutting our losses, we spare ourselves needless frustration. Typically, Emerson is willing to commend strategic thinking only when it serves as a check upon strategic thinking.

But instrumentalism of this kind is really not the sole or even primary target of Emerson's concern. Those who follow the lead of "the base estimate of the market" in their ethical dealings—who vainly try to maximize the benefit and minimize the cost—may exhibit a "low prudence," but they seem healthy when compared to those gripped by what seems the opposite predisposition—the tendency to magnify the cost and to discount the benefit. In these cases, the failure fully to grasp the idea that "every thing has two sides" works to the detriment or diminishment of the self and not just its designs. Sometimes this may be explained in terms of a simple lack of imagination, as in the example of the farmer who gazes with envy on "the power and prestige" of the President, while overlooking the more degrading aspects of life in the White House. And yet as further examples of this pattern are presented, it becomes increasingly clear that something more is involved than the exposure of such cognitive shortcomings. Dwelling on the loss to the exclusion of the gain appears, in his view, to be driven by a broader, more diffuse tendency on the part of individuals, a tendency to view themselves as weak, slighted, or in some way aggrieved. A kind of moral hypochondria obsessed with the "struggles, convulsions, and despairs" of seeking virtue provides one instance of this syndrome, while a more general preoccupation with fairness or seeing justice done represents another.

In response, Emerson administers a series of good-humored expostulations that carry an edge of impatience. His brisk manner of deprecating misfortune and putting catastrophe in its place occasions some of the most spirited writing in "Compensation." In particular, he is anxious to disabuse us of the idea that we can receive serious or permanent harm from another. For example, "Men suffer all their life long, under the foolish superstition that they can be cheated. But it is as impossible for a man to be cheated by any one but himself, as for a thing to be and not to be at the same time." "Nothing can work me damage except myself," he adds, "the harm that I sustain I carry about with me." As we have seen, Emerson is nothing if not consistent in following through on the implications of his logic: if you accept the "stern ethics" of compensation and understand that every evil brings with it a good, then you will see that the only way you can receive harm is by deceiving yourself into believing that someone has actually succeeded in harming you. In this respect, I "never am a real sufferer but by my own fault." On the other hand, harm, adversity, or persecution is to be welcomed, not shunned, for "blame is safer than praise." Accordingly, "the wise man throws himself on the side of his assailants," whereas the thoughtless man presumably deceives himself into believing that his assailants are truly assailants. A preoccupation with fairness only acts to subvert and not serve one's interest.

The suggestion that the only kind of deception worth taking seriously is self-deception receives fuller treatment in the second half of "Spiritual Laws," which follows "Compensation" in *Essays: First Series*. (Both pieces come directly after that volume's best-known essay, "Self-Reliance.") In "Spiritual Laws," Emerson expounds on the "dreadful limits" to "the powers of dissimulation."

> Human character evermore publishes itself. The most fugitive
> deed and word, the mere air of doing a thing, the intimated

purpose, expresses character. If you act you show character; if you sit still, if you sleep, you show it. You think, because you have spoken nothing when others spoke, and have given no opinion on the times, on the church, on slavery, on marriage, on socialism, on secret societies ... that your verdict is still expected with curiosity as a reserved wisdom. Far otherwise; your silence answers very loud.

"All curiosity concerning other people's estimate of us" is "very idle," Emerson continues; "the world is full of judgment-days, and into every assembly that a man enters, in every action he attempts, he is gauged and stamped." Deception is not immoral so much as pointless—"concealment avails ... nothing, boasting nothing." The doctrine that justice is always just demands that we see that character is always transparent. Insisting that "we can only be valued as we make ourselves valuable," "Spiritual Laws" scoffs at the notion that people are generally misunderstood, misjudged. "A man passes for what he is worth," we are told, in a phrase repeated twice for good measure, for "the world must be just." Fears that true merit goes unacknowledged or that genuine worth is too easily counterfeited are greatly exaggerated; indeed, "there need never be any doubt concerning the respective ability of human beings." Just as mere pretension never achieved "an act of real greatness," so the greatness of the act itself is defined by the reverence it excites in others.

Coming from the author of "Self-Reliance," this is a surprising report. For the whole point of that more celebrated essay is to insist on the opposition of worldly judgment to private judgment. Indeed, "to be great is to be misunderstood." And yet an essay like "Spiritual Laws," with its remarks on the involuntary disclosure of personality ("A man cannot speak but he judges himself"), makes clear that this opposition has become overdrawn and needs to be resisted. Evidently, people need to be coaxed out of the habit of presuming that some part of them is hidden from public judgment, that what is most compelling or worthy about them stands outside the appreciation or understanding of their peers. "Spiritual Laws" is merciless in kicking away the props that support such assumptions. To say "the world must be just" is simply to say "it leaves every man, with profound unconcern, to set his own rate." In the end we all get the judgment we deserve, for worldly opinion of our worth is nothing but a mirror that impassively reflects our own true sense of self-worth. Of that opinion Emerson writes "it will certainly accept your own measure of being and doing, whether you sneak about and deny your own name, or whether you see your work produced to the concave sphere of the heavens, one with the revolution of the stars."

By now it should be obvious that Emerson's interest in compensation is not an intellectual interest, narrowly understood. Though scholars are pretty much the only audience left for an essay like "Spiritual Laws," the essay itself wasn't written for them. Emerson's remarks are directed at a particular kind of social psychology. The fictions his conception of justice claims to unmask—the temptation of thinking that we control moral outcomes, the self-deception about the ubiquity of deception and other kinds of hidden injuries, the fixation on unacknowledged or neglected merit—keep circling back to a culture whose expectations about what justice should be are constantly colliding with what, in Emerson's view, justice actually is. The dogmas and doctrines of Church and State may abet such expectations, but ultimately they seem part of a more general problem; in order to understand compensation and its spiritual laws properly, Emerson tells us, we need to "unlearn" nothing less than the "wisdom of the world." Even behavior that might otherwise look purely idiosyncratic or aberrant has widespread currency: thus the habit of clinging to the negative and overlooking the positive, a constant theme in the two essays, is made to appear systemic and entrenched, as if it were the distinguishing feature of a culture that seems to gravitate helplessly toward feelings of entitlement and resentment.

In "Self-Reliance" the great threat is conformity, the mindless impulse to curry favor with the mindless multitude. "Compensation" and "Spiritual Laws" apprehend a different kind of threat, one that resists easy labeling. If Emerson's manifesto on behalf of nonconformity celebrates individual dissent, the two essays placed directly after it champion a theory of objective justice that operates independently of the individual will. What, if anything, is the nature of the connection here? By definition, an objective justice is one that repudiates the subjectivizing or relativizing of justice—the idea that what may be fair for one is not fair for the other. But why should Emerson be so anxious to press this theme and what does it have to do with his interest in a self-reliant individualism? To answer these questions, we need a richer account of the social psychology Emerson engages than can be provided by sketchy references to a culture of entitlement and resentment. To help fill in the picture, we can turn to Tocqueville and his reflections on the centrality of envy to democratic life, an emotion apt to arise in the perceived gap between private and public estimates of worth, between the justice we feel is owed to us and what we actually receive.

Though they are scattered throughout the second volume of *Democracy in America*, Tocqueville's reflections on this theme are not difficult to summarize. As so often in this book, his account involves two main protagonists, equality and mobility, and their story might be summarized as follows: a belief in egalitarian ideals renders comparisons among one's peers easy to make, while the loosening of certain legal barriers to social mobility, combined with a fluctuating market economy, makes departures from the norm easy to see. "In democracies," Tocqueville explains, "private citizens see men rising from their ranks and attaining wealth and power in a few years; that spectacle excites their astonishment and their envy; they wonder how he who was their equal yesterday has today won the right to command them." Where equality is the presumed norm, success for one brings humiliation to others, which is why the less successful are reluctant to ascribe the good fortune of the more successful to the latter's "talents or virtue, [for that] means admitting that they are less virtuous or capable than he. They therefore regard some of his vices as the main cause thereof." Downgrading the envied person is one way to cope with the damage done to self-esteem in such cases; downgrading the envied object is another, perhaps one reason why parables of the poor rich man, oppressed and made miserable by his wealth, dominate the literature of this period, highbrow and lowbrow alike. This is not to say that Tocqueville's analysis is confined to questions over the distribution of wealth; calling envy "the democratic sentiment," he plainly considers it a pervasive phenomenon, influencing everything from political elections to the salaries of public officials. He is especially sensitive to the thin line between aspiration and resentment in antebellum America and at one point uses the concepts interchangeably, observing that "in America no one is too poor to cast a glance of hope and envy toward the pleasures of the rich or whose imagination did not snatch in anticipation good things that fate obstinately refused to him." Democracy, by opening new vistas of opportunity, also opens up new and unprecedented territory for self-reproach to explore.

Essays: First Series, published one year after Tocqueville's commentary, has no theories to offer on the relation between envy and democracy. Indeed, it doesn't have much to say about democracy and its political institutions at all. But it does have a lot to say on the topic of overidealization, a dominant theme in the collection. Thus in the essay on "Love," directly following "Spiritual Laws," we learn that "each man sees his own life defaced and disfigured ... each man sees over his own experience a certain stain of error, whilst that of other men looks fair and ideal." One essay later, in a meditation on friendship, it is said of the friend that "his goodness seems better than our goodness, his nature finer, his temptations less. Every thing that is his,—his name, his form, his dress, his books, and instruments,—fancy enhances." Without compiling individual cases at length, it can be said that in these essays interpersonal comparisons of worth tend to leave many feeling empty-handed, especially when it comes to comparisons among one's near equals. "This over-estimate of the possibilities [of others and] this under-estimate of our own," as "Spiritual Laws" puts it, does not constitute envy, but neither is it all that far from it—one need not be a neo-Nietzschean to see that "whoever is continually dissatisfied with himself is ready for revenge." Indeed, when Emerson concludes the passage I have just cited from "Friendship" with the observation that "our own thought sounds new and larger from his mouth," we cannot help but wonder at the inherent instability of such infatuation, especially when drawn against the imperative, stated three paragraphs later, that "I ought to be equal to every relation."

As we have seen, it is the belief in equal relations that, for Tocqueville, makes envy so prevalent. It is also what makes envy so shameful—to be envious is obviously to betray the fact of one's inequality. That's why Tocqueville's democratic citizen says: it's not fair that they have X and I don't; they must have gotten X unfairly. What makes such cases typical is of course the tendentious appeal to justice, here used as an instrument for transmuting contempt for oneself into contempt of others.

As we have also seen, an Emersonian justice—universal, impersonal, inflexible—renounces such manipulation. The only kind of justice worth affirming is an absolute justice, one that leaves no place for competing evaluations of the good—indeed, no place for evaluation of the good or the just at all. By implication, then, the injustice of ordinary justice would seem to be that it shields its adherents from their weaknesses by colluding in their self-deceptions. The injustice of ordinary justice is that it protects us from the experience of conflict, which is to say that it puts us at a further remove from the lessons of compensation.

If these last points seem somewhat abstract, Emerson helps us focus them in a key passage from "Compensation." There he takes up the issue of envy in order to show how it too has its compensations and how realizing this may help forestall it.

> In the nature of the soul is the compensation for the inequalities of condition. The radical tragedy of nature seems to be the distinction of More and Less. How can Less not feel the pain; how not feel the indignation or malevolence toward More? Look at those who have less faculty, and one feels sad, and knows not well what to make of it. He almost shuns their eye; he fears they will upbraid God. What should they do? It seems a great injustice. But see the facts nearly, and these mountainous inequalities vanish. Love reduces them, as the sun melts the iceberg in the sea. The heart and soul of all men being one, this bitterness of His and Mine ceases. His is mine. I am my brother, and my brother is me. If I feel overshadowed and outdone by

great neighbours, I can yet love; I can still receive; and he that
loveth maketh his own the grandeur he loves. Thereby I make the
discovery my brother is my guardian, acting for me with the
friendliest designs, and the estate I so admired and envied is my
own. It is the nature of the soul to appropriate all things. Jesus
and Shakspeare are fragments of the soul, and by love I conquer
and incorporate them in my own conscious domain. His virtue,—
is not that mine? His wit,—if it cannot be made mine, it is not
wit.

This effort at preempting envy takes the paradoxical form of ratifying
it, of embracing its deepest impulses. To the murmured resentment that says,
"His should be mine," Emerson replies without hesitation that "His is mine";
to the hollow pride that protests, "I am as good as he," Emerson affirms the
radical equality of all souls. The point is not to call envy's bluff but to bring
out its hidden compensation, here given the name of love. To admire and to
cherish the talents and privileges of the superior is, after all, to be faithful to
envy's initial prompting, and this in effect is what Emerson asks the envious
to honor. In so admiring and in so cherishing, they are invited to see how
their love ennobles them with a "grandeur" that places them on an equal
footing with those they had thought were superior. In claiming equality, they
let go of resentment. They move on.

Ultimately, then, the point of the passage is not to censure
covetousness so much as to transfigure it, so that its purely reactive or passive
character may be exchanged for an active receptivity that "conquer[s] and
incorporate[s]." Emerson contrasts this response and its brash, outrageously
confident manner ("see ... these mountainous inequalities vanish") to the
hand-wringing and impotence of the more cultivated, who react to the plight
of the envious with condescension and fear. Indeed, the arch impersonations
and adroit manipulations of perspective make the paragraph, as a whole, a
rhetorical tour de force. If in one sentence we are initially afforded a glimpse
of the suffering of the less fortunate ("How can Less not feel the pain; how
not feel the indignation"), in the next we are invited, by way of direct address,
to share the consternation of More over how to respond to such distress
("Look at those who have less faculty"). But no sooner is this shared
viewpoint suggested than it is withdrawn by the distancing device of the
third-person pronoun ("He almost shuns their eye") as More piously voices
anxieties over the godlessness of the Less. By the time we reach the question
"What should they do?" we are unsure whether the proper referent for
"they" should be Less, as the immediate context would seem to require, or
More, as their muddled sympathy would seem to suggest. This blurring of

the line between the envious and the envied culminates in a sentence both can agree on, a sentence that, in its almost comic haplessness ("It seems a great injustice"), only makes vivid the remoteness, so far as each is concerned, of any viable solution. By making the division between More and Less a little harder to see and by confusing our own sense of affiliation through the rapid cross-cutting of perspectives, Emerson rhetorically anticipates the burden of the message he goes on to relate, with its dissolution of personal boundaries and emphasis on the interchangeable nature of the soul.

Of course, to put the point this way merely underscores what many readers today will find most objectionable about Emerson's response. For the appeal to a spiritual equality in the face of social inequality looks indeed as if it were nothing more than a rhetorical gesture. We have what appears to be a textbook case of how Emerson's religiosity can lead him astray, his invocation of the radical oneness of all souls being transparently a betrayal of bad faith, if not outright escapism. Thus one critic warns against "the temptation to political quiescence" that "compensation presents us with," while another denounces the "barbarous idealism" of this passage, which trivializes the sufferings of the less advantaged and "sanctions the drama of social injustice by denying its existence." It seems to me that such judgments are compelling only to the extent that we agree to regard a phenomenon like envy as unreal or inconsequential—in which case it is not really Emerson who is being evasive. What could be more "quiescent," politically or otherwise, than a life given over to "indignation or malevolence"? Why should we think that the pain of envy is any less acute or intolerable than other afflictions? In bringing Emerson to the bar of social justice, such readings look past Emerson's main object of concern, driving back underground what he tries to bring to light and use. Despite themselves, they help clarify why Emerson might be drawn to consider the imperatives of conventional justice to be not just an encumbrance but an obstruction.

By dwelling on envy, I do not mean to give undue prominence to one theme. Just as "Compensation" can and does recognize cases where resentment is a legitimate response to social inequality (see the remarks, a few pages earlier, on "the unjust accumulations of power and property" and the "hatred" and class enmity they are sure to inspire), so it imagines other "calamities" whose devastation may be offset by awareness of compensation's laws. Still, envy has, I think, a special resonance in Emerson's writings, all the more so given what we have seen of his interest in making use of it. In this light, the critical extent to which his concept of self-reliance necessarily *incites* this particular emotion is worth noting. Though some readers of "Self-Reliance" may recall the comment that "envy is ignorance [and] imitation is suicide," they are even more likely to remember the declaration that comes three sentences before it: "in every work of genius we recognize our own rejected thoughts; they come back to us with a certain alienated majesty." The inspiration we take from "works of genius" is made inseparable from the recognition that something has been taken away from us, or, more exactly, that we have allowed something to be taken away. The impression, in other words, that a gain for one counts as a loss for the other not only clings to such passages but helps account for their appeal. Tocqueville's insight into the nearness between hope and envy in democratic culture is relevant here, for while "Self-Reliance" does not have much to say about civic equality it is very much committed to a radical or "aboriginal" equality of the soul. Where the thought that "it could be me" may so easily change places with the suspicion that "it should have been me," a self-reliant individualism reveals its own compensatory burdens. No doubt it is with such burdens in mind that Emerson concedes his rather daunting expectations for self-reliance, admitting that it "demands something godlike in him who has cast off the common motives of humanity, and has ventured to trust himself as a taskmaster."

Seeing signs of such linked oppositions everywhere, "Compensation" propounds the laws of universal justice. It is a justice that leaves off where others begin, in the sense that it provides no court of appeal for restoring public rights or for redressing private grievances. It offends our moral judgment on two counts, first by putting true justice beyond our reach and second by insisting that when it comes to suffering prolonged injustice we have nobody to blame but ourselves. Like the god of his Puritan ancestors, Emerson's compensation leaves us nowhere to hide. It does so not, of course, out of some fantasy of "surveillance" or yearning for covert control. If Emerson wants to leave the self, ethically speaking, undefended, that is in keeping with his wish to expose our moral and political self-representations to antagonism and conflict, the vicissitudes of compensation. In his theodicy there is ultimately nothing to fall back on but the knowledge that "all things are double, one against the other." In the end, it is the irreducibly conflictual nature of experience that identifies the essential feature of justice for Emerson, just as its denial or refusal marks what he takes to be unjust.

The idea that Emerson considers conflict and justice to be more compatible than opposed may seem hard to reconcile with his infamous, supposedly incurable optimism, samples of which are abundant in both "Compensation" and "Spiritual Laws." Thus we are called upon to admire how "things are arranged for truth and benefit" or how "the sure years reveal a deep remedial force that underlies all facts" or to see that "our life might be easier and simpler than we make it" if we ceased from "interfer[ing] with the optimism of nature." But if such assurances overflow with "the saccharine principle," as Emerson rather self-mockingly puts it in "Circles," that is in part because the culture he finds himself addressing so overwhelmingly renounces it. The popular image of antebellum America as filled with bumptious energy and rollicking adventurers does not fit the imagined audience of these essays, whose timidity, resentment, self-contempt, and stubborn pessimism have already been documented. This is not to claim that Emerson's optimism is purely strategic, as if it were adopted in a crudely tactical sense. Rather, my point is that his investment in optimism, so far from seeking to evade contrast and conflict, works in these essays to advance and insist upon it. For pessimism and resentment have their complacencies too. The objection to states of mind such as envy is, as we have seen, that they despair of the truth that "every action admits of being outdone." In this saying, we find not only the motive for his optimism but the first and last word on what justice is to Emerson.

HAROLD BLOOM

Afterthought:
Reflections in the Evening Land

Huey Long, known as "the Kingfish," dominated the state of Louisiana from 1928 until his assassination in 1935, at the age of 42. Simultaneously governor and a United States senator, the canny Kingfish uttered a prophecy that haunts me in this late summer of 2005, 70 years after his violent end: "Of course we will have fascism in America but we will call it democracy!"

I reflected on Huey Long (always mediated for me by his portrait as Willie Stark in Robert Penn Warren's novel, *All the King's Men*) recently, when I listened to President George W Bush addressing the Veterans of Foreign Wars in Salt Lake City, Utah. I was thus benefited by Rupert Murdoch's Fox TV channel, which is the voice of Bushian crusading democracy, very much of the Kingfish's variety. Even as Bush extolled his Iraq adventure, his regime daily fuses more tightly together elements of oligarchy, plutocracy, and theocracy.

At the age of 75, I wonder if the Democratic party ever again will hold the presidency or control the Congress in my lifetime. I am not sanguine, because our rulers have demonstrated their prowess in Florida (twice) and in Ohio at shaping voting procedures, and they control the Supreme Court. The economist-journalist Paul Krugman recently observed that the Republicans dare not allow themselves to lose either Congress or the White House, because subsequent investigations could disclose dark matters indeed. Krugman did not specify, but among the profiteers of our Iraq crusade are big oil (House of Bush/House of Saud), Halliburton (the vice-president), Bechtel (a nest of mighty Republicans) and so forth.

All of this is extraordinarily blatant, yet the American people seem benumbed, unable to read, think, or remember, and thus fit subjects for a president who shares their limitations. A grumpy old Democrat, I observe to my friends that our emperor is himself the best argument for intelligent design, the current theocratic substitute for what used to be called creationism. Sigmund Freud might be chagrined to discover that he is forgotten, while the satan of America is now Charles Darwin. President Bush, who says that Jesus is his "favorite philosopher", recently decreed in regard to intelligent design and evolution: "Both sides ought to be properly taught."

I am a teacher by profession, about to begin my 51st year at Yale, where frequently my subject is American writers. Without any particular competence in politics, I assert no special insight in regard to the American malaise. But I am a student of what I have learned to call the American Religion, which has little in common with European Christianity. There is now a parody of the American Jesus, a kind of Republican CEO who disapproves of taxes, and who has widened the needle's eye so that camels and the wealthy pass readily into the Kingdom of Heaven. We have also an American holy spirit, the comforter of our burgeoning poor, who don't bother to vote. The American trinity pragmatically is completed by an imperial warrior God, trampling with shock and awe.

These days I reread the writers who best define America: Emerson, Hawthorne, Whitman, Melville, Mark Twain, Faulkner, among others. Searching them, I seek to find what could suffice to explain what seems our national self-destructiveness. D.H. Lawrence, in his *Studies in Classic American Literature* (1923), wrote what seems to me still the most illuminating criticism of Walt Whitman and Herman Melville. Of the two, Melville provoked no ambivalence in Lawrence. But Whitman transformed Lawrence's poetry, and Lawrence himself, from at least 1917 on. Replacing Thomas Hardy as prime precursor, Whitman spoke directly to Lawrence's vitalism, immediacy, and barely evaded homoeroticism. On a much smaller scale, Whitman earlier had a similar impact on Gerard Manley Hopkins. Lawrence, frequently furious at Whitman, as one might be with an overwhelming father, a King Lear of poetry, accurately insisted that the Americans were not worthy of their Whitman. More than ever, they are not, since the Jacksonian democracy that both Whitman and Melville celebrated is dying in our Evening Land.

What defines America? "Democracy" is a ruined word, because of its misuse in the American political rhetoric of our moment. If Hamlet and Don Quixote, between them, define the European self, then Captain Ahab and "Walt Whitman" (the persona, not the man) suggest a very different self from the European. Ahab is Shakespearean, Miltonic, even Byronic-Shelleyan, but his monomaniacal quest is his own, and reacts against the Emersonian self, just as Melville's beloved Hawthorne recoiled also. Whitman, a more positive Emersonian, affirms what the Sage of Concord called self-reliance, the authentic American religion rather than its Bushian parodies. Though he possesses a Yale BA and honorary doctorate, our president is semi-literate at best. He once boasted of never having read a book through, even at Yale. Henry James was affronted when he met President Theodore Roosevelt; what could he have made of George W Bush?

Having just reread James's *The American Scene* (1907), I amuse myself, rather grimly, by imagining the master of the American novel touring the United States in 2005, exactly a century after his return visit to his homeland. Like T.S. Eliot in the next generation, James was far more at home in London than in America, yet both retained an idiom scarcely English. They each eventually became British subjects, graced by the Order of Merit, but Whitman went on haunting them, more covertly in Eliot's case. *The Waste Land* initially was an elegy for Jean Verdenal, who had been to Eliot what Rupert Brooke was to Henry James. Whitman's "Lilacs" elegy for Lincoln became James's favorite poem, and it deeply contaminates *The Waste Land*.

I am not suggesting that the American aesthetic self is necessarily homoerotic: Emerson, Hawthorne, Mark Twain, Faulkner, Robert Frost after all are as representative as are Melville, Whitman and Henry James. Nor does any American fictive self challenge Hamlet as an ultimate abyss of inwardness. Yet Emerson bet the American house (as it were) on self-reliance, which is a doctrine of solitude. Whitman, as person and as poetic mask, like his lilacs, bloomed into a singularity that cared intensely both about the self and others, but Emersonian consciousness all too frequently can flower, Hamlet-like, into an individuality indifferent both to the self and to others. The United States since Emerson has been divided between what he called the "party of hope" and the "party of memory". Our intellectuals of the left and of the right both claim Emerson as ancestor.

In 2005, what is self-reliance? I can recognize three prime stigmata of the American religion: spiritual freedom is solitude, while the soul's encounter with the divine (Jesus, the Paraclete, the Father) is direct and personal, and, most crucially, what is best and oldest in the American religionist goes back to a time-before-time, and so is part or particle of God. Every second year, the Gallup pollsters survey religion in the United

States, and report that 93% of us believe in God, while 89% are certain that God loves him or her on a personal basis. And 45% of us insist that Earth was created precisely as described in Genesis and is only about 9,000 or fewer years old. The actual figure is 4.5 billion years, and some dinosaur fossils are dated as 190 million years back. Perhaps the intelligent designers, led by George W. Bush, will yet give us a dinosaur Gospel, though I doubt it, as they, and he, dwell within a bubble that education cannot invade.

Contemporary America is too dangerous to be laughed away, and I turn to its most powerful writers in order to see if we remain coherent enough for imaginative comprehension. Lawrence was right; Whitman at his very best can sustain momentary comparison with Dante and Shakespeare. Most of what follows will be founded on Whitman, the most American of writers, but first I turn again to *Moby-Dick*, the national epic of self-destructiveness that almost rivals *Leaves of Grass*, which is too large and subtle to be judged in terms of self-preservation or apocalyptic destructiveness.

Some of my friends and students suggest that Iraq is President Bush's white whale, but our leader is absurdly far from Captain Ahab's aesthetic dignity. The valid analogue is the Pequod; as Lawrence says: "America! Then such a crew. Renegades, castaways, cannibals, Ishmael, Quakers," and South Sea Islanders, Native Americans, Africans, Parsees, Manxmen, what you will. One thinks of our tens of thousands of mercenaries in Iraq, called "security employees" or "contractors". They mix former American Special Forces, Gurkhas, Boers, Croatians, whoever is qualified and available. What they lack is Captain Ahab, who could give them a metaphysical dimension.

Ahab carries himself and all his crew (except Ishmael) to triumphant catastrophe, while Moby-Dick swims away, being as indestructible as the Book of Job's Leviathan. The obsessed captain's motive ostensibly is revenge, since earlier he was maimed by the white whale, but his truer desire is to strike through the universe's mask, in order to prove that while the visible world might seem to have been formed in love, the invisible spheres were made in fright. God's rhetorical question to Job: "Can'st thou draw out Leviathan with a hook?" is answered by Ahab's: "I'd strike the sun if it insulted me!" The driving force of the Bushian-Blairians is greed, but the undersong of their Iraq adventure is something closer to Iago's pyromania. Our leader, and yours, are firebugs.

One rightly expects Whitman to explain our Evening Land to us, because his imagination is America's. A Free-Soiler, he opposed the Mexican War, as Emerson did. Do not our two Iraq invasions increasingly resemble the Mexican and Spanish-American conflicts? Donald Rumsfeld speaks of permanent American bases in Iraq, presumably to protect oil wells. President

Bush's approval rating was recently down to 38%, but I fear that this popular reaction has more to do with the high price of petrol than with any outrage at our Iraq crusade.

What has happened to the American imagination if we have become a parody of the Roman empire? I recall going to bed early on election night in November 2004, though friends kept phoning with the hopeful news that there appeared to be some three million additional voters. Turning the phone off, I gloomily prophesied that these were three million Evangelicals, which indeed was the case.

Our politics began to be contaminated by theocratic zealots with the Reagan revelation, when Southern Baptists, Mormons, Pentecostals, and Adventists surged into the Republican party. The alliance between Wall Street and the Christian Right is an old one, but has become explicit only in the past quarter century. What was called the counter-culture of the late 1960s and '70s provoked the reaction of the '80s, which is ongoing. This is all obvious enough, but becomes subtler in the context of the religiosity of the country, which truly divides us into two nations. Sometimes I find myself wondering if the South belatedly has won the civil war, more than a century after its supposed defeat. The leaders of the Republican Party are Southern; even the Bushes, despite their Yale and Connecticut tradition, were careful to become Texans and Floridians. Politics, in the United States, perhaps never again can be separated from religion. When so many vote against their own palpable economic interests, and choose "values" instead, then an American malaise has replaced the American dream.

Whitman, still undervalued as a poet, in relation to his astonishing aesthetic power, remains the permanent prophet of our party of hope. That seems ironic in many ways, since the crucial event of Whitman's life was our Civil War, in which a total of 625,000 men were slain, counting both sides. In Britain, the "Great War" is the First World War, because nearly an entire generation of young men died. The United States remains haunted by the Civil War, the central event in the life of the nation since the Declaration of Independence. David S. Reynolds, the most informed of Whitman's biographers, usefully demonstrates that Whitman's poetry, from 1855-60, was designed to help hold the Union together. After the sunset glory of "When Lilacs Last in the Dooryard Bloom'd," the 1865 elegy overtly for Abraham Lincoln, and inwardly for Whitman's poetic self-identity, something burned out in the bard of *Leaves of Grass*. Day after day, for several years, he had exhausted himself, in the military hospitals of Washington D.C., dressing wounds, reading to, and writing letters for, the ill and maimed, comforting the dying. The extraordinary vitalism and immediacy departed from his poetry. It is as though he had sacrificed his own imagination on the altar of those martyred, like Lincoln, in the fused cause of union and emancipation.

Whitman died in 1892, a time of American politics as corrupt as this, if a touch less blatant than the era of Bushian theocracy. But there was a curious split in the poet of *Leaves of Grass*, between what he called the soul, and his "real me" or "me myself," an entity distinct from his persona, "Walt Whitman, one of the roughs, an American":

> "I believe in you my soul, the other I am must not abase itself to you,
> And you must not be abased to the other."

The rough Walt is the "I" here, and has been created to mediate between his character or soul, and his "real me" or personality. I fear that this is permanently American, the abyss between character and personality. Doubtless, this can be a universal phenomenon: one thinks of Nietzsche and of W.B. Yeats. And yet mutual abasement between soul and self destroys any individual's coherence. My fellow citizens who vote for "values," against their own needs, manifest something of the same dilemma.

As the persona "Walt Whitman" melted away in the furnace of national affliction in the Civil War, it was replaced by a less capable persona, "the Good Grey Poet." No moral rebirth kindled postwar America; instead Whitman witnessed the extraordinary corruption of President U.S. Grant's administration, which is the paradigm emulated by so many Republican presidencies, including what we suffer at this moment.

Whitman himself became less than coherent in his long decline, from 1866 to 1892. He did not ice over, like the later Wordsworth, but his prophetic stance ebbed away. Lost, he ceased to be an Emersonian, and rather weirdly attempted to become a Hegelian! In "The Evening Land," an extraordinary poem of early 1922, D.H. Lawrence anticipated his long-delayed sojourn in America, which began only in September of that year, when he reached Taos, New Mexico. He had hoped to visit the United States in February 1917, but England had denied him a passport. Lawrence's poem is a kind of Whitmanian love-hymn to America, but is even more ambivalent than the chapter on Whitman in *Studies in Classic American Literature*.

"Are you the grave of our day?" Lawrence asks, and begs America to cajole his soul, even as he admits how much he fears the Evening Land:

> "Your more-than-European idealism,
> Like a be-aureoled bleached skeleton hovering
> Its cage-ribs in the social heaven, beneficent."

This rather ghastly vision is not inappropriate to our moment, nor is Lawrence's bitter conclusion:

> "'These States!' as Whitman said,
> Whatever he meant."

What Whitman meant (as Lawrence knew) was that the United States itself was to be the greatest of poems. But with that grand assertion, I find myself so overwhelmed by an uncomfortable sense of irony, that I cease these reflections. Shelley wore a ring, on which was inscribed the motto: "The good time will come." In September, the U.S. Secretary of State Condoleezza Rice was quoted as saying at Zion Church in Whistler, Alabama: "The Lord Jesus Christ is going to come on time if we just wait."

Chronology

1803	Born May 25 in Boston to William Emerson and Ruth Haskins Emerson.
1811	May 12, Emerson's father William dies.
1812	Emerson enters Boston Public Latin School.
1817	Begins studies at Harvard College.
1820	Begins keeping his journal.
1821	Graduates from Harvard. Teaches at his brother William's school in Boston.
1822	Publishes his first article, "Thoughts on the Religion of the Middle Ages," in *The Christian Disciple*.
1825	Enters Harvard Divinity School.
1826–1827	Officially sanctioned to preach as a Unitarian minister. Sails to South Carolina and Florida in an effort to improve his health.
1828–1829	Becomes engaged to Ellen Louisa Tucker. Ordained at Second Church in Boston. Marries Ellen on September 10, 1829.
1831	Ellen dies of tuberculosis on February 8 at the age of nineteen.
1832	Resigns post at Second Church. Travels in Europe.
1833	Meets Wordsworth, Coleridge, and Carlyle during travels abroad. Returns to Boston. Delivers his first public lecture, "The Uses of Natural History."

1834	Settles in Concord, Massachusetts.
1835	Lectures on biography. Marries Lydia Jackson on September 14, whom he renames "Lidian."
1836	Meets Margaret Fuller; helps form Transcendental Club; publishes *Nature* anonymously. Birth of son Waldo.
1837	Delivers "The American Scholar" at Harvard before the Phi Beta Kappa Society. Writes "The Concord Hymn."
1838	Delivers "The Divinity School Address" at Harvard, which causes him to be banned from speaking at Harvard.
1839	Birth of daughter Ellen Tucker.
1841	Publication of first series of *Essays*. Thoreau comes to live with the Emersons. Birth of daughter Edith.
1842	Death of Waldo. Emerson Succeeds Margaret Fuller as editor of *The Dial*.
1844	Birth of son Edward. Delivers "Emancipation of the Negroes in the British West Indies." Publication of *Essays: Second Series*.
1845	Thoreau moves to Walden Pond. Emerson delivers series of lectures on "Representative Men."
1846	Publication of *Poems*.
1847	Travels to Europe for most of the year.
1849	Publication of *Nature; Addresses, Lectures*.
1850	Publication of *Representative Men*. Margaret Fuller dies.
1851	Delivers series of lectures on "The Conduct of Life."
1853	Death of Emerson's mother.
1854	Lectures on poetry at Harvard Divinity School. Thoreau publishes *Walden*.
1855	Whitman publishes *Leaves of Grass*. Emerson writes letter to Whitman in praise of his accomplishment.
1856	Publication of *English Traits*.
1860	Publication of *The Conduct of Life*.
1862	Henry David Thoreau dies.
1865	Eulogizes President Lincoln.
1867	Publication of *May-Day and Other Pieces*. Named Overseer of Harvard College. Delivers "The Progress of Culture" address to the Phi Beta Kappa Society.
1870	Publication of *Society and Solitude*.
1871	Travels to California and meets naturalist John Muir.

1872	Travels to Europe and Mediterranean.
1875	Publishes *Letters and Social Aims*.
1882	Dies of pneumonia in Concord, Massachusetts.

·

Contributors

HAROLD BLOOM is Sterling Professor of the Humanities at Yale University. He is the author of 30 books, including *Shelley's Mythmaking* (1959), *The Visionary Company* (1961), *Blake's Apocalypse* (1963), *Yeats* (1970), *A Map of Misreading* (1975), *Kabbalah and Criticism* (1975), *Agon: Toward a Theory of Revisionism* (1982), *The American Religion* (1992), *The Western Canon* (1994), and *Omens of Millennium: The Gnosis of Angels, Dreams, and Resurrection* (1996). *The Anxiety of Influence* (1973) sets forth Professor Bloom's provocative theory of the literary relationships between the great writers and their predecessors. His most recent books include *Shakespeare: The Invention of the Human* (1998), a 1998 National Book Award finalist, *How to Read and Why* (2000), *Genius: A Mosaic of One Hundred Exemplary Creative Minds* (2002), *Hamlet: Poem Unlimited* (2003), *Where Shall Wisdom Be Found?* (2004), and *Jesus and Yahweh: The Names Divine* (2005). In 1999, Professor Bloom received the prestigious American Academy of Arts and Letters Gold Medal for Criticism. He has also received the International Prize of Catalonia, the Alfonso Reyes Prize of Mexico, and the Hans Christian Andersen Bicentennial Prize of Denmark.

STEPHEN WHICHER wrote *Freedom and Fate: An Inner Life of Ralph Waldo Emerson* and edited *Selections from Ralph Waldo Emerson: An Organic Anthology*, which presents Emerson's major essays arranged chronologically and interspersed with excerpts from his journals, letters, and poetry.

LAWRENCE I. BUELL is Professor of English at Harvard University. His many distinguished books include *Literary Transcendentalism*, *New England Literary Culture*, and, most recently, *Emerson*.

DAVID M. WYATT teaches in the English Department of the University of Maryland. He is the author of *Five Fires: Race, Catastrophe, and the Shaping of California*; *Out of the Sixties: Storytelling and the Vietnam Generation*; and *Prodigal Sons: A Study in Authorship and Authority*, among other books.

BARBARA PACKER is Professor of English at the University of California, Los Angeles. She specializes in 19th-century American literature and has written numerous essays on Emily Dickinson and Ralph Waldo Emerson, as well as a book-length study, *Emerson's Fall: A New Interpretation of the Major Essays*.

SHARON CAMERON is William R. Kenan Jr. Professor of English at Johns Hopkins University. She specializes in 19th- and 20th-century American literature and is the author of many books, including *Lyric Time: Dickinson and the Limits of Genre*, *Thinking in Henry James*, *Beautiful Work: A Meditation on Pain*, and the forthcoming *Impersonality: Seven Essays* (Chicago 2006), in which "Representing Grief" is also reprinted.

DAVID BROMWICH teaches at Yale University, where he is Housum Professor of English. His books include *Hazlitt: The Mind of the Critic*, *Disowned by Memory: Wordsworth's Poetry of the 1790's*, and *Skeptical Music*, which collects his essays and reviews of modern and contemporary poetry.

DAVID M. ROBINSON is Oregon Professor of English at Oregon State University, where he also directs the American Studies program. His publications include *World of Relations: The Achievement of Peter Taylor*, *Emerson and the Conduct of Life*, and *Apostle of Culture: Emerson as Preacher and Lecturer*.

GEORGE KATEB is Emeritus Professor of Politics at Princeton University. His books include *Utopia and Its Enemies* and *The Inner Ocean: Individualism and Democratic Culture*, which won the 1994 Spitz Book Prize awarded by the Conference for the Study of Political Thought.

PAMELA SCHIRMEISTER is Associate Dean of the Graduate School at Yale University. She is the author of *Consolations of Space: The Place of*

Romanticism in Hawthorne, Melville, and James and *Less Legible Meanings: Between Poetry and Philosophy in the Work of Emerson.*

KERRY LARSON is Senior Associate Dean of the Rockham School of Graduate Studies at the University of Michigan, where he is also Associate Professor of English. He is the author of *Whitman's Drama of Consensus.*

Bibliography

Anderson, Quentin. *The Imperial Self: An Essay in American Literary and Cultural History*. New York: Knopf, 1971.

Arnold, Matthew. *Discourses in America*. London: Macmillan, 1885.

Bishop, Jonathan. *Emerson on the Soul*. Cambridge: Harvard University Press, 1964.

Bloom, Harold. *Ralph Waldo Emerson*. Modern Critical Views Series. New York: Chelsea House, 1985.

———. *Agon: Towards a Theory of Revisionism*. New York: Oxford University Press, 1982.

———. *The Breaking of the Vessels*. Chicago: University of Chicago Press, 1982.

———. *Figures of Capable Imagination*. New York: Seabury Press, 1976.

———. *Poetry and Repression: Revisionism from Blake to Stevens*. New Haven: Yale University Press, 1976.

———. *A Map of Misreading*. New York: Oxford University Press, 1975.

Brantley, Richard E. *Coordinates of Anglo-American Romanticism: Wesley, Edwards, Carlyle and Emerson*. Gainesville: University Presses of Florida, 1993.

Brown, Lee Rust. *The Emerson Museum: Practical Romanticism and the Pursuit of the Whole*. Cambridge: Harvard University Press, 1997.

Buell, Lawrence. *New England Literary Culture from Revolution through Renaissance*. New York: Cambridge University Press, 1986.

———. *Ralph Waldo Emerson: A Collection of Critical Essays*. Englewood Cliffs, New Jersey: Prentice-Hall, 1993.

———. "Reading Emerson for the Structures: The Coherence of the Essays." *The Quarterly Journal of Speech* 58, no. 1 (February 1972): 58–69.

Burkholder, Robert E., and Joel Myerson, eds. *Critical Essays on Ralph Waldo Emerson*. Boston: G.K. Hall, 1983.

Cadava, Eduardo. *Emerson and the Climates of History*. Stanford: Stanford University Press, 1997.

Cameron, Kenneth Walter. *Emerson the Essayist*. Hartford: Transcendental Books, 1972.

———. *Emerson's Reading*. Hartford: Transcendental Books, 1962.

Cameron, Sharon. "Representing Grief: Emerson's 'Experience.'" *Representations* 15 (Summer 1986): 15–41.

Carpenter, Frederic Ives. *Emerson and Asia*. Cambridge: Harvard University Press, 1930.

Cavell, Stanley. *Conditions Handsome and Unhandsome: The Constitution of Emersonian Perfectionism*. Chicago: University of Chicago Press, 1990.

———. *Philosophical Passages: Wittgenstein, Emerson, Austin, Derrida*. Oxford: Blackwell, 1995.

Cayton, Mary Kupiec. *Emerson's Emergence: Self and Society in the Transformation of New England, 1800–1845*. Chapel Hill: University of North Carolina Press, 1989.

Chai, Leon. *The Romantic Foundations of the American Renaissance*. Ithaca: Cornell University Press, 1987.

Cheyfitz, Eric. *The Trans-parent: Sexual Politics in the Language of Emerson*. Baltimore: Johns Hopkins University Press, 1981.

Colacurcio, Michael. *Doctrine and Difference*. New York: Routledge, 1997.

Cowen, Michael H. *City of the West: Emerson, America, and Urban Metaphor*. New Haven: Yale University Press, 1967.

Duncan, Jeffrey L. *The Power and Form of Emerson's Thought*. Charlottesville: University Press of Virginia, 1973.

Ellison, Julie. *Emerson's Romantic Style*. Princeton: Princeton University Press, 1984.

Fredman, Stephen. *The Grounding of American Poetry: Charles Olson and the Emersonian Tradition*. New York: Cambridge University Press, 1993.

Gelpi, Donald L. *Endless Seeker: The Religious Quest of Ralph Waldo Emerson*. Lanham: University Press of America, 1991.

Gilmore, Michael T. *American Romanticism and the Marketplace*. Chicago: University of Chicago Press, 1985.

Harris, Kenneth Marc. *Carlyle and Emerson: Their Long Debate*. Cambridge: Harvard University Press, 1978.

Hertz, David Michael. *Angels of Reality: Emersonian Unfoldings in Wright, Stevens, and Ives*. Carbondale: Southern Illinois University Press, 1993.

Hopkins, Vivian C. *Spires of Form: A Study of Emerson's Aesthetic Theory*. Cambridge: Harvard University Press, 1951.

Howe, Irving. *The American Newness: Culture and Politics in the Age of Emerson*. Cambridge: Harvard University Press, 1986.

Hughes, Gertrude Reif. *Emerson's Demanding Optimism*. Baton Rouge: Louisiana State University Press, 1984.

Johnston, Kenneth R., Gilbert Chaitin, Karen Hanson, and Herbert Marks, eds. *Romantic Revolutions: Criticism and Theory*. Bloomington: Indiana University Press, 1990.

Kateb, George. *Emerson and Self-Reliance*. Thousand Oaks: Sage, 1995.

Kazin, Alfred. *An American Procession: The Major American Writers from 1830–1930—The Crucial Century*. New York: Knopf, 1984.

Larson, Kerry. "Justice to Emerson." *Raritan* 21, no. 3 (Winter 2002): 46–67.

Leary, Lewis. *Ralph Waldo Emerson: An Interpretive Essay*. Boston: Twayne, 1980.

Leverenz, David. *Manhood and the American Renaissance*. Ithaca: Cornell University Press, 1989.

Matthiessen, F.O. *American Renaissance: Art and Expression in the Age of Emerson and Whitman*. New York: Oxford University Press, 1941.

Michael, John. *Emerson and Skepticism: The Cipher of the World*. Baltimore: Johns Hopkins University Press, 1988

Miller, Perry. *The Raven and the Whale: The War of Words and Wits in the Era of Poe and Melville*. New York: Harcourt, Brace, 1956.

Myerson, Joel, ed. *Emerson: Centenary Essays*. Carbondale: Southern Illinois University Press, 1982.

Neufeldt, Leonard. *The House of Emerson*. Lincoln: University of Nebraska Press, 1982.

Newfield, Christopher. *The Emerson Effect: Individualism and Submission in America*. Chicago: University of Chicago Press, 1996.

Packer, B. L. *Emerson's Fall: A New Interpretation of the Major Essays*. New York: Continuum, 1982.

Paul, Sherman. *Emerson's Angle of Vision: Man and Nature in American Experience*. Cambridge: Harvard University Press, 1952.

Poirier, Richard. *Poetry and Pragmatism*. Cambridge: Harvard University Press, 1992.

————. *The Renewal of Literature: Emersonian Reflections*. New York: Random House, 1987.

Porte, Joel. *Representative Man: Ralph Waldo Emerson in His Time*. New York: Oxford University Press, 1979.

————, and Saundra Morris, eds. *The Cambridge Companion to Ralph Waldo Emerson*. New York: Cambridge University Press, 1999.

Railton, Stephen. *Authorship and Audience: Literary Performance in the American Renaissance*. Princeton: Princeton University Press, 1991.

Robinson, David. *Emerson and the Conduct of Life: Pragmatism and Ethical Purpose in the Later Work*. New York: Cambridge University Press, 1993.

Rowe, John Carlos. *At Emerson's Tomb: The Politics of Classic American Literature*. New York: Columbia University Press, 1997.

Scheick, William J. *The Slender Human Word: Emerson's Artistry in Prose*. Knoxville: University of Tennessee Press, 1978.

Schirmeister, Pamela. *Less Legible Meanings: Between Poetry and Philosophy in the Work of Emerson*. Stanford: Stanford University Press, 1999.

Staebler, Warren. *Ralph Waldo Emerson*. New York: Twayne, 1973.

Van Leer, David. *Emerson's Epistemology: The Argument of the Major Essays*. New York: Cambridge University Press, 1986.

Wagenknecht, Edward. *Ralph Waldo Emerson: Portrait of a Balanced Soul*. New York: Oxford University Press, 1974.

Whicher, Stephen. *Freedom and Fate: An Inner Life of Ralph Waldo Emerson*. Philadelphia: University of Pennsylvania Press, 1953.

Wolfe, Cary. *The Limits of American Literary Ideology in Pound and Emerson*. New York: Cambridge University Press, 1993.

Wyatt, David. "Spelling Time: The Reader in Emerson's 'Circles.'" *American Literature* 48, no. 2 (May 1976): 140–151.

Yannella, Donald. *Ralph Waldo Emerson*. Boston: Twayne, 1982.

Acknowledgments

"Circles" by Stephen Whicher. From *Freedom and Fate: An Inner Life of Ralph Waldo Emerson*, pp. 94–105. © 1953 by the University of Pennsylvania Press. Reprinted by permission of the University of Pennsylvania Press.

"Reading Emerson for the Structures: The Coherence of the Essays" by Lawrence I. Buell. From *The Quarterly Journal of Speech* 58, no. 1 (February 1972), pp. 58–69. © 1972 by the Speech Communication Association. Reprinted by permission of Taylor & Francis Ltd (http://www.tandf.co.uk/journals).

"Spelling Time: The Reader in Emerson's 'Circles'" by David M. Wyatt. From *American Literature* 48, no. 2 (May 1976), pp. 140–151. © 1976 by Duke University Press. All rights reserved. Used by permission of the publisher.

"Experience" by Barbara Packer. From *Emerson's Fall: A New Interpretation of the Major Essays.* © 1982 by B.L. Packer. Reprinted by permission.

"Emerson: The American Religion" by Harold Bloom. From *Agon: Towards a Theory of Revisionism*, pp. 145–178. © 1982 by Oxford University Press, Inc.

"Representing Grief: Emerson's 'Experience'" by Sharon Cameron. From *Representations* 15 (Summer 1986), pp. 15–41. © 1986 by the Regents of the University of California. Reprinted by permission.

"From Wordsworth to Emerson" by David Bromwich. From *Romantic Revolutions: Criticism and Theory*, pp. 202–218. © 1990 by David Bromwich.

"'Here or Nowhere': *Essays: Second Series*" by David M. Robinson. From *Emerson and the Conduct of Life: Pragmatism and Ethical Purpose in the Later Work*, pp. 71–88. © 1993 by Cambridge University Press.

"Friendship and Love" by George Kateb. From *Emerson and Self-Reliance*, pp. 96–133. © 2000 by Alta Mira Press.

"From Philosophy to Rhetoric" by Pamela Schirmeister. From *Less Legible Meanings: Between Poetry and Philosophy in the Work of Emerson*, pp. 59–85. © 1999 by the Board of Trustees of the Leland Stanford Jr. University.

"Justice to Emerson" by Kerry Larson. From *Raritan* 21, no. 3 (Winter 2002), p. 46–67. © 2002 by *Raritan: A Quarterly Review*.

Index